MILLICENT GARRETT FAWCETT

BY RAY STRACHEY

AUTHOR OF "THE CAUSE, A SHORT HISTORY OF THE
WOMEN'S MOVEMENT," ETC.

LONDON
JOHN MURRAY, ALBEMARLE STREET, W.

First Edition . . . 1931

1430

1597

TO

ALL THE MEN AND WOMEN WHO WERE THE COMRADES OF

MILLICENT GARRETT FAWCETT

IN THE WOMEN'S SUFFRAGE CAUSE

" Let thine eyes look right on, and let thine eyelids look straight before thee.

" Ponder the path of thy feet, and let all thy ways be established.

" Turn not to the right hand nor to the left : remove thy foot from evil."

FOREWORD

THIS book is an attempt to portray the life of a woman whose strength lay not in her circumstances but in her nature. Dame Millicent Fawcett's life was, in a way, monotonous and tranquil, in spite of the storms she lived through and the great social movement she led to victory. The changes which she saw in her lifetime, and which she herself was so largely instrumental in bringing about, were indeed dramatic. She saw her sex lifted up from the position of helpless dependents to that of free citizens, and in the course of her work she lived through intensely exciting hours, and was the central figure in scenes of passionate enthusiasm and equally passionate despair. But in the midst of it all she remained unaltered. She showed the same even judgment, the same quiet conviction and the same humorous breadth of outlook from beginning to end, and there were no dramatic developments in her character and none in her history. An unshaken reasonableness was evident in everything she did, whether great or small, and consequently her biography contains nothing sensational. She knew how to work and how to wait, but she did not know how to give way. " Hold fast, hold firm, hold OUT," she used to say ; and it was what she instinctively did herself.

Such a character is easy to describe in outline, but difficult to portray in detail, and I know that I must have failed to give a complete picture of her individual life. I have, however, tried to do it, partly because I so much loved and admired her, but also because it was her own wish. " If ever my life comes to be written," she wrote to me, " I would rather you did it than anyone. Your knowledge is not mugged up out of books, but comes from our having worked together, and been in tight places together." She underlined the IF, thinking there was nothing, apart from her cause, which would be worth the telling ; but in that she was wrong. I shall always be proud to remember that it was with her approval that I have had the task of recording her example for the generation which follows her.

In the preparation of this book I have been helped by a very great number of Dame Millicent's friends, and it is not easy to express my sense of what I owe them. I have to thank her daughter, Miss Philippa Fawcett, for full access to all the letters and papers, and also for her own personal co-operation. Also Dame Millicent's friend, Dr. Jane Walker, who has not only let me see a great many letters which are in her possession, but has discussed this book with me in detail. I had hoped to include a Preface by her in this volume ; but I am glad to know that instead Dr. Walker is writing the fuller story of her friendship with Dame Millicent, which is to be published as a separate book at a later date.

There are forty-seven other people who have kindly allowed me to use extracts from letters or photographs in their possession, or who have told me anecdotes of Dame Millicent. I wish to thank them all, and particularly the late Lady Frances Balfour, Miss B. A. Clough, Mr. J. F. Dryhurst, Miss Gwen John, Miss Lucas, Mrs. Marson, Miss Merrifield, Miss Edith Miller, Mrs. Henry Sidgwick, Miss Frances Sterling, Mrs. Hew Stevenson, Mrs. Cobden Unwin, and Miss H. M. White.

Finally, I want to make special mention of Dame Millicent's fellow workers in the National Union of Women's Suffrage Societies, to whom I have dedicated this book. I know well that she would have wished me to refer to them all individually and by name, but I have not done so. My reason is that they were too numerous, and threatened to destroy the unity of the subject. I cannot exactly apologise for an omission which is deliberate ; but I can, and do, ask them to forgive me.

RAY STRACHEY.

1929–1930.

CONTENTS

CHAPTER I

GIRLHOOD

CHAPTER II

MARRIAGE, 1867

CHAPTER III

POLITICS AND ECONOMICS IN THE 'SEVENTIES

CHAPTER IV

THE WOMEN'S COLLEGES

CHAPTER V

HENRY FAWCETT'S WORK AND DEATH

ix

CHAPTER VI

THE "MAIDEN TRIBUTE"—THE LIBERAL UNIONISTS

CHAPTER VII

ABOVE THE SENIOR WRANGLER, 1890

CHAPTER VIII

WOMEN'S SUFFRAGE IN THE 'NINETIES

CHAPTER IX

THE SOUTH AFRICAN WAR

CHAPTER X

THE SUFFRAGE REVIVAL AND THE MILITANTS

CHAPTER XI

THE STRUGGLE WITH THE LIBERAL PARTY

CHAPTER XII

THE EUROPEAN WAR

CHAPTER XIII

THE SUFFRAGE VICTORY, 1918

CHAPTER XIV

STANDING AND STARING

CHAPTER XV

THE FINAL VICTORY, 1928, AND DEATH

LIST OF ILLUSTRATIONS

CHAPTER I

GIRLHOOD

Mr. and Mrs. Newson Garrett—Aldeburgh in the 'sixties—The school at Blackheath—Elizabeth's efforts to become a doctor—Early influences—Music—John Stuart Mill's election meeting.

THE Eastern Counties, with their low-lying fields, their tidal estuaries and their gorse-grown commons, are not typical of the whole of England ; but the people who live in Essex, Suffolk and Norfolk are English through and through. Radical of thought, positive of speech, but cautious and empirical in action, honest, kindly, shrewd, humorous, and deeply, if secretly, imaginative, these Anglo-Saxons have lived the same quiet life for generations past. They have fished their shallow, stormy seas and tilled their rich lands and prayed to God in their windswept flint churches without much change or discontent. They have bred their scholars and their eccentrics, their learned divines, their hunting squires, their merchants, their fishermen and their yeomen ; and they have been proud of them all. There, perhaps more than in any other part of the country, the people have clung obstinately to their ancient liberties and preserved their civic rights. It was from the Eastern Counties that Oliver Cromwell drew the thousand " men of religion " who formed his famous troop, and that region was his stronghold. Later on, it was in Ipswich, Colchester and Norwich that the Quakers and Unitarians congregated, when the days of toleration came, and something of the Puritan hatred of emotion went deep into the habits of the people. Independence was as dear to them as loyalty ; and England stood for both.

Into this atmosphere and among these people Millicent

Garrett was born in 1847. Her parents, and their parents before them, were of East Anglian stock, in and about Snape, Saxmundham and Aldeburgh. Her father was a merchant and shipowner, building his own ships and brewing his own malt, and sending his sailing vessels from the dangerous little harbour of Aldeburgh up and down the coast with the produce of the farms and markets. An active and enterprising man, Newson Garrett stood out prominently in all the affairs of the countryside. Brave, even to rashness, vehement, quarrelsome, and full of fun, he was foremost in everything practical or political which was afoot. If there were wrecks, as there often were on the treacherous sands at the river mouth, he was out in the surf with the rescue parties ; if there was a new railway to be laid, a new Mayor to be elected or a new house to be built, Mr. Garrett was in the thick of it all ; and his ten children, as they grew up, became intimately familiar with the realities of Suffolk life. To them business undertakings and civic responsibility were real and tangible things, known at first hand. They saw for themselves the connections of trade, agriculture and the perils of the sea ; they knew the ways and speech of simple people. And this knowledge was their inheritance.

Millicent Garrett had four elder and one younger sisters, and two elder and two younger brothers, those closest to her in age being her sister Agnes and her brother Sam. Among this large family there was always stir and movement and much laughing ; there were riding expeditions, when a whole cavalcade went out on Shetland ponies with their father, or adventurous drives with him across-country, regardless of roads or dykes. There were boating parties on the Alde and skating on the flooded meadows, and now and then there were dances and Christmas parties, when the house would be overflowing with guests and the whole place would ring with merriment.

Mrs. Garrett, to whom fell the management of all this big household, was an extremely orderly and methodical woman, who had every department of her work thoroughly under her own control.

" If such things had come her way," her daughter wrote, " she would have proved a very capable organiser of a big business. But the management of her house and her correspondence with her ten children completely absorbed and satisfied her. She used to say with a happy smile, ' The lines have fallen to me in pleasant places, yea, I have a goodly heritage.' " Her occupations were, indeed, her household and her family, and she loved both them and the work they gave her ; but her interests were not theirs. Even from her husband, whom she admired devotedly, she differed profoundly in outlook as well as temperament. The real personal interest of her life lay, not in politics, or enterprise, or business, or strife, but in religion ; and though she was inevitably involved in all sorts of new activities by her enterprising husband and her sons and daughters, it was sorely against her inclinations. She only took part in these things for their sakes ; for herself what absorbed her thoughts was her faith, and its implications ; and prayer and the practice of holiness were, for her, the true objects of human life.

The Garrett family lived in two houses during the years when Milly was a child : one of these was Alde House, in Aldeburgh, and the other was at Snape, few miles up the river. In this tiny village, which consisted of nothing more than a few cottages, the ol stone bridge, the fifteenth-century church and the b red brick granaries of Mr. Garrett's maltings, he ha built himself a large one-storey house. Here the fami lived from October to May, to be nearer to the busine and to the markets, but in summer they moved ba to the more sociable surroundings of the little seasi town. They knew, of course, all their neighbou from the county magnates to the country folk ; l

2

it was among the latter that the children made their grown-up friends. James Cable, the hero of the life-boats, Mrs. Barham, the gardener's wife, and Mary Reeder, the pensioner, were the figures on their stage, and strong, individual figures they were, " characters " in the full sense of the word, whose sayings and doings afforded perennial amusement as well as serious reflection to Millicent and her brothers and sisters. In the reminiscences which she wrote sixty years later, these people are vividly described, and the anecdotes she remembered about them show clearly both their virtues and the force and importance of their example. Modest, determined and independent these stories show them to have been ; blunt of speech and with an element of that quiet East Anglian humour which was so strong in Milly herself—that quiet, ruminating humour which depends not on wit or brilliance, but on a constant observation of the oddities of human character, and its contacts with life.

In the early years of Victoria's reign, life in a little town was absurdly cramped and tied up in the bonds of rigid convention. Newson Garrett indeed broke through everything of the sort, but his children well knew that they existed. Millicent herself has left a picture of the social life of the Aldeburgh of her child-hood in her novel, *Janet Doncaster*. In this book, Norborough, with its narrow little social sets, its depressed gentlewomen, its prosperous and its destitute doctor, and its isolation from the great world, is clearly drawn from the life. Her heroine, Janet, is in some ways very like herself, and the great event of her early childhood, as of little Milly's own, was a trip in the lifeboat for practice on a stormy day. " The incident," the novel says, " supplied for a long time the romantic element in Janet's quiet life " ; and no doubt the same was true for little Millicent Garrett. " It made her love the sea more than ever. She imagined herself in storms and shipwrecks. She got hold of the story of

Grace Darling and made it the theme of a splendid fugue of adventure in which, however, the central figure was not Grace Darling. It was a revelation to her one day accidentally to hear that Grace Darling was still living. What a splendid thing it would be, she thought, to live with her in a lighthouse ! And then the theme of the fugue changed, and there were two Grace Darlings rowing a boat to save shipwrecked mariners, lighting the lamps at sunset, or cast alone on a desolate rock— how and why not particularly explained—knowing that if they didn't have a light there would be a ship-wreck during the night, and desperate straits they were put to to make a light first, and then to find fuel to keep it burning."

All children dream such dreams ; but it is pleasant to know that for little Milly, whose life was to be spent in such different fashion, battling with political and not material storms, and striving to keep burning so intellectual a light, they should have taken this rough and primitive form. And it is pleasant to realise that through all her life in towns, and her labours on dusty platforms and in committee rooms, she kept her love of strong winds and high waves and the rough salt sea. For that, too, like her Puritan reserve and her obstinate individualism, was part of her English inheritance.

That such influences were forming her opinions and her outlook was of course unknown to the child. " To show what a queer little creature I was," the reminiscences say, " I may mention that I remember thinking on my tenth birthday that I had now reached the prime of life, and that henceforward I must expect a descent towards the sere and yellow leaf of old age." This tenth birthday was in 1857 ; but six months later her decline was cheered by the tremendous event of her first visit to London to stay with her eldest sister Louie. Louisa Garrett had married James Smith not long after that tenth birthday of Milly's, and now her father, with Milly and Agnes, went up to see her in her new home. The nearest railway was then at Ipswich, so the journey began with a drive of twenty-six miles in their own carriage, after which came the wonders of the iron road. And then came London, " a sort of fairyland " with the lighted shop windows, and an " evening entertainment," and other glories which were new to the two little girls. No doubt all this set another fugue running in Milly's head, which somewhat drove out, for the time at least, Grace Darling and the shipwrecked mariners.

It must have been about this same time that the real interests of Millicent's life began to open before her, chiefly through the influence of her sister Elizabeth. The three elder girls, Louie, Elizabeth and Alice, had been sent for a year or two each to a school at Blackheath kept by a Miss Browning, who was an aunt of Robert Browning the poet. Louie was thirteen and Lizzie eleven years older than Milly, so that their school days were over well before she reached her childish prime, and Lizzie was a young lady of twenty-one when Louie was married and when the visit to London took place. The whole family was closely united, and what the elder girls were thinking was shared with their parents, and even with the little ones ; and after this great experience Agnes and Milly were able to begin to understand and appreciate what was going on.

The Blackheath school was evidently quite unlike the usual girls' schools of the day, and Louie and Elizabeth and, later on, Alice and the others came away from it not so much with knowledge (for they all left before they were sixteen) as with quickened intellectual interests. They were not taught " accomplishments " nor provided with superficial information. Instead, Literature, Art and Music were turned into real living excitements, and in the Garrett household there was much talk of them, and much reading of

poetry, essays and the like. These were Louie's chief
interests, but what appealed even more to Elizabeth,
as to her father, was politics. The stirring affairs of
the world of the 'fifties were what they thought of—the
Crimean War, the troubles in France, the Indian Mutiny,
and the ups and downs of the Government at home.
Mr. Garrett at that time believed himself (quite
erroneously) to be a Conservative, and he swept his
whole family along in the controversies of the time.
One of Milly's earliest recollections was of a day in
September 1855, when her father came in " at break-
fast time with a newspaper in his hand, looking gay
and handsome, and calling out to all his little brood,
' Heads up and shoulders down. Sebastopol is taken ! ' "
And even those who were too young to understand what
war could be, or why it should be fought, were forced
to realise that something happening far away at the
other end of Europe was important to them, and somehow, obscurely, a cause for rejoicing.

This sort of thing found a special response in Milly's
awakening mind, and a year or two later, when Elizabeth was the eldest daughter at home, this impression deepened. For Elizabeth brought all the younger
children into close touch with her own thoughts. She
became " the leader and friend of the younger half of
the family," and her sister " loved to remember her
deep fund of natural human affection and almost
maternal feeling towards us." " One of Elizabeth's
inventions for our benefit," the reminiscences say,
" was what she called TALKS ON THINGS IN GENERAL,
which took place on Sunday evenings. I can see her
now on the sofa in the Alde House drawing-room :
George, our youngest brother, on her lap, and the rest
of us grouped round her while she talked on just what
was uppermost in her own mind at the time—Garibaldi
and the freeing of Italy from the Austrians, Carlyle's
Cromwell, Macaulay's *History of England*, and modern
political events and persons, such as Lord Palmerston

and the chances of a Reform Bill, Louis Napoleon and the Haynau incident, etc., etc. I remember taking the most lively interest in the 1857 campaign in Italy against the Austrians, when the French joined forces with the King of Sardinia. From that time Garibaldi, Cavour and Victor Emmanuel became my heroes, and I tried to learn all that I could about them." There is little doubt that Florence Nightingale, too, figured in these talks, and probably she jostled Grace Darling somewhat in Milly's secret imagination.

All this was new and delightful ; but Elizabeth added to it another more direct and immediate interest, and one which appealed irresistibly to her sister, and that was the startling novelty of the idea of women's rights. In the Garrett family, indeed, the question did not present itself in the form of any acute grievance. The girls were not made to feel themselves inferior—they rode and talked with their father as the boys did, and were not discouraged from thinking ; but in spite of this there was no idea of settling them in life in any other way than by marriage, and Elizabeth did not feel quite satisfied with the prospect. Louie had married and had gone to London, and presently Alice married and went to India, but Elizabeth's energies were not satisfied with the duties of a daughter at home. She liked and admired her brothers-in-law, but she thought there might be something more to be made of life over and above the pleasures and duties of being a wife, and from 1851, when she left school, to 1860, when she left home, she pondered the matter in her mind.

The Blackheath school had brought Elizabeth more than stimulus to education, it had brought her friends ; and it was through these friends that a definite direction was given to her vague aspirations. On one of the visits which she and Louie paid to their schoolfellows, Sophie and Annie Crowe, at Usworth, near Durham, they met Emily Davies, the only daughter of the Rector of Gateshead. Emily Davies was six years older than Elizabeth, and at the time when they first met she had already formed very positive and coherent views as to what was the important thing to be done in the world, and she soon swept Elizabeth along with her in the same course. The five girls who were there at Usworth together were all between the ages of fifteen and twenty-one ; they knew nothing of the world or of the difficulties of reform ; and they talked, of course, of everything in heaven and earth, but mostly of themselves and what they were to do in life. It was easy for Emily to show them that the whole of their social and political position, as young ladies, was fundamentally and flagrantly wrong, and from that starting-point it was easy and delightful to plan out how it was all to be remedied. So far as any of them knew, they were alone in this opinion of the universe. None of them had as yet come in contact with any of the others who at that date were criticising the position of women. All they had to go by was the circumstance of their own lives and the limited range of things they had personally encountered. But that was quite enough to establish the position, and all five of them agreed that the structure of society must be reformed from top to bottom. All five agreed, but to Emily and Elizabeth this agreement meant action ; and these two became firm and congenial friends in their determination. Both of them dedicated themselves and all their powers to this cause, both of them burned with enthusiasm to be at work, and both were made of the hard enduring stuff which pioneering requires.

For all their eagerness and their certainty of aim, it was not easy to see how they could begin. They were young and inexperienced, without money or influential friends ; they were both daughters at home, with family claims and domestic duties, and the whole world was against them. But none of these things really mattered. They were earnest, and they were right ; and though they had to be patient for a few years their chance was coming, and the life's work which they planned out in their girlhood awaited them.

Emily Davies was Elizabeth's friend, but the younger children did not like her. She came many times to stay at Alde House, but the children dreaded her visits. She was too positive and rational, too severe and dry. She snubbed Agnes and Milly and Sam unmercifully, took their beloved Lizzie away from them, or talked over their heads, and they were glad when she went away. But her ideas were another matter. Transmuted through Lizzie's voice, they became the most natural and obvious things, so that the children grew up with them and found them simple and inevitable. Slavery was wrong, liberty was desirable, and the position of women must be changed ; there was no question about these doctrines in their minds.

All this was happening while Milly was a small child. She grew up to the great age of twelve and went away in her turn to the school at Blackheath before the way opened out for Elizabeth ; but then everything came with a rush. In 1859 Elizabeth went up for one of her precious visits to her sister Louie. Perhaps it was the same visit when she took Agnes and Milly to school —" in lovely sky-blue silk dresses "—as a schoolfellow remembered sixty years later, " when they told us you were both so very clever."

Emily Davies was in London then, just back from a winter in Algiers with her brother Henry, and she and Elizabeth met constantly. In Algiers Emily had made the acquaintance of Barbara Bodichon, and through her the two girls were now introduced to the group of feminists which—though they had not known it—had already been in existence for four years. They went together to the little office in Langham Place, where Isa Craig and Adelaide Ann Procter and Jessie Boucherett and Bessie Rayner Parkes were boldly carrying on the

Women's Employment Bureau ; they read with rapture
the back numbers of the *Englishwoman's Journal*
(which had been started two years before), and they
talked, endlessly and happily, with the congenial
spirits whom they had found. They learnt all about
the unsuccessful effort which had been made four years
earlier to secure a Married Women's Property Bill,
they came in contact with the Social Science Association ; and at last the world opened out before them.
Emily, with her characteristic caution, was afraid some
of these new friends of theirs were going ahead too fast,
but Elizabeth had no qualms. It was so refreshing
to be up and at work ; and her only trouble was which
aspect of the cause to select for her own onslaught.

And then, just at this moment, a new revelation came
her way, and in a few hours the decision was made.
For she met Dr. Elizabeth Blackwell. This lady,
who had qualified as a medical practitioner in the
United States, came to settle in London, and succeeded
in getting her name inscribed upon the British Medical
Register in this same year, 1859; and, of course, like
Emily Davies and Elizabeth Garrett, she gravitated to
Langham Place and found friends and supporters there.
They were all thrilled and inspired by her achievement
and the possibilities it opened out, and among them
they decided that the time was ripe for some public
lectures upon the suitability of the medical profession
for women. On March 2nd, 1859, the first of these
lectures was given in the Marylebone Hall. " My good
friends, the Misses Leigh Smith," Dr. Blackwell wrote
in her autobiography, " supported by their generous-
hearted father and Miss Bessie Rayner Parkes, interested
themselves actively. . . . Our young friends brought
up primroses and other lovely flowers and green wreaths
from Hastings to ornament the reading desk, and
warmly supported me by their ardent sympathy. . . .
I well remember the tears rolling down the benevolent
face of Miss Anna Goldsmid, who sat immediately in

front of me. But the most important listener was the
bright intelligent young lady whose interest in the
study of medicine was then aroused—Miss Elizabeth
Garrett."

It is easy to imagine the talks which Elizabeth and
Emily must had have after this momentous lecture ;
they went, at once no doubt, to see Dr. Blackwell,
they collected what information they could about the
actual legal possibilities, and they went over the chances
of failure. They must have considered, too, the bearing
of the enterprise on the whole cause, and satisfied
themselves that it was the right direction in which to
make a move. Emily herself was determined to begin
with the problem of education, since that lay at the
root of it all ; but health was fundamental too, and
what might not women doctors do directly through
their profession, as well as indirectly through their
existence ! The idea was exactly what they had been
waiting for, and Elizabeth fairly jumped at it. At last
she knew what to be at ; and nothing in heaven or
earth would stop her.

Elizabeth needed every scrap of her determination,
for the task in front of her was truly formidable. Not
only did it mean submitting herself to a discipline and
a course of study which might, for all she knew, be
beyond her powers, but it also meant flying in the face
of all the conventions and outraging all the proprieties.
Except to the very few of the elect she would henceforth be an outcast—and, what was perhaps worse, a
figure of fun ; and it was well that she knew she could
count on support in her own home circle. Even here
it was not all smooth, however, for her mother was
wholly unsympathetic. She had no interest in the great
cause, and grieved terribly over Elizabeth's decision.
She could not feel that such a course of action was
anything but a disgrace to the whole family, and she
shrank almost with agony from the notoriety and the
criticism which it involved. But Elizabeth's father

was different. Not only did he share his daughter's
view about the position of women in general, but he
also loved a real stand-up fight. He was ready to back
her therefore in every way against prejudice at home
and against enemies abroad. When she needed him
he was ready to come to London to help her to interview doctors or University authorities, and he loved
to share with her the humours and the indignations of
the campaign. He found her the money and the moral
support she needed, and stood out, with her, against
the discouragement of the difficult start. Sometimes,
indeed, he wavered. " I don't think I can go on with
it," he would burst out to the other children, " it will
kill your mother." But then another setback from
the outside would come, and he would rush back again
into the fray.

Neither Elizabeth nor her father knew, when they
first took up the project, how tremendous the opposition
would be. They could in some degree measure the
intangible difficulties, the social prejudices and the
ridicule ; but what they did not know, and had to learn
by experience, was the weight of the practical legal
obstruction and the bitter enmity of a wealthy vested
interest. These things, however, were soon apparent.
For six years Elizabeth tried in every conceivable way
to find an opening into her chosen profession, going
from one to another, from hospitals to examining bodies,
from professors to lawyers, learning what she could
here and there, and growing more and more determined
every year ; and at last, in 1865, she found a crack by
which to enter in, and, through the discredited Apothe-
caries' Licence, she got her name safely and legally
inscribed on the British Medical Register.

The tale of these early struggles belongs to Elizabeth's
life, and not to her sister's. But it is important to
remember that all through Milly's schooldays, and
through the young lady period which followed, this
adventure was going on. It lit and kept burning

Millicent's enthusiasm for a cause which might without it have seemed too natural and straightforward to deserve much attention ; and it made her familiar, from the very first, with the dragons which were to stand in her own path.

But the fight for medical education was not Milly's. Although she followed every stage of it with intense interest, and sympathised with every move, she was mainly busy, in the years when it was going on, with her own intellectual development and with the difficult and absorbing task of growing up.

There is no record of what Milly was like at school. Her sister Alice had been a prodigy at mathematics, but no such pre-eminence is recorded of Milly, and her own reminiscences seem to show that she was more interested in what she was learning out of school than in her actual lessons. There were occasional week-ends with her dear sister Louie, who lived in Manchester Square ; and from that centre all sorts of new joys were provided for the young sister. " On these week-end visits Louie and her husband usually took me to some fascinating entertainment on Saturday afternoon or evening, and on Sunday to hear the Rev. F. D. Maurice preach at St. Peter's, Vere Street." . . . " I hold myself fortunate to have heard Maurice repeatedly at a time when my own mind was in process of formation. He had the voice, the look, the inspiration of a prophet ; and spiritual things were to him the greatest realities of the universe. . . . He awakened in me new thoughts and, I hope, partially at all events, new reverences."

Until this time the religious influences of Millicent's life had not been very greatly heeded. Her mother was indeed of a profoundly religious temperament, but she was strictly evangelical, and a rigid Sabbatarian ; and though her children, of course, conformed to her standard, they did not appreciate much beyond the strictness and dullness of the outward form, and they hardened their little hearts and closed their little ears, so that her words flowed over them like water. Now, however, this attitude changed. Under the influence of Maurice, and the more liberal tone of the people Louie knew, Millicent began to think seriously of the problems of life and death, of belief and human conduct. She began to read poetry, looking only, as young people do, for the meaning and the inspiration, and she began to think and dream. Dogmatic belief had no attraction for her, but goodness, that was the real thing ! Tolerance, kindness and honest practical effort, with the pure spiritual impulse behind them, these were the things she reverenced ; and it was in these terms, from the very first, that she interpreted righteousness.

But Millicent was still very young. Real and lasting as the influence of Maurice was, there were many other things to be attended to. There were friends, for example, such as her own special sister Agnes, and her cousin Rhoda, who came to the school while she was still there ; and there were all the daily happenings of life. There is no doubt that Milly was popular at school ; one of her companions recalled, after sixty years, how kind she used to be to shy little new-comers, and they all joined together to give her a parting present when she was, rather suddenly and unexpectedly, sent for to come home.

This abrupt ending to her schooldays, which came when Milly was fifteen, was due to some temporary financial stringency in the family, which, however, did not last very long, and seems to have made no other difference in their way of living. Even in this most advanced family the education of the girls was the first and not the last thing to be economised ; but as it turned out Milly did not suffer from the change.

" I was bitterly sorry to leave school," the reminiscences say, " but my parents were very good in making it up to me as well as they could by allowing me undisturbed use of our old schoolroom for reading and study in the morning. . . . So I did not regard myself as a martyr, though I did miss the good teaching I had had at Blackheath. I had a little bedroom to myself, and there I stored my favourite books."

A room of one's own, in the 'sixties, was a thing very few young ladies had, and as to the undisturbed mornings, they were unparalleled. But Mrs. Garrett, even if she did not sympathise with the women's movement, did sympathise with her daughters ; and so Milly's desire to go on studying was respected.

But now, for all the uninterrupted mornings, young ladyhood began for Milly. Agnes, who was two years older, had come home from school before, and the two sisters were always together. They took turns in reading aloud Mill or Buckle, or whatever was the serious book of the moment, and they vied with each other in learning Browning by heart. They went off on picnics and expeditions, too, and there was one exciting day when Milly came upon *Swift's Journal to Stella* in an inn parlour, and persuaded the innkeeper to let her buy it from him. Life was full of interest for these sisters, and besides interest there were all the gaieties and sociabilities proper to their age. There were plenty of dances, which they loved, and of course the riding and the boating or skating which they had enjoyed as children. And now, too, there was music. Their father's shipbuilding business was extending, and he brought a Mr. Metcalfe, from the Tyne, to help him. " He it was," the reminiscences say, " who introduced us to the great world of music—Bach, Mozart and Handel. He was less enthusiastic about Beethoven ; and Wagner, I think, he had never heard of. Mozart was the god of his idolatry, and Spohr. I can hear now my sister Agnes singing Spohr's ' Who calls the Hunter to the Wood ? ' with the piano accompaniment in Mrs. Metcalfe's rather inadequate hands, Mr. Metcalfe playing the horn obligato, taking the horn from his lips from time to time to say to his wife quite good-naturedly, ' What a fool you are, my dear ! ' He

MILLICENT AND AGNES GARRETT.
Aged 16 and 18.

opened a new world of music for us, and gave us a
perennial spring of consolation, hope and endurance
which has never failed us." As with poetry, so with
music : it was in terms of human and, so to speak,
moral emotion that Millicent appreciated the arts.
She wished to find, and did find, strength and courage
in lovely sounds ; but there is no doubt that she found
sheer æsthetic pleasure too. For Milly was very
musical, and though she did not play any instrument,
or sing, as Agnes did, she carried the sounds about in her
head, and was seldom without a private orchestra of
her own, playing away in secret. From this time she
added London concerts to the splendid things she got
from her visits to Louie, and then, and all through her
life, she derived much happiness from listening to music.

With all her varied pleasures, and with the serious
self-improvement which still went on in the uninterrupted mornings, and the long Sunday afternoons when
she read Shakespeare in her bedroom—so as not to
distress her mother's Sabbatarian conscience—Milly
did not lose sight of the women's movement. Elizabeth's struggle was at its height, and Emily Davies
was just succeeding in opening the Cambridge Local
Examination to girls ; and all the ins and outs of these
campaigns were discussed, raged at or laughed over
at Manchester Square and Alde House. At this time,
too, a little incident happened to Milly herself, which
broke through, as little incidents sometimes do, the
outer shell of her defences and made her realise the
depth and strength of her feelings. It was at a time
when there was a ball at Alde House, and the place
was packed with gay young people, intent on enjoyment—" three in a bedroom with a fire," as she described it, " and two of our guests and myself sitting
over it before dressing for the dance. I was by far
the youngest of the three. My two companions were
talking, and presently took up the subject of the failure
of a recent marriage in our immediate circle. The

young husband and wife were estranged, and no one exactly knew the reason why; after pursuing this interesting theme for some time, one said to the other, ' I cannot see what she has to complain of. Look how he dresses her!' I fumed inwardly, but said nothing. I thought I would like to try to make that sort of talk impossible. I kept on thinking about it, and the degradation of it, which seemed to be accepted by my companions as a matter of course. I did not know anything at that time about ' kept women,' but ' Look how he dresses her ' was of its essence.''

Millicent was a young woman of determination, and the things she '' kept on thinking about '' included not only the intolerable position but the problem of how it was to be remedied ; and about this same time John Stuart Mill showed her the way. It was in 1865, when Milly was nearly eighteen, that he received an invitation to stand for Parliament for the City of Westminster, and Louie and all the Langham Place circle were active in his campaign. He had expressed clearly in his election address his strong approval of Women's Suffrage, and this action really brought the subject for the first time into the political world. Milly, who was in London staying with her sister, was taken to one of his meetings, and it made a lifelong impression upon her.

'' The room where the meeting was held,'' she wrote in her reminiscences, '' was not large, but it was densely crowded. I do not remember Mill's speech, but I do remember the impression made by his delicate, sensitive physique, united as it was with a very unusual degree of moral courage. I also remember very distinctly that when the heckling began a man rose in the audience and said he had a question to ask. He then proceeded to read a passage from a book in his hand, in which the statement was made that the characteristic fault of the British working man was untruthfulness. The heckler then personally addressed Mr. Mill and said ' The question I wish to ask is, Did you write this ? ' Mill instantly rose and simply said ' I did,' and sat down again. The effect was instantaneous and electrical. The meeting cheered itself hoarse. Mill's candour and directness were such a delightful contrast to the usual shiftiness of Parliamentary candidates. His personality added to the effect he produced ; and I heard it stated afterwards that those two words ' I did ' won him the election." . . . " This meeting," she added, " kindled tenfold my enthusiasm for women's suffrage."

It was not only women's suffrage which excited Milly's enthusiasm at this time, however. All the political questions of the day were tremendously alive and important to her. She read and accepted Mill's philosophy, and shared the hopes and beliefs of the Radicals, and followed with intense interest the progress of the American Civil War, being herself, of course, an ardent Northerner. The progress of public events, and the principles which ought to underlie public action were, for her, the things which really mattered, and she felt that it was among these problems that her lifework lay. Philanthropy, which absorbed the attention of so many able and vigorous women at that time, had little appeal for her. It was but a patching up at the best. Art, literature, music—these were delightful and uplifting ; but they were not the real thing. It was the structure of the State, the principles of human government, and the adjustment of man to society which seemed important ; and every year, as she grew older, her mind turned more and more to these subjects.

There was something very simple and direct in her way of looking at life, and everything she did chimed in with it. Goodness—industry—self-control—all these blended together for her into an ideal which it seemed natural and obvious to seek after in every action of life, and which she assumed, as a matter of course, must be equally sought after by everyone else.

3

And so, with these interests and that background, Millicent Garrett grew up. Serene, self-contained and thoughtful, with intense vitality and perfect health and an irrepressible sense of fun, she approached her eighteenth birthday. The whole world was before her, but she knew what she wanted from it—and that was a chance to do her share, in her own day and generation, for the political enfranchisement of her own sex.

CHAPTER II

MARRIAGE, 1867

Party at Aubrey House—Henry Fawcett—The engagement—Marriage
—Friends at Cambridge—Life in London—Birth of Philippa.

ON the night when the news of the assassination of
Lincoln reached London, in May 1865, Milly and her
sister were invited to a party at Aubrey House, Campden
Hill. This was the home of Mr. and Mrs. Peter Taylor,
and it was one of those places where the Radicals and
Reformers of the day were accustomed to meet. Mr.
Taylor was a Member of Parliament, and Henry Fawcett,
who had just become Member for Brighton, was one of
his friends. Milly, like all their circle, knew of Henry
Fawcett, and of the splendid way in which he faced his
blindness. She knew that everyone liked him, and
she was ready to admire him to the full. But until
that night she had never seen him. When she and her
party arrived there was already an excited buzz of
conversation about the tragedy of Lincoln's death,
and Milly joined in it at once, expressing without
hesitation what she felt, and speaking with characteristic earnestness and decision. She said that the
loss of Lincoln was the greatest misfortune which could
have befallen the world from the death of any one man,
and when challenged to particularise, she added that
it was " greater than the loss of any of the crowned
heads in Europe." " There was nothing but what
was obvious in this," she comments in her reminiscences ; but it did not seem so to the blind man who
was then hearing her voice for the first time. He
decided then and there that he must know more of the
young lady who had spoken these words, and immedi-

ately asked Mrs. Taylor to introduce them. What
else they said that night is nowhere recorded, but
before the evening was over Henry Fawcett had fallen
in love with Millicent Garrett, and henceforward took
every possible opportunity of being in her company.

Henry Fawcett was at that time thirty-two years
old, and he had been blind for eight years. He was
the son of Mr. William Fawcett of Salisbury, a man
who had made his own way in the world, and who had
begun life as assistant to a draper, had then set up in
business for himself and prospered, and had been
elected Mayor of Salisbury in 1832. He was an ardent
Liberal politician and a man of splendid health and
strong physical and mental energy, greatly respected
and beloved in the town.

Henry was his second son ; and very early in life
the boy had realised in what direction his interests lay,
and had marked out for himself the career which he
intended to follow, and the course of preparation which
seemed most fitting. From his schooldays he had
devoted himself to hard and serious study, with the
intention of understanding political and economic
problems and of entering Parliament later on ; and
when he went on to Cambridge with a scholarship he
still followed the same course. He was eighth wrangler
in 1855, and held a Fellowship at Trinity Hall ; and
it was when he had reached this point in his steady
progress that his terrible misfortune befell him. He
was out shooting near Salisbury in the autumn of 1858
when an accidental shot from his father's gun struck
him, and from that moment he did not see the light
again. He was not otherwise hurt, but it seemed as
if his whole career must be cut short, and his life ruined ;
and his father's agony of distress can be imagined.
But the son was not to be daunted. Almost as soon
as he realised what had happened, and long before he
was sure that all hope had gone, he made up his mind
that he would prove to his father that the accident had

neither ruined nor even altered his life. He determined to go straight on, just as if he could still see,
neither changing his occupations nor abating his enjoyments, and living neither as a hero nor as a martyr,
but as himself, just as he had been before.

He was not given to speaking of this calamity in
later life, and indeed gave the impression of thinking
less of it than his companions ; but he once told a
friend, in a single sentence, the whole history of that
time. " Morgan," he said, " it took me one night to
decide whether the loss of my sight should make any
difference in my life or not ; I decided it should not."
That was all. Just as simply as he described it, so he
seemed to do it, and the courage and strength of purpose
which this decision showed did not fail him all his life
long.

Henry Fawcett was, as can be seen, a resolute man,
with a strong will and serious convictions, and a liking
for dry and difficult subjects. But these qualities by
no means make up a complete picture of the man.
For he was also the most genial and most expansive
of companions, genuinely interested in every detail of
the concerns of his friends, always ready to be sociable,
and exceedingly fond of gossip, jokes and good stories.
He was very popular at Cambridge, both before and
after his blindness, and he had a host of intimate friends,
of whom Leslie Stephen was among the closest, who
all saved up their best stories and their happiest jokes
for his benefit, and enjoyed them over again to the
accompaniment of his ringing laugh. He was a very
tall, large man, with a liking for a great deal of exercise
which he took both on the river and by immense long
tramps over the countryside ; and he was so wedded
to this pastime that Leslie Stephen declared that he
was inclined to measure a man's moral excellence by
his love of walking.

In 1860, five years before he met Millicent Garrett,
he unsuccessfully contested Southwark as an unofficial

Radical candidate, and in 1863 he had done the same
thing in Cambridge itself, but in spite of this unorthodox
proceeding, he was in the same year elected Professor
of Political Economy, a position which he continued
to hold until his death.   In the following year he stood
again for Parliament, this time for Brighton, and it
was to a meeting summoned by the local Liberal
Selection Committee that he made what was almost
his only public reference to his blindness.   The following account of his speech is taken from Leslie Stephen's
Life of Henry Fawcett :

" Then Fawcett came forward, and won probably
the greatest oratorical triumph of his life. He began
amidst great interruption ; but after a few sentences,
says the reporter in a hostile paper, the vast body of
electors ' listened with breathless attention.' You
could have heard a pin drop, as a hearer told me.
Fawcett began by pointing out that the committee
was appointed not to decide but to recommend, and
that it was pledged to give the candidates an opportunity of speaking to the electors—a matter of the
most critical importance in his case. And then he told
them his story. ' You do not know me now,' he said,
' but you shall know me in the course of a few minutes.'
He proceeded with the account of his accident, during
which, says the reporter, ' a deep feeling of pity and
sympathy seemed to pervade the meeting.' He told
them how he had been blinded by two stray shots
' from a companion's gun ' ; how the lovely landscape
had been instantly blotted out ; and how he knew that
every lovely scene would be henceforth ' shrouded in
impenetrable gloom.' ' It was a blow to a man,' he
said simply ; but in ten minutes he had made up his
mind to face the difficulty bravely. He would never
ask for sympathy, but he demanded to be treated as
an equal. He went on with the story of his previous
attempts to enter Parliament, and ended with a profession of his political principles. I do not think that

Fawcett ever again referred to his accident in public, except in speaking to fellow sufferers. His blindness was apparently being made an insuperable obstacle, his best and most natural answer was to tell the plain story of his struggle, and he told it with a straightforward manliness which completely overpowered the audience."

These words not only touched but convinced his hearers that it was possible for him to be a Member of Parliament, and he was officially adopted as the candidate, though, of course, there were still some who had misgivings. However, a band of his Cambridge friends then came upon the scene, and the energetic and novel electioneering methods of these young men, combined with the increasing respect which the candidate himself was winning, were enough to make his ultimate success certain, and though defeated at the by-election, he was triumphantly returned in 1865. At thirty-two years old, therefore, Henry Fawcett had realised his early ambition, and had brought himself to the place where he believed his talents and his energies could best serve his country.

As soon as he got into Parliament Henry Fawcett joined himself to the group of Radicals of whom John Stuart Mill was the leader, and with them he criticised, while in the main he supported the Liberal Government. And the first subjects to which he devoted his attention were education, land tenure, and the position of agricultural labourers in England, Ireland and India.

This is not the place to give details of his political career ; but its main outline is important, for it was a community of tastes and a similarity of outlook which first drew Henry Fawcett and Millicent Garrett together. And though, of course, a great deal more was presently added, that congeniality remained, and was a source of deep happiness all through their married life.

It was eighteen months after their first meeting that these two became engaged. In that interval Harry had made friends with Louie and her husband, and had succeeded in being with Milly herself several times ; but it was not until he had the opportunity of meeting Mr. Garrett, at one of the gatherings of the British Association, that he made real progress. Mr. Garrett liked him at sight, and asked him to come down to Alde House for a few days' visit. It is reported that someone warned him, " If you invite Fawcett to stay with you he will want to marry Milly," and that he answered, " Stuff and nonsense." But it was a true warning, for it was there, in October 1866, that he and Milly became engaged.

Milly was very deeply in love, but she seems to have taken this, and the prospect of marriage, steadily and almost quietly. She knew her own mind, and his, and had no hesitation. His blindness, which was the only possible objection anyone could raise, seemed no objection to her. The simple way in which he took it, and the courageousness of character which this revealed, were part of his worth ; and in the only letter of hers which remains from that time, there is no mention of it at all.

The engagement, curiously enough, was followed by a few weeks of uncertainty. In the 'sixties it was almost impossible, however straightforward a marriage might be, for the preliminaries to be gone through without some obstruction ; and even Mr. Garrett, open-hearted and impetuous as he was, could not reconcile himself to Milly's decision at the first asking. A delay was imposed, and a period of probation ; and it was during this interval that the following letter was written by Milly to her sympathetic eldest sister :

ALDE HOUSE, ALDEBURGH,
October 24, 1866.

" DEAREST LOUIE,—
       " Your letter to Mother this morning was welcome to me as flowers in May, more especially as I have been rather heavily jumped upon by dear old Liz and

ELIZABETH GARRETT, 1866.

MILLICENT GARRETT, 1866.

the parents during the last few days. The jumping, I am happy to say, reached its worst on Sunday, and has since been proceeding much more gently. I had a most awful letter from Lizzie on Sunday morning, and all that day, whenever I was a moment alone with Mother, she would say, ' Dear, I am tormented by the idea that very likely, now he has had a little quiet time to think of what he has done, Mr. Fawcett may heartily regret what has passed ' ; at this point Father, if within hearing, would first grunt and then groan heavily. And then too it seems so long since I had seen Mr. Fawcett and the remembrance of his great and tender love would grow dim, and like Sir Hugh Evans, I had to struggle against ' great inclinations to cry.' On Monday afternoon Mother had a letter from Mr. Fawcett that quite set her doubts at rest on the subject of his repentance, and that quite made me ashamed that she had been able to infect me with her suspicions. The result of Mr. Fawcett's letter was that Mother wrote to him to say that she would be very glad to see him in a week or ten days, and that meantime we might write to each other.

" I think from the tone of Lizzie's letter that she could not have known how much had passed between Mr. Fawcett and myself ; this month of entire separation was instituted and ordained by Father only and for his sole pleasure. I shall be not one whit more bound than I am now when all the world and his wife know of our engagement. I am bound now by truth and love, and nothing but purer truth and deeper love, which I trust may come in after years, can bind me closer. Lizzie also offered to get for me Mme Bodichon's, Miss Crowe's and others' opinions of Mr. Fawcett. I don't know Mme Bodichon—if I did, of course I cannot say what weight her opinions might have with me ; but at present, judging from Dr. Bodichon's appearance, I should say that it was improbable that we should agree in the choice of husbands. Dr. Bodichon is more like a he-hag than anyone else I can recall just at present. I have not written to Lizzie, for I am afraid of vexing her, which I should be dreadfully sorry to do, for I know that it is out of pure love for me and anxiety for my happiness that she wrote as she did. If you

see her before Saturday give her my love, and try to
talk her over, at least so far as to refrain from further
jumping when she comes down here. I really think
she would consider we were throwing ourselves away
' without sufficient cos ' if we married the archangel
Michael with twenty thousand a year. One of Lizzie's
strong points is, by the way, that if I marry Mr. Fawcett,
we shall be miserably and grovellingly poor. I do not
know if she knows what Mr. Fawcett's income is, but
I should say we could live very comfortably on £800 a
year, which he told Father his income from various
sources was. If, as Lizzie says, we have twelve or
fifteen children, I shall become an ' orfus ' seeker ;
but as Mrs. Bloomfield says, ' We must leave that to
the Lord.'

"Mr. and Mrs. Maurice Cowell are staying here now :
he is a *deppitation* from the —— Society, and accordingly
goes about holding forth at the villages round about.
Mother took a party (not including your humble servant)
to the Reading Room to hear him dilate on the advantages of sending moral pocket handkerchiefs to the
Andaman Islanders ; I don't think he was quite so
eloquent on the subject as might have been anticipated,
but his hearers comforted themselves by reflecting that
grace was better than gifts, and that they need not go
to hear him again.

"You will let me hear from you soon."

The letter which Mrs. Garrett had received on the
Monday afternoon, and which so much eased matters
for Milly, was preserved among her treasures. Harry's
inability to write with his own hand must have been,
at that time, especially grievous ; and this letter, which
is written with many abbreviations, was obviously
dictated, in agitation, to a college friend. It is dated
Trinity Hall, October 21, 1866, and runs as follows :

" MY DEAR MRS. GARRETT,—
          "After what I said to you and Mr. Garrett I
consider myself bound for the present, unless I receive
your permission, not to write to M. But I cannot tell
you the comfort which I should receive if you would

send me a line to tell me how she is. I am sure you have too kind a heart to withhold this satisfaction from me. I am most desirous that you should try, as I tried, to place all the disadvantages connected with my blindness in as strong a light as possible before M., but if after doing so you find, as I am convinced you will, that her mind remains unchanged, I do then earnestly entreat you, my dear Mrs. Garrett, to write to me, as this complete separation from her whom I love so intensely is indeed hard to bear. I will leave it entirely to your own discretion to say anything about this letter to Millicent.

"Remember me most kindly to Mr. Garrett, and assuring you that I already feel a warm attachment for every member of your family,

"Believe me to be,

"My dear Mrs. Garrett,

"Yours very sincerely,

"H. F."

The sky was not long in clearing. Louie, who had no doubt long suspected what was coming, sent an immediate answer to Milly's letter.

"MY DEAR DEAR DEAR TROTTY," she said, "(this for the last time, but for this once I must use the old baby name) I am so happy about you. I believe that dear old Lizzie is as wrong as ever she was right in being afraid. And I am quite sure that no one will be more glad than she will to have the results prove it so. I have just been writing to Mr. Fawcett. I only asked him to come and see me, for I couldn't talk when Edward made a necessary third.[1] By the by, Madam, how do YOU manage ? For I suspect that your objection to a discriminating audience is even greater than mine. And that reminds me that I think you ought to come up to London as soon as you can. . . . I cannot tell you how much I should like to have you here, and par conséquence to see a great deal of Mr. Fawcett, and to like him more and more." . . .

---

[1] Edward was Mr. Fawcett's secretary and guide until the time of his marriage.

This visit took place, but there is no record of the exact months. Certainly it was not long before Lizzie's approval was entirely won, and the engagement welcomed on all sides. In less than the stipulated month it was public property, and Leslie Stephen was writing to Miss Thackeray (to whom he was not yet quite engaged) to tell her how " Old Fawcett " poked fun at him from the security of his own happiness, and how important it was that his re-election to the Professorship, which was due in December, should be successfully pulled off. That it was so, an old telegraph form handed in at Cambridge on December 28 bears witness —sent off, no doubt, with a very thankful heart to tell Millicent that one of the various sources of income still stood firm.

There is one other letter from this time which must be quoted, a letter sent to Miss Garrett by one of Fawcett's leading supporters in Brighton, Mr. Willett. In spite of the stilted language and the formality, this letter shows something of the affection which Henry Fawcett inspired, and it shows, too, the tone of thought of the people among whom Millicent was now to live.

" MY DEAR MISS GARRETT," the letter runs, " I hear from Professor Fawcett that there is a probability that his choice of a companion and helpmeet in life may not be rejected, and he writes asking me to address my congratulations to you.

" This must be my excuse for commencing my note to a perfect stranger in so familiar a manner ; and being a stranger to you I naturally feel some little restraint and hesitation in acceding to his request. And indeed to marry a poor blind man would be to many young ladies a source of sympathetic commiseration rather than rejoicing, for I fear that the desire of most ladies is to live an easier life, and by marriage to gain a protector and companion whose position will leave them more free for the claims of Society and amusement, and often thus they ' prevent men leading nobler lives.'

" Now as an old married man I must I fear be rather

a bore in thus stating that I know many enthusiastic and shallow-minded girls would not hesitate to marry a Professor of Political Economy and an M.P. without a thought of how the very responsible duties (which in my friend's case MUST follow or his life MUST be a wreck and disappointment to himself and all his friends) are to be performed.

" And yet from all I hear of you I do sincerely hope and believe that he has met with the rare treasure of a companion whose delight would be in duty, and who has faith to ' bear, hope, endure and believe all things ' from him to whom she gives her heart and hand. And so indeed the congratulations should rather be to him than to you ; but not alone, for I am sure a devoted wife might be most happy with him, warm hearted and full of noble desires and earnest compassion, bracing him up to crush his sad affliction and forgetting himself, determined to use his utmost powers in the cause of his neglected and ignorant countrymen and women and to help forward the ' good time coming.'

" No happier or more contented lot could I desire for either of my own daughters, even had he never been either a professor or an M.P., and therefore in conclusion pray accept my most sincere and earnest and heartfelt congratulations and with them the hope that I and mine are about to gain another true and worthy friend, whom we hope ere long to know personally."

That was, indeed, the way in which Millicent looked at her future married life. There was to be another side to it, too, in which her husband helped her work, which Mr. Willett did not yet realise. But Harry did. And in that understanding, with strong love and confidence, they were married on St. George's Day, 1867.

Millicent's marriage made a great change in her life. From living quietly at Aldeburgh, with occasional glimpses of the excitements of London life, she now lived in the centre of political interest, with occasional holidays in the country. And the change was much to her taste.

The most immediate and intimate expansion of her

life was of course that she now became a member of
her husband's family with a new and ready-made set
of interests and connections in Salisbury. She was
welcomed there with great cordiality, and she formed
with Harry's sister Maria in particular, an intimate and
lifelong friendship which was based on mutual affection
and respect. With his father and mother too she was
on excellent terms ; and years later, long after they
were all dead, Salisbury remained one of the places
she most loved to visit. For all her recollections of it
were coloured by the enjoyments and the happiness of
her early married life.

Besides Harry's family, there were all Harry's friends
for her to learn to know, both in London and at Cambridge. Owing to his Professorship it was necessary
for him to live in Cambridge from October to February
every year, but since Parliament did not at that time
meet in the autumn there was no difficulty in combining
this with his political career. It meant, however,
keeping up two houses, and as their means were not
great, both these establishments were small, and Milly
became, as she said herself, " a dragon over unnecessary
expenditure."

They took, at first, a small house in Bessborough
Gardens, fifteen minutes' walk from the House of
Commons, at the bottom of Vauxhall Bridge Road, and
though it was not very comfortable or commodious,
they lived there for eight years. At Cambridge during
the same period they took such furnished houses as they
could find, and in both places, though they entertained
a good deal, their style of living was very simple. But
it was not the outward circumstances of life which
interested either of them, but rather the things they
were doing and the people they met, and in these they
were very rich.

Very soon after their marriage Prof. Fawcett took
his bride to Cambridge, to the summer meeting
of the Fellows of Trinity Hall. The Long Vacation

was beginning, and the University was not in full swing, but there was enough of its characteristic flavour and oddity to amuse Milly exceedingly. H. A. Morgan, at that time Fellow, and later Master, of Jesus happened to be there, and as he and Fawcett were intimate friends, they met almost daily. Morgan had a tremendous stock of stories characteristic of all their friends and acquaintances, and he was besides an " inimitable mimic " ; and of course his friend set him on to describe Dr. Kennedy, Dr. Bateson, and all the other " characters " to his wife, with the result that she began to know them even before she met them in reality. When therefore in the autumn she had to take her place in Cambridge society, she knew a little what to expect.

The Cambridge of the 'sixties was a quaint and rather comic place, where manners and conventions survived which had long vanished elsewhere. In *What I Remember* Mrs. Fawcett gives many amusing examples of what it was like, glimpses of social absurdities and of odd characters which entertained her greatly at the time, and came back to her memory sixty years later in all their grotesque charm. There were many among the dons to whom the idea of the possible freedom of women was wholly unfamiliar, and Mrs. Fawcett recalled sixty years later how angry this sometimes made her. In one of the speeches she made in 1928, when the victory had been won and the struggle was over, she told of an incident which had made a deep impression on her mind. " About 1867," she said, " in my early married life in Cambridge, I met a friend of my husband's who had just returned from a great International Exhibition in Paris. I asked him to tell me about it, and what were the most interesting things he had seen, but he excused himself from replying to me by saying he had not had time to visit the silk department."

Such encounters were infuriating ; but on the whole

the Fawcetts were not much troubled by reactionary
people nor by the dying University conventions. Their
friends were among the younger men, the reformers
of the day—James Stuart, Henry Sidgwick, J. F.
Moulton, the Peiles and Mr. Sedley Taylor and the
rest. There was plenty of eccentricity among them,
too, and much poking of fun at each other, but there
was none of the ponderous conventionality of the old
régime. Not that there were not unexpected doings
there at times. A letter from Prof. Fawcett's friend,
H. D. Warr, of Trinity Hall, gives such a ludicrous
if perhaps fanciful description of a University quarrel
that it must be included. It is dated September 1870 :

" MY DEAR FAWCETT," it runs, " there have been
such extraordinary doings here that I think you certainly ought to know them. It is a long time since
anything so scandalous has happened in Cambridge as
the row which has just taken place between Porter and
Perkins. About a fortnight ago there was a dinner-
party at Downing at which Perkins sat at the head of
the table with Porter and XXX of Emmanuel on either
side of him. I am not sure that you know XXX ; he
is a long, narrow, rather elegant person, with a weak
fluid sort of look, and he talks a great deal, but what
he says is very vague. The three got on well enough
till XXX brought up religion and made some remarks
of a heterodox nature—in his weak way—whereupon
Perkins, who is very orthodox, fired up. ' I'll just
tell you what it is '—this is the universal proscenium
of Perkins when he means mischief—' if I have to choose
between the Bible and a jabbering jackass like you, I
had a damned sight rather have the Bible.' Of course
this floored poor XXX ; and then Porter very naturally
remonstrated. ' Really—really—now, Perkins—that's
a har-ble har-ble thing to say to a man ! Really—
really—no—no—no gentleman would say such a har-ble
thing.' ' I'll just tell you what it is, Porter,' Perkins
returned, ' I don't care much whether a gentleman
would say such a har-ble thing or not, but I'll be damned
if I am so little a gentleman that I have been engaged

to a gal for seven years and haven't the pluck to marry
her.' ' Really—really—now—you know, Perkins, that's
a most extrar-ordinary, extrar-ordinary most har-ble,
har-ble, indecent thing to say, you know, Perkins, I,
really, really, you know I can't stand it, Perkins,' said
poor Porter. ' Well, I don't know about standing it ;
but I'll just tell you what it is, Porter,' Perkins replied,
' if you haven't named the day to that gal by this day
fortnight I'll be damned if I don't set a dog on you.'
Then the other guests intervened and peace was made.
About a week after this I happened to see Perkins on
Parker's Piece with a large savage-looking white bulldog which he was coaxing with a bit of liver and teaching
it, so far as one could see, tricks ; of course I thought
nothing of this at the time. However, a few days
ago, just when the fortnight which Perkins had allowed
Porter to propose within had expired, I was surprised
to see Perkins sauntering about near Peterhouse with
this big dog ; and, sure enough, out came Porter before
I had passed. I was close to him and saw all that took
place. Perkins went up to Porter, told him that the
time was up and that there was the dog, and asked him
if he had proposed. I did not hear Porter's answer,
but it was evidently unsatisfactory, for Perkins at once
set the dog on him. It pinned Porter by the calf of
the leg and bit him furiously while Perkins called to it,
' Give it him in the bone, Bingo ! good dog, Bingo, give
it him in the bone ! ' Poor Porter roared with pain,
but Perkins only said, ' Well, will you write to that gal
to-night ? Good dog, Bingo ! Good dog, Bingo ! '
At last, when Porter was half dead with terror, Perkins
tried to drag the dog off, but could not do so, and at
last only released him in this way—HE KNELT DOWN
IN THE ROAD AND BIT THE DOG'S TAIL TILL, OPENING
ITS MOUTH TO HOWL, IT RELEASED PORTER.

" This is what took place the other day between two
Cambridge tutors in broad daylight in King's Parade.

" Next day Perkins called to know whether Porter had
hydrophobia. There are no symptoms of it as yet."

To be introduced into a society where incidents of
this kind were still possible, and yet where her own
associates were brilliant men, as broadminded and

reasonable as her own husband, was very entertaining to Milly. And it was all made additionally pleasant by the fact that everyone was well disposed towards herself. A friend, writing more than fifty years later, described how he was present in the Senate House when Mrs. Fawcett first appeared. " As you well know," he says, " the Professor was ever a great favourite with the undergraduates, but the hearty cheers that rang through the House that day were meant for the Professor's bride as much as for himself. And it was whispered, ' What a pity the Professor cannot see what a pretty bride he has won.' "

Even more than the undergraduates, because with better knowledge, Henry Fawcett's intimates welcomed his wife, and from the very first she was able to share his friendships. They were a very sociable couple, in a simple way, and dined out very frequently ; and it was a familiar sight to see the little lady walking home with her tall husband through the moonlit streets of Cambridge, both of them talking as hard as they could, and rejoicing in the strict economy which made a carriage drive impossible.

Millicent Fawcett was very nice to look at, and it was not only the undergraduates, but Harry himself, who regretted that he could not see her. She was very small, and looked all the smaller beside her huge husband ; but she was, and appeared to be, in radiant health. She had a lovely complexion, and masses of shining brown hair, and a certain calmness of expression which corresponded to the serenity of her mind. Her voice, which was very clear, was all that Harry could judge ; but he was always asking his friends how Milly was looking, and begging them for descriptions of her face. He took, too, the greatest interest in her clothes ; and though Milly herself was not by nature fond of fine raiment, there is no doubt that she dressed to please her blind husband. In the old letters and memories of early days which now survive, there

PROFESSOR AND MRS. HENRY FAWCETT, 1867.

36]

is a constant reference to what she wore—the " lovely
plum-coloured dress with puffed sleeves," " the beautiful
pink-lined cloak," " the sage green and gold brocade,"
and " the white satin," and, even more often, " the
daintiness and neatness of her appearance." And
though Milly herself might be quite indifferent to it all,
every time that Harry was told that she looked lovely
he glowed with pride and pleasure.

When February came the pleasant Cambridge life
was exchanged for the equal, though different, enjoyments of London. Millicent was young and, as she
said, her " political education was just beginning."
From the time of her marriage until 1871 she acted as
her husband's secretary, and naturally had to read and
write for Harry. " I grappled with newspapers and
Blue-books," she says, " and learned more or less to
convey their import to him." Indeed, she did more
than that ; for they discussed together everything
that was happening, and as time went on she was able
to add helpful criticism to her other functions, and to
contribute directly to his essays, lectures and speeches.

The London life, of course, left Henry Fawcett less
leisure for being sociable than that at Cambridge, for
he was a very regular attendant at the House, and,
though he always dined at home, almost the whole of
his afternoons and evenings were occupied. However,
there were Saturdays and other days off ; and political
dinners and evening parties both at their own house
and elsewhere, which they both greatly enjoyed. At
one of these parties, however, it happened that Harry
was left for a long time to the mercies of an intelligent
bore, and when his wife at last came near to him he,
not knowing of course who was in earshot, was heard
to murmur, " Milly, Milly, your voice is the voice of an
angel "—as indeed for him it always was.

One of the most interesting of their friends was of
course John Stuart Mill. There is a letter from him
to Henry Fawcett, written after his defeat in the elec-

tion of '68, which shows the great similarity of their outlook.

" You will, I am sure," he says, " understand that my not having acknowledged your letter of November 20 until after I have nearly brought up the arrears of my correspondence, was not because I felt little, but because you do not need any fresh assurance to know how much I do feel. I am not the less touched at the regrets of my friends because I myself have no need of consolation. On the contrary, we are in the first flush of enjoyment of our recovered freedom, and in better cue than we have been for a long while for working hard and efficiently for our opinions. The elections, though so unfavourable to candidates of advanced opinions, have given us a House capable of the immediate work it had to do, viz. to make Gladstone Minister and disestablish the Irish Church. Between this and the next General Election the working classes will have time to organise their political action, and to insist upon having an equal share of influence in the choice of candidates ; and it is then, and not before, that Chadwicks will prevail over Bouveries, and Odgers over Henry Hoares. Meanwhile, it is a great satisfaction to me that you are still in the House to assert great principles, and that you are as unlikely as anyone there to be easily discouraged. I need hardly say that I am always at your command for any help I can give you out of the House, and that not meeting you there, I shall hope to see you oftener at Blackheath.

" Mrs. Fawcett's article has given us as much pleasure in the Fortnightly as it did when we first had the opportunity of reading it. Pray give her Helen's and my kind regards."

" I regarded it as a very great honour," Mrs. Fawcett's reminiscences say, " when we were invited from time to time to dine with Mr. Mill and his stepdaughter, Miss Helen Taylor, at Blackheath. These were delightful evenings, when we met Mr. and Mrs. Grote, Prof. Cairns and other celebrities, and heard, I suppose, some of the best talk from some of the best talkers in England."

They heard it, and they contributed to it ; for Henry Fawcett was always ready for an argument ; and even Milly, young as she was, knew exactly what she thought and was not afraid to say it.

The woman question, of course, cropped up constantly on these occasions, and though for the most part the people the Fawcetts met were sufficiently sympathetic for the discussion to be more of ways and means than of principles, opponents were sometimes unearthed and great battles royal engaged. Mrs. Fawcett records one such occasion, when Mill and Herbert Spencer attacked each other, and Herbert Spencer based his arguments upon the heavy handicap Nature imposed upon women.

" Mill's reply," she says, " took my fancy exceedingly. ' You look upon Nature as something we should do well to follow. I look upon Nature as a horrid old harridan.' "

No doubt this did not " convert " Herbert Spencer ; but it fitted in exactly with Milly's own somewhat austere outlook, and rejoiced her heart.

This, then, was the background of life for the first years after Millicent's marriage. Her daughter, Philippa, was born in 1868, and added another to the interests and joys of her mother and father ; but Millicent saw no reason why the presence of a baby in the house should entirely interrupt and break up its mother's life. She attended devotedly to the infant, she knitted its garments (at what her friends considered an astonishing pace), and she watched most carefully over its health, but she continued to do other things as well.

Philippa, though quite healthy, was a noisy baby, and years afterwards her mother, writing to a friend whose baby showed the same tendencies, explained her views about this :

" About your baby," she wrote, " I think I may perhaps be able to console you a little, because I always

say that Philippa screamed incessantly for many
months in her babyhood. Probably it has something
to do with health, and may be modified by hitting upon
just the right sort of feeding ; but I think it also has
to do with nervous organisation, a highly strung nervous
baby being the victim of it, while a stupid one does
nothing but digest, sleep and grow fat. That is where
my consolation comes in—it may be a sign of nascent
mental activity, and you are nursing into life and
strength someone who will leave an impression on the
history of the world. So cheer up, dear C., and try to
' bear with patience.' . . . Make your husband hold
the baby sometimes while you write me a letter to say
how you all are."

No doubt at the time, when Philippa " screamed incessantly for many months," her mother was less philosophical about it, but she was never in a state of foolish
worry. She used to take the baby with her, without a
nurse, when she stayed at Aldeburgh or Salisbury, and
she played with it, and carried it about in her arms,
as all mothers do. She watched most eagerly for signs
of developing intelligence, and no doubt she secretly
thought it the most wonderful baby in the world ; but
she was careful not say so too openly, and she did not
forget that there were other things as well as her own
baby in the world. And undoubtedly, she loved her
daughter all the better for this fact.

CHAPTER III

POLITICS AND ECONOMICS IN THE 'SEVENTIES

First Women's Suffrage Petition—John Stuart Mill's amendment—First Women's Suffrage Committee—Early meetings—Local government—Josephine Butler's crusade—*Political Economy for Beginners—Janet Doncaster*—Elizabeth's marriage—Agnes and Rhoda—Amusements and travel.

DURING the first years of her marriage a great deal of Millicent's time was necessarily taken up with her work for her husband, with the management of her two houses, with her baby, and with intercourse with her own and her husband's family and with their many friends. Nevertheless, she did not delay to take up her own special task, and she fitted it in with everything else.

Eighteen sixty-seven, the year that Millicent was married, was the year when Women's Suffrage first came prominently forward in public. Barbara Bodichon, who was always the most daring and enterprising of the Langham Place group, had asked Mr. Mill whether he would present a Women's Suffrage petition in the House of Commons, and he had replied that if she could get together a hundred signatures he would certainly do so. Delighted with this encouragement, she had at once formed a little committee of herself, Emily Davies, Elizabeth Garrett and one or two others, and they had gone to the outstanding women of the day, such as Florence Nightingale and Harriet Martineau, and found them perfectly ready to sign. They had then gone on to the ladies of the radical circles in which they chiefly moved, and to some of the others whom Emily Davies had succeeded in interesting in female education, and what with one

41

and another, although Milly was still too young to be included, they had obtained 1,399 names in a fortnight.

The story of the taking of this document to the House of Commons has been often told ; how Elizabeth and Emily, exceedingly shy and self-conscious, took it there in a cab, and how they hid it under the apple-woman's stall in Westminster Hall while Mr. Fawcett went off to find Mr. Mill for them ; and how they all rejoiced and congratulated each other upon the splendid names it contained. Nothing came of the presentation of the petition—nothing ever came of petitions—but a few months later Mill's amendment to the Reform Bill brought the subject into the full blare of publicity, and launched it definitely upon the political field.

Milly was in the Ladies' Gallery when this great debate came on. " Of course," she wrote in description, " the heavy brass trellis which then screened off these galleries, and their bad ventilation made them quite unnecessarily tiring and even exhausting, but the whole scene was new to me and very interesting. . . . I heard Mill's speech when he moved the Women's Suffrage amendment to the 1867 Reform Bill ; its terms were to omit the word ' man ' from the enfranchising clause and substitute the word ' person.' The speech was a masterpiece of close reasoning, tinged here and there by deep emotion. It thrilled me to hear my sister and her successful efforts to open the medical profession to women referred to. But perhaps what interested me most of all was the evidently powerful impression the speech made on the House. This was particularly shown in the case of Mr. John Bright. His brother Jacob, and all his sisters with whom I was acquainted, were Suffragists, but they had not succeeded in taking the most distinguished member of their family with them. As soon as Mill rose to speak, John Bright entered the House and flung himself into the corner seat below the gangway on the left of the

Chair, just below where Mill was speaking. Bright had a mocking smile on his face, which everyone who remembers it will recall had a strong natural capacity in the curve of the mouth, even in repose, for expressing contempt. He crossed his legs, and swung the one that was uppermost backwards and forwards. His whole figure suggested a strong mixture of dislike and scorn ; but as Mill developed his arguments this gradually changed. The swinging leg became still, the mocking smile vanished, and when the division was taken Bright's name was actually among the seventy-three who voted for Mill's amendment. Bright, however, soon had a relapse ; he was by nature an ardent Anti-Suffragist, and this was the one and only time that he gave a vote in favour of extending the representative institutions to women. Though the amendment had been defeated by more than two to one, we were elated by the success, much greater than we had expected, of Mill's speech, and were especially glad that the division had not been on party lines. . . ."

The immediate consequence of this Parliamentary event was the formation of a regular Women's Suffrage Committee in London, and in July 1867 its first meeting took place in Mrs. Peter Taylor's house on Campden Hill. Mrs. Henry Fawcett was one of those who were present, though of course she was not yet a leader, but merely the youngest recruit, no more inexperienced indeed than the other ladies, but younger than they were. Years later, on her eightieth birthday, Mrs. McLaren, one of John Bright's sisters, who had been a member of the original committee, wrote to Millicent recalling those early days.

" I sometimes tell my children," she wrote, " how when you first came to our Women's Suffrage Committees, those held in Mrs. Peter Taylor's at Aubrey House, you looked like a schoolgirl rather than a married woman, and how you listened to opinions and suggestions as they fell from different members, and would then throw in your own counsel, which always seemed the right thing for us to accept."

Even at that early stage the whole movement was hedged about with difficulties. It is true that most of its supporters thought the victory would come in a very short time, and that they did not in the least realise the strength and bitterness of conventional people's opposition. It was not from these directions that the difficulties came, but from their own ranks. In the first place it was exceedingly unusual for women to be doing public business of any kind, and even these pioneers, bold as they were, did not quite know how far they could go. They had to try to avoid shocking people as far as possible, and they even discovered unexpected timidities in themselves and their husbands and fathers. Then in the second place, they were so politically innocent, and so excessively scrupulous and high-minded, that they created tangles and confusions for themselves where none really existed. And so the internal affairs of the Society were intricate, involved, and much befogged with personal feelings and ignorance of procedure. From the first, however, Mrs. Fawcett was on the side of good sense. With her husband's experience at call, and with her own native steadiness and pertinacity to guide her, she seemed to sail through the storms with considerable equanimity, and even as early as 1870 her advice was being sought from all sides.

There were plenty of real difficulties for the Women's Movement to face, as well as those which its creators invented. The first of these was the problem of how far it would be injurious for the political side of the movement to be avowedly connected with its other aspects. It was obvious, of course, to all the suffragists that the education movement and the political movement and the medical women's movement were all part of the same thing. But each of these reforms was separate, and all were battling against prejudice and obstruction ; and it seemed rather dangerous to

let the general public see what a close connection there
was between them all. Some would support girls'
schools who would not face political enfranchisement ;
and it seemed to Emily Davies, and to many more,
that it would be a mistake for the same people to appear
prominently in support of more than one reform.
Elizabeth Garrett, passionate believer in the franchise
as she was, felt this same hesitation, and a letter of hers
to Milly, dated 1867, makes this quite clear.

" I shall be very glad to subscribe £1 1s. a year to
the Franchise Society," she wrote, " but I would rather
not have my name advertised on the General Committee.
I think it is wiser as a medical woman to keep somewhat
in the background as regards other movements. . . .
I particularly do not wish my name to appear in public
advertisements."

In spite of all these hesitations, however, the committee got under way, and similar committees were
almost immediately started in Manchester, Edinburgh,
Bristol and Birmingham. The Parliamentary friends
had to be backed up, and there were plenty of women
eager—though rather incompetent—to do so.

The first step they took, in 1868, was to endeavour
to prove in the Courts that women householders were
already entitled to vote in Parliamentary elections.
A test case was taken, but it was lost, and the committees
realised that they would have to try and spread an
organisation over the country as widely as possible.
Pamphlets were printed, and petitions signed, and
before long it became evident that public meetings
would have to be held. This was regarded as a most
terribly bold and dangerous thing in the 'sixties and
'seventies. Women hardly ever spoke in public, and
it was thought dreadfully " advanced " and likely to
be " unsexing " ; besides, no one believed that a
woman's voice could be heard. All the committee
members were afraid of this duty, and the Press howled
with laughter at the mere idea. But for all that, the

meetings began, first in drawing-rooms, and then in small halls, and then here, there and everywhere where an audience could be secured. The first big meeting was in Manchester in 1868, and the second was in London in the Gallery of the Architectural Society in Conduit Street. At this meeting Mrs. Peter Taylor took the chair, and here, for the first time, Mrs. Henry Fawcett appeared on a public platform. She made only a short speech, for Mill, and Charles Kingsley, and Morley, and Dilke and Stansfield, as well as Henry Fawcett and six others were also speaking ; but even a short speech was a severe ordeal, and she confessed to being " terrified." Whatever she may have felt, she certainly did not appear to be nervous. Her voice was clear and audible, her sentences were finished and simple, and her whole air one of perfect calm. The impression of her early speaking, recorded again and again by her hearers, was always the same : clear, logical, self-possessed, and pre-eminently " ladylike," as the phrase of the period ran. She looked charming and " modest," she was beautifully dressed, her voice could be heard distinctly, she made reasonable remarks in a natural manner, and she sometimes made excellent jokes. The whole performance was completely disarming, and even the most hostile person in the room could find no fault with her, beyond the unpardonable fault of appearing there at all. These impressions—which are taken from the reports of her speeches in the 'seventies— were certainly true of the first speech of all, though poor Milly herself, in her agony of nervousness, could not know that this was the impression she would inevitably make, or believe that she was destined to spend so much of her life in this very hateful occupation. All she thought of then, no doubt, was " scraping through," and then going home to talk it all over with the others, and to reckon up how much good had been done, and how far, if at all, the thing would have to be repeated.

The effect of this public meeting was not quite all that the promoters had hoped. Most newspapers were shocked at the appearance of women on a platform, and public discussion of Women's Suffrage revealed what deep-seated opposition there was. Instead of finishing things off by one stroke, the committees saw that they would have to undertake regular speaking campaigns and even to tour the country. With great reluctance they took up the work.

Mrs. Fawcett herself made her next speech at Brighton, in her husband's constituency, in 1870. Here, of course, there was even more to overcome than there had been in London. The local Liberals were considerably alarmed. It was one thing for their Member to hold these odd views himself, and this might be overlooked ; but for his wife to come down and gratuitously make a display of herself on a platform in support of women's rights was most unwise, and certain to do harm. However, they could do nothing. Both Henry Fawcett and his wife were clear that it was their duty to hold the meeting, and if his supporters could not accept their judgment, they could not but respect their integrity. Moreover, the three chief Brighton friends stood by them. Mr. Willett— he who had written to Miss Garrett before her marriage —Mr. Carpenter, who agreed to take the chair—and Mr. Merrifield (who, as Mrs. Fawcett said, " would have been a woman suffragist if he had been born on a desert island ")—all these three backed them up, and on March 23, 1870, the meeting took place, without, of course, any of the evil consequences which had been expected, but, on the contrary, with a degree of enthusiasm and support which surprised the faint-hearted. A vote of thanks to the Member for " allowing his wife to lecture " was unanimously passed, and no evil consequences in the constituency followed.

The work had got to be done, and there were all too few people to do it ; and so when calls came from

Bristol, from Birmingham, from Scotland, or from anywhere else, Millicent responded. Sometimes alone,
sometimes with her cousin Rhoda, or with Miss Becker
or Miss Ashworth, or others of the workers, she went
forth to encounter the varied fortunes, the physical
weariness, the comic episodes and the heavy burden
of pioneer public speaking. Sometimes there were
pleasant things, new friends, successful meetings, good
jokes ; sometimes there were angry sneers, open
hostility and uncomfortable inns. They laughed over
the reports which said, "The lecturer was youthful
but composed, feminine but intelligent," and neither
the good fortune nor the bad made any difference ; the
job had got to be done, and they did it.

In these early years of her life, Mrs. Fawcett did not
devote her whole time to this work. She would speak
perhaps half a dozen times, and go on one or two short
tours in the year, from which she would bring home
the most entertaining tales, but that was the extent
of her public appearances. For she had a great many
other things to do as well. One of these was the writing
of pamphlets and letters to the Press, at which she was
exceedingly efficient, and another was the mobilisation
of friends in Parliament. This side of the movement,
in which before the end she grew immensely experienced,
was at first inspired by the brightest hopes.

The debate on the Reform Bill had revealed eighty
friends, and the attempts at organisation had revealed
others. A very large number of the individual Members
of the Parliament of 1868–73 said that they believed
in Women's Suffrage, and the committees innocently
assumed that this meant that it would become law.
It seemed that success was only a matter of waiting
for the opportunity, and when, in May 1870, Mr. Jacob
Bright secured time to bring in a Private Members'
Bill, they thought their cause was as good as won. He
brought it in, and gained a second reading victory,
and then the trouble began. In the Committee stage

Mr. Gladstone opposed it on behalf of the Government, without giving any reasons, it is true, but effectively for all that. He said, " It would be the greatest mistake to pass this Bill," and it was not passed. And so, with nothing more to it than that, the Parliamentary opportunity was over.

Mrs. Fawcett was no doubt less surprised by this reverse than some of the others, for she moved in political circles, and knew how the machinery worked ; and, moreover, she had a settled opinion about Gladstone. This opinion was expressed in a concrete shape in the family. Baby Philippa possessed a wooden horse, which ran on wheels, and was pulled along by a string. She had discovered that if you pulled the string gently the horse would not move at all, but if you pulled hard it would come with a great rush ; and her father, on hearing of this peculiarity, had named the horse Gladstone !

But in spite of the lesson of the wooden horse, and in spite of knowing many political people, even Mrs. Fawcett did not realise that the defeat of 1870 was to be so lasting, or that accepting an adverse decision was to be an experience she would go through so often again. For forty-seven years after that first defeat she was destined to be busy with the details of Parliamentary tactics, the selection of leaders in the House, the terms of Bills and resolutions, the ways of securing Parliamentary time, presenting petitions, focusing public opinion and the like. All this was then hidden from her, but even in the early years she went frequently to the House of Commons, and, with Miss Lydia Becker, who came to be the political secretary of the Suffrage Societies, she discussed tactics and expedients, each of which in the beginning seemed to offer some slight hope of advance, and none of which in the end ever seemed to come to effective action. Year after year this went on, but neither Miss Becker nor Mrs. Fawcett grew discouraged. They were not exactly hopeful, but they were determined to miss no chances ; and, as their experience of disappointment grew, so did their determination to succeed.

All was not disappointment, however. Women's Suffrage did not get forward, but other related causes did, and Mrs. Fawcett took a leading part in them. In 1869 an Act giving the Municipal Franchise to women ratepayers was passed without any special agitation or difficulty, and in the following year the Education Act created School Boards, for which women were eligible, and at once the suffragists seized upon the chance of doing practical public work.

The first women candidates were the pioneers of the women's movement, and in London the two who came forward were Emily Davies and Elizabeth Garrett. There is no record now remaining of their election campaign, but it is easy to imagine how thrilling and exciting it was, and with what energy and amusement Milly threw herself into it.

Elizabeth was by then a practising doctor, with a small infirmary in the Euston Road. She was known to the working people of Holborn, and she was loved by them. Her meetings must have been crowded and enthusiastic, and the canvassing which her sisters certainly carried out on her behalf must have brought them home with charming and touching tales to send back to Aldeburgh and to tell over to each other. Certainly, when the voting came, all this found public expression, for both these women candidates were elected, and Elizabeth had a greater majority than anyone had ever secured in a municipal election in London before, having polled, with the aid of the " plumping " device, 47,858 votes.

There is a letter from Mrs. Grote, commenting on this election, and referring to one of Mrs. Fawcett's articles upon the Education Act, then being hotly discussed. It is dated December 16, 1870, and runs as follows :

" Dear Mrs. Fawcett,—

"As a veteran labourer in the field of social philosophy, permit me to offer you my cordial congratulations on the masterly essay which appeared in *The Times* of the 14th inst. It exhausts the subject—which is tossed about and handled in all its bearings with a searching knowledge and variety of points of view, which, if mankind were only open to *reason*, would lead to our retracing our mischievous course. I have from the first looked with something more than indifference on the new Education Act. The perusal of your paper confirms and enhances my dislike of its tendencies, whilst I am assisted in discerning remote ramifications of evil which promise to corrupt the innermost sources of a healthy social system.

" I was pleased at the success of Miss Garrett and Miss Davies, on account of my sympathy with female activity in administrative matters—and I only hope that those estimable women may lay to heart your admirable lessons, when they come to exercise the functions they have assumed.

" Believe me, dear Mrs. Fawcett, with my compliments to Mr. Fawcett

Yours very sincerely."

Mrs. Fawcett's article, and Mrs. Grote's opinions were, needless to say, not directed against the main principle of the Education Act, for they were both ardent advocates of the spread of education as widely as possible. The point they criticised was the proposal that the education should be not only compulsory but free of charge. They saw in this a weakening of parental responsibility, and a dangerous dependency upon the State, and they believed that a service which was not directly paid for would not be appreciated.

That was one aspect of the Radical Individualist view of the 'seventies, when the Franco-Prussian War was going on, and when Karl Marx was at the height of his career. Politically it was not destined to prevail, but it remained part of Mrs. Fawcett's general outlook to the end of her life.

5

The year 1870 saw a fresh complication of the Suffrage work in the beginning of Josephine Butler's Crusade for the Repeal of the Contagious Diseases Acts. This movement was of immense importance to the ultimate Women's Suffrage victory, and it was one which Mrs. Fawcett supported with her whole heart ; and yet it finds no place in her biography, for it occupied no place in her life. Deliberately, and after careful consideration, she stood aside from it, and though this decision cost her a great effort, she believed to the end of her life that it had been right. The reasons which actuated her were reasons of policy, and they were reflected in the great storm which shook the suffrage committees at that date. Mrs. Butler's Crusade was one which shocked and outraged public opinion, and by its nature and subject roused up the fiercest opposition ; and Mrs. Fawcett and many others believed that it would seriously damage the Suffrage cause if the two movements appeared to be too much connected. It was a very difficult time, and there were passionate and heated differences of opinion among the workers in the women's movement. Everyone agreed that the educational workers must keep out of it, but among the rest a double set of cleavages arose. There were some, of whom Emily Davies and Elizabeth Garrett were examples, who actually disagreed with Mrs. Butler, and believed that the C.D. Acts were a necessary evil ; there were others, like John Stuart Mill and Mrs. Fawcett, who strongly supported Mrs. Butler's views, and yet felt it unwise to take an active part in her work ; and there were others still, like Rhoda Garrett and Mr. Jacob Bright, who went boldly forward and supported both. The London Suffrage Society split into two parts, and the same sort of thing happened elsewhere, and everyone was disturbed and anxious. But Mrs. Fawcett, though greatly troubled over all this, was quite clear in her own mind. She was herself only twenty-three, but she was already closely associated with Women's Suffrage in the minds of political people ; and, after talking it all over with Mill and with her husband, she took her stand and adhered to it. The fact that in action Milly disagreed with Rhoda, and in opinion with Elizabeth, was a great trial for all three of them. They all loved each other so much, and met so often, that the years from '70 to '74 must have been difficult and trying ; but these three were able to carry their friendship through them unimpaired, and to respect, even though they disagreed with, each other's opinions.

Things did not really perplex Milly, nor depress her. She could be sad, but she would not be discouraged ; for she truly believed, without any effort of faith, that all was for the best, and that good must triumph over evil. And so, with ups and downs, but with steady and unfaltering purpose, she fitted the women's movement into the pattern of her life.

Although the women's movement occupied so large a share of Millicent's thoughts, it would be a mistake to suppose that she worked at nothing else.

Prof. Fawcett spent much time in the preparation of his Cambridge lectures and his speeches in the House, as well as in writing a number of weighty articles on Politics and Economics ; and his wife naturally helped him in these tasks, read the necessary authorities to him, and discussed in detail the problems he was considering. From the very first, however, he urged and encouraged her to write on her own account, and her very first article, " The Lectures for Women in Cambridge," appeared in *Macmillan's Magazine* in the year after her marriage. This article brought her £7—the first money she had ever earned (though, as the law then stood, it belonged to her husband !), and she sent it to the fund which was being raised for Mr. Mill's election expenses. Other articles soon followed on various questions.

Milly wrote easily and well ; what she had to say

was always clear and reasonable, and expressed with a certain grave simplicity of style ; and her work was so successful that Mr. Macmillan, the publisher, who was one of their close friends, began to press her to write a book on Political Economy for Beginners. Harry took up the idea with enthusiasm ; the book was badly needed, and Milly was exactly the person to write it, and between them they persuaded her to undertake the task.

Nothing is so difficult as to condense and popularise a complicated subject, and the task was really a hard one. However, Millicent had the simplifying mind as well as the knowledge which was needed, and, more-over, she had a natural distaste for elaboration. She used the plainest words and the homeliest illustrations, and the little book, which appeared in 1870, was an immediate success. It brought her appreciative letters from all sides, and rapidly went through ten editions, being carefully revised and improved by the author each time. The outline of the book, of course, sets forth the doctrine according to John Stuart Mill, though with some characteristic variations. Mrs. Fawcett was a convinced believer in Mill's philosophic individual-ism, and shared her husband's view that sound govern-ment and sound economics depended on the encourage-ment of the spirit of self-help, and accordingly her little book went somewhat out of fashion at the end of the nineteenth century. It remains, however, a very lucid piece of work, which reveals the ability and the outlook of its young author. It has, moreover, been many times reprinted since its early editions in the 'seventies, and it is used by students to this day.[1]

In 1872, two years after the first edition of *Political Economy for Beginners* had appeared, a volume of *Essays and Lectures on Social and Political Subjects* was brought out, which was made up of four essays by Henry Fawcett

[1] *Political Economy for Beginners*, by Dame Millicent Fawcett. Macmillan & Co., fcap. 8vo, 3s.

and eight by his wife. This volume was very well received, and much discussed at the time.

" I have just been reading your essays," wrote Frances Power Cobbe, " and I felt as I did so the strongest *concern* to tell you how greatly I admire them, and how heartily I thank you for striking such good, strong, well-delivered blows in our battle. There is not a word in which I do not agree—and many of your points are novel and telling, while the tone of the whole is beyond praise."

These essays were followed by a number of others, which Millicent contributed to *Macmillan's* and other Reviews, and then in 1875 she embarked upon a new kind of writing, and published her novel, *Janet Doncaster*. Her friends all liked this story, and it is in fact a very pleasant little book, but it had no great success. It is not very effective as a novel, having little action, and a marked tendency to be a tract against drunkenness. In spite of these drawbacks it is full of charming bits of description and observation, and its heroine is thoroughly alive, and displays many of the characteristics of the author herself. Janet—like Milly—was of unshakeable will. She followed her own judgment remorselessly, and, like her creator, her actions and her inner life were lit up by an unfaltering impersonal passion. Such a character was not very usual in the fiction of the 'seventies, nor very likely to be popular ; and, moreover, it must be admitted that the book as a whole was not written with the skill of a great novelist. Such as it was, however, it sold a little and was reviewed a good deal ; and Elizabeth wrote that she expected it would make Milly a rich woman : " We shall see you and Harry careering in the Park every day on steeds of your own buying and feeding." But Milly suspected that her name and her friends were the chief element in the flutter her book made, and she determined to test the matter properly. She accordingly wrote a second novel, without letting anyone into the secret, and published it under another name. It fell perfectly flat—as she had feared it might—and she was satisfied —if naturally disappointed—that the career of a novelist was not for her.

Unfortunately, all traces of this novel, even to its name and date of its publication, are lost. We cannot now judge, except from *Janet Doncaster*, if her decision was justified ; but in any case—in the light of all she did accomplish—it is impossible to regret the career which she abandoned in the 'seventies.

Mrs. Fawcett's work for the Women's Movement, the political work with her husband and her own literary work does not by any means complete the tale of what occupied her in the early years of her married life, for besides all their solid activities, Milly and her husband had a great deal of play, and they had besides a large and very congenial family, of which they saw a great deal.

One of the pleasures of the Cambridge terms was the opportunity of seeing Sam, who was an undergraduate, and he and his sister were much together. He came also to Bessborough Gardens, where there was room for any of the Garrett tribe, and where also Harry's father and mother, and his sister Maria often stayed.

There is a story of one of these visits, when Millicent took her father-in-law to a play, which happened to be exceedingly moving. Mr. Fawcett was unused to London theatres, and was soon in tears, and presently, as the tragedy piled up, he was heard to say, in a sort of howl, " Milly, Milly, why did you bring me here to be miserable ? "

Misery, however, was not the predominant note of a visit to Bessborough Gardens, where there was always a great deal of coming and going, and where everyone brought their best jokes to provoke Harry's hearty laugh; and the family reunions there were thoroughly enjoyed.

Mrs. Smith, dear sister Louie, died in 1867, soon after Milly's marriage, and this was a terrible grief to the whole family. She had been the intimate friend and confidante of her sisters, a sort of second mother to the younger ones, and the two little daughters she left became a very special charge to their aunts.

In 1870, three years later, Elizabeth startled and astonished them all by getting engaged to be married. She was then thirty-four years old, and had been successfully conducting a dispensary in the Euston Road for several years. She had just been elected a member of the London School Board and was in the full tide of her practice as a medical woman. And yet she committed the terrible irrelevance of falling in love, and her friends began to fear that her career was over. This, however, was not Elizabeth's idea, nor that of her future husband ; and the letter in which she announced her engagement to Milly makes this extremely clear. It is dated from Aldeburgh, on Christmas Day, 1870, and runs as follows :

" On Friday night my horizon was suddenly changed by Mr. Anderson asking me to marry him. I do hope, my dear, that you will not think that I have meanly deserted my post. I think it need not prove to be so, and I believe that he would regret it as much as you or I would. I am sure that the woman question will never be solved in any complete way so long as marriage is thought to be incompatible with freedom and with an independent career, and I think there is a very good chance that we may be able to do something to discourage this notion. . . . Father was, I fancy, a little disappointed that I should marry at all. . . ."

So far the apology goes, and then follows the natural Elizabeth, with none of the doubts or hesitations she had had in her sister's case :

" I hope you will like him and that Harry will too when you meet. I am very happy, dear Milly. I think we shall be married at Easter. There is nothing to wait for, as our joint income will be a good one, and we are both certainly old enough. We think of looking at once for a large house in my own or the Grosvenor Square district. We have agreed not to be married by the Church of England Service and to have no Service unless we can find one we like. I dare say it will end in our using the Scotch form and bargaining beforehand for no catechism as to obedience. . . . There is no reason for keeping my engagement a secret."

The prediction came true—as indeed also did Elizabeth's hope that she would be able to prove that marriage and a career could go together. She and Mr. J. G. Skelton Anderson were married at the Scotch Church in Upper George Street, as is proved by a little note to Milly telling her that it was to be at 8.30. in the morning. " Do come, my dear one, and get Harry up in time too ! "

In the summer of 1871 another family event, of great importance and interest to Milly, took place in connection with her sister Agnes. These two had been very particularly devoted to each other as children, and their special friendship had continued unimpaired. And now Agnes, who was twenty-six, was thinking, like her sister Elizabeth, that the time had come to set out on an independent career. Agnes Garrett, ever since her schooldays, had been devoted to her cousin Rhoda ; and Rhoda, by the circumstances of her own family, had been earning her living for some time, though without as yet settling down to any single occupation. These two friends discussed, just as Emily Davies and Elizabeth had discussed, the best way to help forward the great cause and at the same time win their personal independence. Agnes thought perhaps the best way would be by going into business, since that was a great sphere in which women as yet had but a tiny part. Her father, still as radical as he had been ten years earlier, suggested taking her into the family maltings at Snape. But this was too much for her brothers. Newson, the eldest, had not much ground for objection, since he was in the Army ; but Edmund, who was in the business himself, was a different matter, and Agnes felt it would not work.   She therefore went off to London to consult with Rhoda, and they decided to become house decorators.   They found an architect, Mr. Cottier, who was willing to give them some training in his studio, and they made up their minds to live together in London and to build up, if they could, a real business partnership.   Her father and mother were for the moment displeased by this decision, and there is a letter to them dictated by Harry and written in Milly's handwriting upon the subject.

" MY DEAR MR. GARRETT," it begins, with all the formality of the 'seventies, " I was very sorry to find from your letter received this morning that Milly and I have caused you and Mrs. Garrett any pain.   You seem annoyed because you say we have countenanced Agnes's recent course of action.   I am quite sure you would have been the first to have felt that we had acted towards her with great unkindness if, when she had determined to settle in London, we had not done our best to make her as comfortable as possible by offering her for a time a home at our house.   It was certainly nothing more than she might fairly expect from a brother and sister.   I do not feel that I have in any way influenced Agnes ; she is old enough and has ability enough to judge for herself without inter- ference from me.   I think it is quite as laudable on her part to desire to make her own living as it was for Lizzie to do the same.   Agnes was chiefly influenced in her desire to obtain something to do in London from a very proper motive that she did not like to be the cause of a family disagreement, and from the tone Newson and Edmund adopted with regard to her entering the malt- ing business she felt only too certain that if you had carried out your intention to take her into your business, family discord would be the inevitable result.   The only advice that I gave Agnes was that she should write to you before anything was settled ; this I know she did, as she told you about Cottier, when all she knew was that he was willing to entertain the idea.   I further advised her that as Skelton Anderson had great business experience, that in the event of your not coming to London she should consult him in all business matters. I have never even seen Cottier. I do not precisely know the arrangement which has been made with him, and therefore do not know whether so far as my opinion is concerned I should approve of it or not ; but whether I might approve of it or not really seems to me not to make any difference in the circumstance that Milly and I could not have acted wrong, but on the contrary that we were bound to offer to a sister any hospitality in our power."

Mr. Garrett was soon reconciled, and the partnership began, and proved to be just what best suited both the cousins. They soon had plenty of work, and they began to make money. They found themselves, without difficulty, on the very happiest terms with the painters and workmen they employed, and they gained a reputation for the excellence of their materials and the thoroughness of their work. Everything went well, and they enjoyed themselves greatly ; and not the least of their advantages was that they were their own masters. They were not tied down to days and hours, but could go off, when the call came, on Suffrage speaking tours and other political campaigns ; and Rhoda in particular frequently did so. She was in every way a brilliant young woman, easily the most eloquent and convincing of all the early speakers, and popular wherever she went. And after she and Agnes settled together in London they saw a great deal of Milly and her husband, and of Elizabeth and hers, so that the three households were in constant communication. And it was not only in London that they met. Elizabeth and her husband had a house at Aldeburgh, and Agnes and Rhoda had a delightful cottage at Rustington, where they loved to forgather ; and there, while their elders talked, Philippa and Rhoda's young brother Edmund played and paddled by the sea.

Sir Hubert and Lady Maud Parry were their neighbours at Rustington, and the whole family soon made great friends with them, finding themselves congenial in ideas, in jokes, and in love of music. Sir Hubert, like everyone else who met Henry Fawcett, was impressed by the way in which he ignored his blindness.

" Paid the Garretts a visit this morning," he wrote in his journal in 1879, " and went down to bathe with Prof. Fawcett. It is extraordinary how he gets through things. I led him into the water, and though there were considerable waves going, he dashed fearlessly in, and plunged under and swam about a little. He is marvellously handy. He climbed over an awkward wall and walked in the most awkward places by the beach with very little help."

That was, of course, just Harry's normal behaviour, which gradually ceased to surprise, though it never ceased to excite the admiration of his friends. There seemed to be in fact very little that anyone needed to do for him, and the chief call he made upon the good offices of his friends was to require them to bring him every joke and good story they came across. These, as they came, were at once passed on to go the round of Harry's immediate circle ; and what with the things Milly noticed and the things Rhoda invented, and the things which the Cambridge dons collected, there was always something fresh to retail.

There is another letter of H. D. Warr's, for example, dated January 1872, which must have given rise to a great deal of laughter, although of course the unkind rumours which it reported were both discouraging and troublesome.

" MY DEAR FAWCETT," it runs, " I really cannot help dropping you a line to warn you of two slanderous imputations on Mrs. Fawcett's character and good sense which have, during your absence in Cambridge, obtained a miserable currency in London society. I met with them both at a party last night, and I need hardly say that I used my best efforts to silence upon the spot the vipers who uttered them ; but calumny is strong—and I think it will need some forcible measure, such for example as an advertisement in *The Times*, to extract the sting.

"The first slander is that Philippa is boarded out, Mrs. Fawcett having peremptorily refused to undertake her early education. This statement was calmly advanced by a person who is well known to you both, and who evidently fully believed what he was saying and spoke in perfect good faith. Leslie Stephen, who was at this school for scandal with me, was so taken aback that he could find nothing to say, but I fought for Mrs. Fawcett's good name as well as I could. I could not get anyone to believe that Philippa was NOT boarded out—the company insisted that they knew for a fact that she had been boarded out since her birth —but I am proud to say that by a series of highly circumstantial fiction I managed to get it believed that the foster-mother to whom Mrs. Fawcett is supposed to have delegated her duties is a very clean and respectable person, and that the place in which she lives with her charge is healthy and well drained.

"The second slander, for the propagation of which no less a person than Miss Cobbe is, I regret to say, responsible, resembles an invention of Mr. Morgan's with regard to the propriety of burning down all the chapels in Cambridge. Miss Cobbe states that at a party at your house given towards Christmas, the conversation turned upon the Tichborne Trial, and someone quoted Lord Westbury's famous sarcasm, ' Poor Coleridge ! There are TWO IMPOSTORS who have been found out in that case'; whereupon Mrs. Fawcett said, ' Well, in my opinion the claimant is the greatest impostor that has appeared for the LAST EIGHTEEN HUNDRED YEARS.' As this period coincides with the commencement of the Christian era and the remark was made shortly before Christmas, there could be no doubt about the innuendo ; and Miss Cobbe was moved almost to a shower of rich tears at the heartlessness of the satire. Pray do not acknowledge this line, but take the necessary steps for denying the slanders. It makes me perfectly misanthropical to think that so good a woman as Mrs. Fawcett should apparently have received Ophelia's ' plague for her dowry.' "

This kind of malicious report was part of the penalty which all the pioneers of the cause had to face ; but Mrs. Fawcett herself took it all very calmly, realising that it was not so much personal to her as directed against the new, startling and dangerous doctrines she represented. Indeed, from the very first she managed to extract a good deal of fun from her opponents ; and being unshakeably sure of the rightness of her opinions, she had no difficulty in keeping her temper.

There is a story in her reminiscences which illustrates her way of dealing with this situation which is especially characteristic, because it shows not only her good humour but also the remorselessness which never allowed her to pass over in silence an insult directed through her to the cause. In describing the results of her first public speech she says :

" A few days later a then well-known Member of Parliament, Mr. C. R., referred publicly in the House of Commons to the appearance of Mrs. Taylor and myself upon a platform to advocate votes for women, as ' two ladies, wives of members of this House, who had disgraced themselves,' and added that he would not further disgrace them by mentioning their names.

" It so happened that a very short time after this, my husband and I were spending the week-end in Cambridge, and that most hospitable of men, Mr. James Porter, of Peterhouse," [the victim of Mr. Perkins's bulldog !] "asked us to dine with him. What was my amusement to see Mr. C. R. among the guests : this amusement was intensified into positive glee when he was asked to take me in to dinner. I could not resist expressing condolences with him on his unfortunate position. Should I ask Mr. Porter to let him exchange me for some other lady who had not disgraced herself ? But after we had let off steam a little in this way, I found him quite an agreeable neighbour at the table, and so far as I know, he never again publicly held up any woman to contempt for advocating the enfranchisement of her own sex. After all, what he had said was very mild compared to Horace

Walpole's abuse of Mary Wollstonecraft as ' a hyena in petticoats.' "

Opportunities for this sort of retaliation came frequently in Mrs. Fawcett's life, and she never missed them. Often, of course, they made her enemies more furious than ever, but she did not mind that. They had deserved a rap over the knuckles, and they received it.

But, after all, life was not entirely composed of the women's movement, or even of politics and serious problems. Milly was never idle, but some of her activities had no more solemn motive behind them than the simple desire to enjoy herself. It was in this spirit that she read novels and poetry and all the current books of the day, and it was for fun, and not from any sense of duty, that she persuaded her friend Emma Miller to read Dante with her in the mornings. For the same reason, too, she arranged many informal concerts in her own drawing-room, and asked Mr. Sedley Taylor to play to her when they were in Cambridge, or went off to the big orchestral concerts when they were in town. She enjoyed these things with the serenity of a good conscience ; but the truth is that she enjoyed the whole of her life. An atmosphere of happiness radiated out from the Fawcetts which made everyone glad to be with them, and they were both so generous and so eager to share the good things they had that even the shyest could not feel embarrassed in their company.

The devotion between Harry and his wife was apparent to everyone who knew them. He was, indeed, dependent on her, but not in the sense one would suppose from his blindness. Sometimes she led him, of course, and often she read to him and smoothed his way ; but that was external. It was her companionship, her counsel and her advice upon which he really depended. He would call to her in his great voice, " Milly, Milly, where are you ? Are you enjoying yourself ? " as he went about the house or garden, or as they took their walks ; and Milly always *was* enjoying herself, so he could be contented.

One of the many things they had in common was a love of physical exercise, and they arranged their lives so as to take a great deal of it. When they were in Cambridge Millicent went regularly to the gymnasium in the town, which a bold innovator opened to women on some hours of the week. One of the other " Cambridge ladies " who went with her recalled with pride, fifty years later, that she was always able to beat her at the high jump and in vaulting the horse ! Besides this, there was, of course, walking, which was Harry's favourite pursuit, and rowing, which he regularly practised with an eight of dons who called themselves the Ancient Mariners, and which his wife also enjoyed, though in a less strenuous way. Then there was riding, which they both loved, and of which they managed to get a great deal, especially at Cambridge ; and in fortunate winters there was skating, which was another joy. As soon as there was a frost the Professor and his wife would drop everything, and make for the Fens, dragging all their household and as many friends as they could catch with them, and there they would stay more or less continuously until the thaw came. Mr. Fawcett was a magnificent skater, and he would go about either holding the end of a friend's stick or else entirely by himself, guided by the sound of the skates of his companions ; and in this way he made several long expeditions which became famous in Cambridge. On one occasion, when the frost was very severe, he skated all the way to Ely and back with a friend. In places the going was rough, and his companion remarked on the heaps of snow, whereupon Fawcett said, in perfect simplicity and unconsciousness, " Yes, I should not like to come along here in the dark." This remark, of course, was passed about among his friends, and it made them realise afresh how deep was his disregard for his infirmity.

Fishing was another thing which Henry Fawcett

loved, and many of his holidays were spent in Scotland or by the trout streams of Wiltshire in this sport. It was almost the only thing which his wife did not share with him, but she could not endure it ; and while he was so employed she generally went abroad for a few weeks with Elizabeth, or her friend Emma Miller. Italy and Switzerland had, in the 'seventies, a special romance and glory, and there was then a thrill in the pilgrimage to Rome, to Florence, or to the high Alps which nothing else equalled. Millicent was a very devout tourist, and a very thorough one. She saw sights with the straightforward enjoyment with which she approached everything else, and she diligently read up the proper authorities beforehand so as to miss nothing important. She let herself be guided by Ruskin, and by Augustus Hare ; she took *Romola* to Florence and all the correct books, and found great refreshment from the complete change of thoughts and interests which her foreign journeys brought her. She came home from these travels with the usual tourists' trophies of the period, with photographs and little leather or china objects to be distributed to her friends, and in this, as in all else, she tried to spread out as widely as she could the things she had enjoyed.

Even on her travels, however, she could not resist political interests when they came her way. She was taken to see Garibaldi when he was living near Rome in 1874 and, as she said, it became one of her " most cherished memories to have stood in that noble presence, to have heard that voice, and to have pressed his hand."

Only once did she attempt to make Harry share these pleasures. Inspired, no doubt, by Leslie Stephen's passion for mountaineering, she induced him to go to Switzerland with her, but, as she said, " this was not a success. He was ordinarily so completely cheerful that I had misunderstood the degree to which he would suffer in a place where hardly anything but external beauty and grandeur was spoken of ; I had extolled

the mountain air, but he scoffed at it, and said he preferred the shady side of Regent Street. Two of our
Cambridge friends were our companions who, of course,
helped him to the utmost of their power. With one
of them, Mr. J. F. Moulton (afterwards Lord Moulton),
I made the ascent of Monte Rosa from the Riffel Alp,
with the usual escort of guides and porters. We had
perfect weather and encountered no difficulties. I
immensely enjoyed the expedition, but Harry was in
a fever of anxiety during every hour of my absence,
and I felt on my return that I ought not to have gone.''

This was the only time in all their life together when
she could even imagine that she had failed him in his
blindness. Once again, indeed, she caused him terrible
anxiety, but it was not her own fault. It was during
the election contest at Brighton, in 1874, when, as they
were starting for a ride together, her horse fell with her,
and she was thrown with great force and rendered
unconscious. Harry could not see for himself what
had happened, and thought that she had been killed,
and Leslie Stephen reports that eye-witnesses told him
of Fawcett's terrible agony, and of his pathetic weeping.
She was not seriously hurt, and was soon herself again,
but the next day, when Prof. Fawcett was speaking
to the electors, he could not resist referring to what
had come so forcibly into his mind, namely, the value
and worth of his wife. He thanked the voters for
having supported him in the past, and told them that,
if he had overcome obstacles, it had been by the assistance of others, and because he had '' a helpmate whose
political judgment was much less frequently at fault
than my own.'' It was a remote, reticent way of
referring to her accident, but his hearers understood
him ; and Milly, too, knew that what he was saying
was that if he had lost her it would not only be as a
husband losing his beloved wife, or as a blind man
losing his guide, but as a worker losing his partner, and
a friend his friend.

6

CHAPTER IV

THE WOMEN'S COLLEGES

The Lawn—Philippa as a child—The higher education movement—
The beginning of Newnham—The Graces, 1881—Married women's
property.

BY 1875 the finances of the Fawcetts were somewhat
easier, and there remains a letter from Henry Fawcett's
father written in this year which is interesting, because
it shows the full confidence and trust which existed
between them on all subjects. In this letter the father
thanks his son for offering to reduce by £50 a year the
allowance which was made to him, but assures him
that it will still be paid as usual, as it can well be spared.

" We are delighted," he writes, " to find that your
income is so flourishing, and we sincerely hope that it
may continue to increase. You both deserve good
fortune, for no two work harder than you and Millicent."

This increased prosperity made possible an improvement in the outward circumstances of their lives, and
Millicent found two delightful houses, one in London
and one in Cambridge, in which they were able permanently to settle. One of Prof. Fawcett's friends,
who was to go for a walk with him on the day when
the London house was found, remembers how eagerly
Milly joined them, and how graphically she described
it all to her husband as they went along, telling him
just what the rooms were like, and all about the large
garden and the trees ; and how they walked so far that
they were able to have tea in a farmhouse, and the
Professor suddenly said, " Milly, I think my mouth
must be made of cast iron, I can drink my tea so hot ! " ;
and how they all laughed and enjoyed themselves, and
covered the ground at a tremendous pace.

This London house was at No. 51 The Lawn, South Lambeth Road, and its garden was an unending pleasure to Harry, for he was able to walk freely in it at all hours of the day and night, and, in spite of the fact that it was but a few hundred yards from Vauxhall Station, he was able to hear real birds, and the sound of wind among real leaves.

The Cambridge house was No. 18 Brookside, and although both were still small houses, they were made very delightful by the decorations which Agnes and Rhoda carried out. It was the height of the Morris period, and so it is easy even now to know what these rooms looked like, with the blues and greens, and the chintzes and wall-papers of the period, and the plates, and the Arundel prints on the wall. Mrs. Fawcett found good old furniture in out-of-the-way places in Salisbury, and with this and their many books and flowers, the two houses were delightful, and became famous among their acquaintances for their beauty no less than for the good talk and the good people to be met there.

No description of these houses would be complete without a mention of Oddo, the dog, to whom the whole family was devoted. Oddo was a Dandie Dinmont, and he was supposed to converse extensively with Philippa in a broad East Anglian dialect, and to take a keen interest in current events. He decked himself out in red bows when any of his lady friends passed the Tripos, and entertained all sorts of celebrities to tea in the Lawn garden.

By the time this house was taken Philippa was seven. Her mother had herself taught her "at the very beginning of her baby lessons," and later she went to a day school, first with Miss J. Macleod Smith at Cambridge, and then to the Clapham High School. Like most only children, she was often afflicted by the stories which her parents told about her, and was heard to murmur on one occasion, in a resigned way, " Mother makes them and Father sticks to them "; which was probably true.

The Fawcetts were rather " advanced " in their treatment of their daughter, and not only allowed her freedom to say and think and read what she liked, but also to go about alone in a way that was almost unprecedented. When one of the conventional mothers of the period summoned up courage to remonstrate with Mrs. Fawcett about this, she was met with a disconcerting reply. " There is no need to worry about Philippa," her mother said; " I have told her not to get run over, and she won't," a statement which, although entirely true, did nothing to reassure the visitor. But her mother and father were undisturbed by criticism and remonstrance. On one occasion, when Philippa was fourteen, she and her father were staying at Aldeburgh, and went together to visit Edward Fitzgerald, who was living nearby. The poet, wishing to be friendly to the little girl, asked her what stories she liked best to read, but was completely horrified when she answered " Thackeray and George Eliot." Unable to control his dismay he exclaimed, " What can your mother be thinking of to let you read such books ? " and this, of course, Harry reported to his wife, to her great entertainment ; and no doubt they talked over again together what they *were* thinking of in regard to education and Philippa's future. There was, even then, no doubt about her ability or her special gifts. When she began to have mathematical coaching at Cambridge her teachers quickly recognised that she was an exceptionally good pupil, and it is pleasant to know that her father, though he did not live to see her sensational triumph, was certain that she would be a high Wrangler.

Any account of Mrs. Fawcett's life is necessarily full of her political work and interests and of the women's movement ; but it would be a serious mistake to suppose that these were the only things which occupied or amused her. For the fact was she enjoyed almost everything.

There is a story, for example, of a visit to a copper-mine in Cornwall, in which both Harry and his father had shares, which illustrates the adventurousness of Milly and her determination to act in every way as her husband's eyes. They had gone down to Liskeard to enquire into the affairs of the company, and Milly insisted on seeing for herself the actual work under-ground. She put on the special clothes used by the manager—white flannel " undergarments " with an outer suit of strong white material, great thick boots and warm stockings, and a hard round hat adorned with a lump of clay in which was stuck a tallow candle. In this outfit she climbed down the ladder which led to the shafts and inspected the workings, coming up again, grimed all over, to describe it minutely to her husband, and make him share her experiences.

Into such adventures, as well as into discussions of Indian finance and Land Tenure, Milly was drawn by her desire to share all that interested her husband ; but after 1871 she no longer acted as his sole secretary. In that year Mr. J. F. Dryhurst became his secretary, and, in Mrs. Fawcett's words, " was from that time invaluable." He remained with them until Henry Fawcett's death, and became the lifelong friend of the whole family.

His appointment naturally left Millicent somewhat freer for her own concerns ; and she could use all the time she had. For the causes in which she was involved were growing, and insatiable, and she cared about them more and more. A conversation which she overheard in the waiting-room at Ipswich station about this time fitted in very aptly with the course of her thoughts.

It was, she tells in the reminiscences, " between two clergymen's wives, who were busy making small articles of lace, which were to be sold for the benefit of the schools in their respective parishes. ' What do you find sells best ? ' said No. 1 to No. 2, who instantly replied, ' OH ! THINGS THAT ARE REALLY USEFUL, SUCH AS BUTTERFLIES FOR THE HAIR ! ' Of course, there was a comic aspect to this which I did not fail to appreciate, but I hoped a time would come before very long when intelligent and active-minded women would cease to regard ' butterflies for the hair ' as ' really useful.' "

The aspect of the movement which was coming into prominence at that very time was indeed directed to that end, for it was the movement for the higher education of women, and its storm-centre was Cambridge.

In 1867, the year when Milly was married, Emily Davies had begun to make public a scheme which she had long cherished for starting a real college for women, and two years later it had actually materialised, with six students, in a small house at Hitchin. All had gone well, the students had been coached by lecturers from Cambridge, and Miss Davies had even persuaded the examiners to allow them to take the Previous Examination (Little Go) papers in an unofficial way. Some of the students had passed this examination in 1870, and in 1873 they took the Tripos papers too, and none of them failed ; and in the same year the little party, now grown in numbers, had moved from Hitchin to Girton, on the outskirts of Cambridge itself, where, with great effort and audacity, a raw new college was being built to receive them.

Elizabeth was one of the strong supporters of this adventure, and Milly, of course, knew and approved of it ; but she was not one of those who took an active part in promoting it, for she belonged to another group of people who were trying to bring about the same result in a somewhat different way. And their activities, which covered the same period of time, must have a fuller description, since it was with them that she was closely associated all her life long.

Miss Anne Jemima Clough was the originator of the plan out of which the scheme developed, and Mr.

James Stuart and Mr. Henry Sidgwick were among its chief early supporters. Miss Clough began by arranging a series of local lectures for ladies in the North of England, and these lectures were so eagerly welcomed, and so crowded, that developments followed very fast. In the country as a whole they led to the system of Higher Local Examinations, to the extramural developments of the Universities, and to other schemes ; but what concerns us here is what they led to in Cambridge itself. In 1869, before they had been going in the north for quite two years, Mr. Sidgwick realised that local lectures could easily be given in Cambridge itself, since there were teachers on the spot, and young ladies who might like to be taught ; and he asked Mrs. Fawcett if she would lend her drawing-room one afternoon for a discussion of the idea. All those who were likely to be interested were invited, and a party collected, consisting of University dons, mostly rather youthful ones, and what are still called " Cambridge ladies," that is to say, wives or daughters of University men living in the town.

It is easy to imagine them as they sat discussing the idea—their enthusiasm, their scruples, and their determination to go discreetly about the business of introducing anything so revolutionary !

Henry Sidgwick and Mrs. Fawcett certainly, and probably some of the others too, saw even then that local lectures in Cambridge would attract students from other places, and that if the scheme worked at all it would lead to some form of residential college ; but some were afraid that it would be going too fast to talk of this, and what they actually discussed at the tea-party was the lectures themselves—how and where they could be held, who could be asked to give them, how people were to be admitted, who was to collect fees, and how it was all to be made known.

It is pleasant to think of the people who were gathered there. There was Prof. Fawcett, with his booming

voice making them all welcome ; and there was Milly,
looking so charming, as bold and resolute as any of
them, but rather quiet and attentive. Henry Sidgwick,
with his candid eyes and his fascinating stammer, was
no doubt the chief spokesman, for, as he told his sister,
he was " violently engaged in the scheme for improving
female education." But he was warmly backed up
by James Stuart, who was able to tell them how well
the thing had worked when he had lectured in Liverpool
and the north, and no doubt he made them all laugh
with his stories of the difficulties he had *not* met with ;
then there was Dr. Kennedy, explosive and excitable,
and his daughters, equally fiery but better behaved ;
and Mrs. Bateson, very sure it could all be done,
and capably willing to give out the lecture tickets
herself and see to the finances ; and Mr. Markby, " a
little over-enthusiastic," as Sidgwick said, and " going
to write a paper very soon which is to change public
opinion, and after that we shall succeed "—Mr. Markby
who had been Secretary to the Schools Enquiry Commission, and who had seen so much of girls' education
that it was no wonder he was eager for change. All
these were there, and Prof. Maurice, too, and Dr.
and Mrs. Peile, and Mrs. Venn and Mrs. Adams, friends
of the Fawcetts already, but destined to come closer
than ever as the scheme took shape, sitting quietly
enough there in the drawing-room, but suspecting, as
they made their plans, that they were really doing
something rather ambitious, and feeling quite certain
that it would be good.

And then tea came in, and with it little Philippa, not
boarded out at all, but dressed in white muslin, with
a little blue sash ; and not too shy to trot round among
the guests so long as her mother was there. And,
though they didn't know it, little Philippa was destined
to be one of those who justified their great audacity
in the most public and startling way. They must all
have felt rather serious as they dispersed after this

party, for they had put their hands to a plough which was going to cut deep.

The lectures began the very next term, in spite of the dilatory traditions of a university town, and between seventy and eighty ladies attended them. Milly herself did so when she was in Cambridge, and when she was in London she worked on their behalf in other ways. She saw Mr. Mill and drew him in, and, as Sidgwick said, he " came forward like a woman " and gave money for a scholarship. This, of course, (as he and Mrs. Fawcett and Sidgwick all intended) opened up the subject of residence, and a whole set of new problems appeared. At first, while the holders of scholarships and other " foreigners " were few in number, they could be disposed of among friendly hostesses in the town ; but they came and came in a steady stream, and it was soon very difficult to provide for them. Nobody wanted to turn them away, and yet, Cambridge being what it was, and the year being 1870, no one could contemplate their being alone in lodgings. The Lecture Committee did not feel able to face the responsibility of providing for them, and finally Mr. Sidgwick, who was unbelievably kindhearted, quietly gave up his summer holiday for 1871, and with the money took a small furnished house for their use. He made light of his action. " I am going to have all the fun of being married without the burden of a wife " ; but, of course, it involved him in a great multitude of worries, and it was not until he had secured Miss Clough's promise to take charge of his venture that he felt any peace of mind.

Once this beginning had been made, the thing grew even more rapidly. More and more students came, a larger house and then another still had to be taken, and finally, in 1874, it was decided to build, and the Newnham Hall Company was formed.

All this meant a great deal of anxious work, in which Mrs. Fawcett was deeply involved. There was money

to raise for the buildings, and the Hall itself to plan.
The thing was still so tentative, that the landlords felt
they must be careful, and actually obliged the committee to adopt plans which provided for the division
of the Hall into two private houses, should the scheme
collapse and the students fall away !

Mrs. Fawcett was not only a member of the Company,
but also of the Lecture Association, which continued
as a separate body until 1880 ; and it all meant time
and anxious deliberation. She attended the committee
meetings very faithfully, and began to accumulate the
experience of how to get business done, which stood
her in such good stead later on, and she kept on bringing
in new friends to the movement. She and Miss Clough
frequently consulted each other upon the problems
of the students' lives, and she did her share in entertaining them, and was always seeking for ways in which
they could be helped and encouraged. To those she
knew well she sent pictures for their rooms, books and
even dresses for special occasions ; she was anxious
about their health, their amusements and their hobbies,
their families and their holidays, as well as their examination results, and there remain many letters of hers
from the early years urging her young friends not to
take things too hard or to worry too much, and to be
sure to eat and sleep enough so as to be prepared to do
themselves credit in the Tripos ordeal. When they
left college, too, her care went on, for, of course, she
took as keen an interest in professional openings for
women as in their education itself.

In a letter, written about 1877, to Mr. J. Carvell
Williams, of the Liberation Society, this interest and
her reasons for it are very lucidly expressed.

" I am afraid," she writes, " I cannot send you anything on the general question of the entrance of women
into professions. I have a great collection of pamphlet
literature on Women's Suffrage, Education, Medical
training, and on special laws relating to women,

but none on the general question of the fitness of women for professions. I think the principal argument is like the argument for Free Trade—train the faculties by a sound and healthy education, and then allow these faculties free scope in whatever direction nature and natural gifts may indicate as the fittest. If everything were open and free I think it is just as absurd to fear that women will, as a body, take up work for which nature unfits them, as it would be to fear that Free Trade would cause the capital and labour of Manchester to be wasted in the cultivation of the vine, or any other plant, for the growth of which she has no natural advantages. The value of the opportunity of free development to the individual is so inestimable that a few mistakes and a few instances of misdirected energy are, in comparison, of no importance."

This general view, which nothing could possibly shake, made her ready not only in the 'seventies, but all through her life, to help and encourage the ambitions of young women. Again and again she urged them to persevere, and to look upon their careers as genuinely important.

" It would be a great pity," she wrote to one of them, " for you to give up work that suits you so well. I do not think women ought to give up their work for anything short of *real* necessity. You say you may be wanted at home ; but if, for instance, you were married, you would not give up your husband to go home, and you ought to feel that you are *married* to your work. That is the way to do justice to it and to yourself."

Advice of this kind was seldom given in the 'seventies, for the whole trend of convention was the other way. The young women who were thinking of journalism, of exploration, of science or of medicine found themselves interrupted by their families on the most frivolous pretexts, and expected to subordinate their own affairs to their brothers' holidays, their nieces' measles or their parents' whims ; and a difficult time their consciences had amid all the conflicting claims. Mrs. Fawcett, however, was perfectly clear. Real necessity, real family emergencies must come first, whether for man or woman ; but for the rest, if they were fit for good work they must do it ; and adventurous girls were always sure of her sympathy and her practical help— introductions, books, sometimes loans to start them off on their careers, so that all over the world there came to be women who owed their success to Mrs. Fawcett. In the 'seventies, however, the preliminary difficulty of getting education and training was still the chief trouble. The students who came to Newnham Hall nearly all did so in the face of serious family disapproval ; and much discussion and persuasion, and much reassuring and pleading went to the arrival of every one. Mrs. Fawcett took her full share in this task, being always ready, because she sympathised so truly with the girls, to try to win over their parents ; and whenever she could make the opportunity she did effective propaganda among them.

There is a letter of hers to Mrs. Merrifield, the wife of Prof. Fawcett's Brighton friend, which throws a good deal of light upon the perplexities of girls of that period. Even in enlightened families, where the main position was accepted without reservation, the practical working out was not easy, and it needed the heavy guns which Mrs. Fawcett could bring to bear to enable the daughter to have her way. The letter is dated February 11, 1877, and is written from The Lawn.

" It has given me the greatest pleasure," she says, " to be allowed a sight of May's delightful letter. The whole tone of it does her immense credit. My own feeling on the subject of the letter is strongly in favour of the Tripos. I always regretted that May did not from the first decide to study for some one Tripos ; partly because of the value as a mental training of the severe concentration which work for a Tripos involves, and also because I was sure that May would make a success that would be most valuable to the cause of women's education. I should most heartily rejoice for May's own sake and for the sake of the cause, if she and you all made the sacrifice of her prolonged absence from home in order to enable her to read for the Classical Tripos. Notwithstanding the keen love of home which May so deeply feels, I feel sure (from the tone of her letter) that she is almost passionately desirous of reading for the Tripos ; and that giving it up, though she might think it her higher duty to do so, would cause her a bitter pang.

" Before deciding finally either way, do you not think it would be a good plan if Mr. Merrifield consulted May's Latin Lecturer as to her chances of a first class in that subject ? She evidently has the true scholar's intensity of love for the Classics ; her progress in Greek must be most wonderful. I believe that, so far as she herself is concerned, she does not hesitate for an instant in her choice ; she longs to read for the Tripos. But she does hesitate because she is not sure whether it is her duty to return home after June 1878. I think the question resolves itself into whether you are willing to make this sacrifice for her sake ; and of this you alone can be the judges. Harry quite concurs in what I have written. He joins me in kindest regards to you all."

This letter, as can be imagined, settled the matter, and May was enabled to feel free to stay for her Tripos, which in fact she passed with great distinction, going on to become a notable classical scholar, the wife of Prof. Verrall, and in her turn a member of the staff of Newnham College, a guide and inspirer of students.

It would be misleading to pretend that all the expansion and development of higher education proceeded with no troubles but those which came from outward opposition. There were two other sources of difficulty, and one of them came from the students themselves, who, though they were wonderfully good as students, and wonderfully patient of restrictions on the whole, did now and then break out a little into impatience.

The first example of this came at the very start, when

the early pioneer students were cooped up together in
the little house which Henry Sidgwick had taken, and
when even he was forced to admit that it had been
" rather a trying term." But he understood what was
the matter. " There is such a strong impulse towards
liberty among the young women attracted by the movement," he wrote, " that they will not submit to maternal
government " ; and though it was clear that they had
to be governed somehow, and though he himself sometimes had to reprove them, he did not in his heart seriously
blame the students. In exactly the same way Mrs.
Fawcett looked at their vagaries.

" You plunged daggers into my heart," she wrote
to her friend Emma Miller in 1880, " by hinting that
everything was not perfect at the Newnham festivity.
The ' perfect law of liberty ' will, when it is supreme,
diffuse sweetness and light about clothes and other
things ; the ugly eccentricities that one meets with now
are similar to the ostentation of the nouveaux riches.
These poor children have only just found a little bit
of liberty, and they give themselves airs over it."

With such sympathy among the governors, and with
the tremendous earnestness of the students, the little
troubles which arose did not grow to difficult propor-
tions ; but the other internal difficulty of the education
movement was more troublesome, and gave more
anxiety on all sides, and that was the divergence of view
between the Girton and Newnham Committees. As
the thing has turned out, the differences have melted
into nothing, and the two schemes have merged into
one achievement ; but in the early days, when it was
all so dangerous and difficult, and when a false step
seemed as if it might wreck everything, it was another
matter.

Miss Davies and the Girton Committee felt that the
only possible line of safety lay in making the young
women adhere strictly to the regulations in force for
young men. They dreaded and distrusted any special

variation designed to " suit women," and they insisted
on compulsory Greek, and the full term of residence
for their students. Henry Sidgwick and his friends
did not care much about this aspect of the business.
What they sought was to give education, the best they
could devise, to young women. They did not want
to impose upon them restrictions which they thought
bad in the case of men, and they were unwilling to shut
out short-time students, who might gain something
from the chance. Even the proposal of special examinations for women did not unduly worry them—though
to Miss Davies they were anathema—and it was therefore evident that the two schemes could not amalgamate
at all. Nevertheless, when both were so struggling,
and when money was so hard to come by, it seemed
dreadful to have two separate efforts going on in the
same University, and more than once attempts were
made to combine them. In spite of great goodwill on
both sides, these well-meant proposals met with no
success.

As Henry Sidgwick wrote to his friend, Frederick
Myers, in 1871, he was " forced more and more into
involuntary antagonism with Miss Davies," and he
added—characteristically for both of them—" She
wrote to me the other day and mentioned affably that
I was the serpent that was eating out her vitals."

This state of affairs made the business more difficult,
and it is a great tribute to the good sense of both groups,
and to their genuine enthusiasm for the cause as a whole,
that friends and lecturers were able to work with both
colleges without feeling treacherous to either.

Mrs. Fawcett naturally had an important part to
play in this delicate situation. Emily Davies, who was
the leader, and indeed almost the whole driving force
of the Girton Committee, was her sister Elizabeth's
friend. Milly still felt a little in awe of her, and still
remembered that she had been a small child when Emily
was already quite grown up ; but she was not going

to give way for that reason. A good deal of quite plain-spoken, though very civil correspondence passed between them, and in the end they agreed to differ. After all, the field was distressingly wide, and there were students enough and there was work enough for both colleges ; and it would be suicidal and small-minded and wrong to keep any quarrel alive.

For all their mutual toleration, cases of difficulty often occurred, since both had to deal with the same unwilling University, and both had to share the same informal position. It was at the instance of Girton, and rather against the advice of the Newnham people, that the petition for official recognition went forward in 1880 ; but once it had started they had of course to stand shoulder to shoulder, and when the preliminaries had all been gone through, and the Syndicate had reported, and the vote in the Senate came on, they were all so anxious and excited that they forgot to be hostile at all. The vote was taken on February 24, 1881, and Mrs. Fawcett, like the rest, did all she could to induce her friends to come up to support the right side.

We can imagine the letters she and her husband sent out, and the anxiety they felt. Everything depended on it, for if the vote were lost even the informal sanction which had hitherto obtained would vanish. Everything hung upon the decision of the M.A.'s ; and no one could tell who was coming up, or what the out-voters would do.

" I shall never forget," Henry Sidgwick wrote to his sister in describing the great day, " the astonishment with which I realised that the Senate House was full of about 400 M.A.'s, and that, so far as I could see, they were all going to vote on the right side. Ultimately, with great trouble, I discovered the Enemy seated in a depressed manner on a couple of benches in one corner, about thirty in number."

So it was. The Graces admitting women to the Honours examinations, though not to the degrees, were passed by 331 votes to 32 ; and we can imagine how Milly and the other ladies waited outside, and how their friends came rushing out with the good news, and what rejoicing and happiness there was that night in the colleges themselves and in the homes of their Cambridge friends.

While Newnham and Girton were starting at Cambridge the other aspects of the women's movement were still struggling on, and the agitation to secure to married women the right to hold their own property was in full swing. In 1870 an Act was passed allowing them possession of their own earnings, but this was of course not enough to satisfy those who believed that women should be really independent people. " My conception of harmony," Millicent used to say, " is not the music of a husband playing a solo on the trombone," and she entered with enthusiasm into the efforts to secure a wider Bill. Early in the 'seventies Mrs. Fawcett brought the subject up at a meeting of the Liberal electors of East Suffolk which was held in her father's house at Aldeburgh.

" Those present were mostly Suffolk farmers," she relates in the reminiscences. " I explained my petition, and asked for signatures, but obtained very few. One old farmer voiced the feelings of the majority. ' Am I to understand you, ma'am, that if this Bill becomes law, and my wife had a matter of a hundred pound left her, I should have to *arst* her for it ? ' Of course I was obliged to confess that he would have to suffer this humiliation, and then I got no more signatures."

This meeting no doubt brought home to Milly the difficulties in the way of the reform, but another experience which befell her in 1877 brought home its importance.

" I was at Waterloo station taking a ticket," she writes. " As I dropped my purse back into my pocket I felt a hand there that was not my own ; I naturally grabbed it and tried to hold it ; naturally also I was

7

unsuccessful : it belonged to a young man who quickly
broke from me with my purse in his possession.   Some
bystanders grasped the situation, and pursued the thief,
who threw my purse on the ground, and ended his
flight in the arms of a policeman.   He and the thief
and I were then marched off to a small office in the
station, where there was a police inspector.   The policeman said, ' This here young gen'leman have been liftin'
a bit off this here young lady.'   The inspector said to
me, ' Do you charge him ? ' and I replied, ' Yes.'   If
I had known then as much as I knew later, I should
have said NO, and contented myself with the recovery
of my purse.   ' But I, being young and foolish,' did
not see that this would have been the best both for me
and for the thief.   He was brought up before a police
magistrate the next day and committed for trial at the
Surrey Sessions.   I had to come up from Cambridge
in about six weeks' time to give evidence against him.
When in the Court I saw the charge sheet, and noted
that the thief was charged with ' stealing from the
person of Millicent Fawcett a purse containing £1 18s. 6d.,
the property of Henry Fawcett,' I felt as if I had been
charged with theft myself."

Feelings of this sort, though they were growing strong
among all kinds of women, would probably not have
been enough, by themselves, to produce a change in
the law ; for, of course, women were still a long way
from enfranchisement.   But the trading community
and the lawyers joined forces with the women, because
of their experience of the inconveniences of the existing
state of affairs, and bit by bit improvements were
brought about, until in 1882 the full Married Women's
Property Act was passed.

Victories, however, did not mean repose for any of
the pioneer women.   As soon as one point was gained,
they passed on to the next ; and Millicent, like the rest,
found a fresh incitement to effort in every advance.
There was still so much to do ; and she felt so strong
and eager to do it.

CHAPTER V

HENRY FAWCETT'S WORK AND DEATH

Open spaces—India—Religious tests—Protective legislation for women—Fawcett and Gladstone—The Post Office—Henry Fawcett's illness—Rhoda's death—The Reform Bill and defeat of Women's Suffrage clause—Henry Fawcett's death.

WHEN old Mr. Fawcett had said to his son that " no two work harder than you and Millicent," he had spoken no less than the truth. But they both loved to do it, for there were dozens of things which seemed to them worth attempting ; and they both felt strong and energetic and eager to use their powers.

Over and above their regular work for the women's movement, and the political economy lectures which were part of Harry's duties as a Professor, they interested themselves in innumerable questions of general political importance, and cared intensely about them. The preservation of open spaces was one of these subjects, and Henry Fawcett took immense trouble, and grudged no effort which might enable him to help to preserve Epping Forest, Wimbledon Common, the New Forest, or the banks of the Thames from destruction. He spared himself no pains, but entered into all the laborious consultations with the Commons Preservation Society and with Miss Octavia Hill, and he also went himself continually to " see " the threatened places and to learn on the spot what was actually going on and become familiar with the local circumstances.

It was sometimes a considerable interruption to his other work ; but Henry Fawcett loved the thought of wide spaces and lovely scenery as much as, or even more than, people who could see them ; and he did not let the matter drop until he had preserved these things for the people. He it was who moved in the House of Commons the injunction which prevented the felling of any more of the New Forest trees till after the Royal Commission should have reported ; and later, when the Commission was sitting, he gave evidence himself, showing a knowledge of the Forest which was truly amazing. It was then over twenty years since his blindness had come upon him ; but he had visited the Forest from Salisbury in his boyhood, and he had walked much there in the course of his investigations, and the whole region seemed to be as dear to him as to many seeing people who had lived there all their lives. To this day Henry Fawcett is remembered as the preserver of the Forest, and the Act of 1877, which followed upon the Report of the Commission, is its Charter.

Another of Henry Fawcett's absorbing interests was India, and on this subject he became so much one of the leading authorities in the House that he came to be known as " the Member for India." In the general election of 1874 he was defeated at Brighton, and when the news of this reached Calcutta the sense of what his loss would mean was so acute that a fund was at once opened and £400 was sent home to defray his expenses in another contest. Before the money reached him he had already been adopted and elected for Hackney ; but the money was used at the next election in 1880 ; whereupon a similar sum was again raised to be ready for another call.

Henry Fawcett confined his work for India mainly to financial aspects. The subject was, of course, highly technical, and Fawcett's mastery of the facts, and powers of cross-examining expert witnesses, which would have been remarkable even in a man who had the use of his eyes, were astonishing in one who was blind. He forced the House, year after year, to give serious consideration to the Indian Budget by the earnestness and lucidity with which he explained it, and though his view of Indian problems did not always prevail, his contention that Parliament must seriously occupy itself with the affairs resulting from its great responsibility came to be not only respected but fully conceded.

Outside Parliament and, ultimately, within it also, another of Henry Fawcett's great interests was University reform. In the intricate problems of college politics, Fawcett had always taken an eager interest, and, with nearly all his Cambridge friends, he was ardent for the removal of religious tests, for the removal of the bar against married Fellows, and for the endowment of research and the changes in University teaching which have since been brought about. The ins and outs of these campaigns are fully described in other places—they do not rightly belong to the story of Henry Fawcett's wife. But it is certain that they occupied much of her time and attention, and that she discussed them often and eagerly, gave her advice as to procedure and tactics, and became immersed, even as Henry did, in the intangible niceties of University politics, and the gossip and amusement which are an inseparable part of all such campaigns.

One pleasant thing which this controversy brought to them both was a visit to Dublin and other parts of Ireland, during the time when the question of religious tests in Dublin University was before Parliament. On this visit, as on all their journeys, they collected a great number of new friends ; and of course this time they also collected a great many good Irish stories to carry home. They did not lose sight of their new friends, and in later years, when Mrs. Fawcett's own work came to be closely connected with Ireland, she returned there again and again.

The effort to secure the removal of all religious tests was one aspect of Henry Fawcett's endeavour to

establish religious freedom.   His own views were those
of an Agnostic rather than an Atheist, and a great deal
of importance attached to the distinction, which Mrs.
Fawcett was very careful to preserve.   There remains
a letter, dated 1874, from one of her friends whom she
had taken to task for " coupling with your husband's
name the term Atheist."

" You were right," the penitent friend admits, " in
saying I was wanting in Christian charity when I used
the words of others in speaking on so very grave a
matter, and I am very sorry."

If Henry Fawcett could not be called an Atheist,
neither could he be called a Christian.   " The three
best men I have known," Mrs. Fawcett told W. T.
Stead in later years, " were not Christians " ; and when
asked to name these, she mentioned her husband, John
Stuart Mill and Henry Sidgwick : and all three held
very similar views.

They felt no certainty about religious doctrines, or
the existence of a future life, and did not base their
belief in the necessity of human virtue and effort upon
those things.   Industry, virtue and high endeavour
seemed to be self-evidently good, and they saw no need
to reinforce these by the sanctions of any faith or dogma.
And there were many men and women in the 'seventies
and 'eighties who shared this outlook.

During the years when Henry Fawcett was in Parliament the question of religious liberty became very
prominent, and he naturally took his stand with the
reformers.   The " secularist " agitation carried on by
Bradlaugh and others was rousing a great deal of
opposition, and the subject was much discussed.
Fawcett gave general support to Bradlaugh's position,
but when in 1877 the famous case which resulted from
his Birth Control pamphlet came on, Fawcett no longer
upheld him.   There is an interesting letter from Mrs.
Fawcett to Bradlaugh written in June 1877 on this
matter :

" I have no doubt that you are aware," she writes, " that I was served last night with a subpœna on your behalf during the absence of my husband at Cambridge. I am surprised at your taking this course, as I thought my husband had already explained to you personally as well as to the messenger whom you sent with the purpose of serving us with subpœnas last Wednesday week, that if we were called as witnesses we should effectually damage your case. Your messenger on that occasion (whose name I think is Mr. Paris), on hearing the very strong opinion which Mr. Fawcett entertains as to the objectionable character of the work you have published, refrained in your interest from serving the subpœnas. So far as my knowledge of the book enables me to speak, I agree entirely with the opinion I have frequently heard Mr. Fawcett express, and this opinion, as I believe you know, is strongly condemnatory of the character of the book.

" I cannot believe it possible that you wish to make either Mr. Fawcett or myself exhibits in the witness box to our great annoyance, and I may add to my extreme pain, without any possible good accruing to yourself ; and I therefore assume that the subpœna is only a precautionary measure on your part, and that we shall not be called to prove authorship which it is impossible to conceive will be disputed by the prose-cution, and the bearing of which, even if it is disputed, I fail to see.

" Mr. Fawcett has not yet returned home, and conse-quently I have not seen him since I was served with the subpœna, but I know enough of his mind on this matter to be confident that he fully concurs in what I have said in this letter.

" I am, Sir, yours obediently,
" MILLICENT GARRETT FAWCETT."

After this letter it is not surprising that neither Mr. nor Mrs. Fawcett was called to give evidence ; but later, when in 1880 Bradlaugh became a Member of Parliament, Henry Fawcett again supported him in the matter of taking the oath. Bradlaugh might be, and indeed was, an uncomfortable champion of liberty ;

but liberty itself, wherever attacked, commanded Fawcett's allegiance.

It was partly on this same ground that Fawcett took up an unpopular stand in 1874, and found himself almost alone in the House in its defence. This was on the occasion when one of the early laws for the special protection of women in industry was brought forward. There had been a Home Office Committee in 1873 which recommended that women's hours should be reduced to a lower legal limit than those for men, and Fawcett opposed the resulting legislation. It was not that he was opposed to all factory laws. In spite of the inherent dislike which all the philosophic Radicals felt for State interference, Henry Fawcett had consistently supported the Factory Acts ; and had repeatedly urged that their provisions should be extended to agricultural workers. He had claimed that one of the chief benefits of a wider franchise would be better factory laws, and he took great pains to make himself familiar both with the general benefits of the Acts and with the difficulties of administration. When, however, this proposal with regard to women came forward, he vehemently opposed it, and although he was almost the only person inside the House of Commons to hold this opinion, he persisted in trying to amend the Bill throughout its course. His view, which his wife fully shared, was that such a law, which classed " women and young persons " together, would impose a handicap both upon the status and upon the opportunities of women workers, and that, within the framework of the factory law, all adult workers should have an equal standing. He relied upon the organisation of the workers themselves to provide the best safeguard against oppressive conditions, and declared that this proposal was, in part at any rate, the work of male Trade Unions anxious to restrict and limit the competition of female labour. All this was unavailing. The Act was passed in 1878, and the hours of work for women have remained to this day legally less than those for men. But it is interesting to know that a controversy in which Mrs. Fawcett was still engaged in 1929 began at such an early date.

Politically, as we have seen, Henry Fawcett was a Liberal ; but he was by no means always orthodox. He was exceedingly anxious to see working men represented in the House of Commons, and did all he could to encourage such independent candidates when they came forward, even if they were opposing official Liberals. In 1870 he supported a shoemaker friend of his, George Odger, at a by-election in Southwark, and did his best to persuade one of the official Liberal candidates to retire in his favour, though without success. Millicent, too, supported Odger, and spoke for him, and she records that this led to the only serious disagreement she ever had with her mother-in-law. Old Mrs. Fawcett was an ardent and very orthodox Liberal, and she did not at all approve of her son's action, though she said nothing about that. " But," as Millicent said, " at that time it was an unheard-of thing for women to speak on election platforms, and that I had done this on behalf of a candidate who was in opposition to the Liberal Party was to her an almost unforgivable sin. I couldn't promise I would never do it again, but I did promise never to speak in Salisbury unless she invited me to do so, and this promise, of course, I kept, and in course of time she did invite me and I accepted the invitation."

It was not only by supporting unorthodox candidates that Fawcett showed his uneasiness under the Party Whip. Throughout his early years in the House, he was very critical of his own Party, and of its leader in particular ; and this feeling was reciprocated by Gladstone. Although later on they worked together, and agreed on many things, Fawcett was never entirely forgiven for the successful stand he made on the Dublin University Bill, which caused Gladstone's fall in 1873 ;

and both men were conscious of the fact. After the election of 1874, however, the Liberals were in opposition, and Fawcett then found it easier to agree with his Party, and was ready to make common cause with them against Disraeli ; and during the next six years, while his own influence and political standing were steadily increasing, his party orthodoxy was quite good. When, therefore, the election of 1880 led to the formation of a Liberal Government, Gladstone offered him a place in it, as Postmaster-General, though without a seat in the Cabinet. The antagonism of the two men was not ended, and could not be ended, because it was founded on their very different characters ; but their politics were close enough together for co-operation to be possible.

Henry Fawcett was unaffectedly glad to accept office. It was, of course, difficult for him to abandon his accustomed position as a critic, and to resign any of his political independence. But he felt that a position in the Government offered a great opportunity for usefulness, and he was, quite simply, pleased to be promoted.

The new appointment brought with it a new source of income, but the Fawcetts did not alter their style of living, or even set up a carriage. One or two developments were, of course, inevitable. Millicent was presented at Court, and had to give some more formal entertainments than she had previously done ; and she also found some unexpected domestic drawbacks in being the wife of the Postmaster-General.

" My cook is going to be married," she wrote to Emma Miller, " but not for about a year. There's many a slip, etc. Her young man may find somebody else to keep company with while she is at Cambridge next autumn. But unfortunately he is a postman, so I expect he thinks all his fortunes here and hereafter depend on his marrying the P.M.G.'s cook."

On the whole, however, nothing was greatly changed, and life went on at Cambridge and at Lambeth as before, except that a new and fascinating interest in the Post Office work was added to all the rest.

It is not necessary here to describe Fawcett's brilliant success as Postmaster-General, nor the way in which he turned his personal qualities and his care for the welfare of the people to the advantage of his administration. All those with whom he came in contact loved him ; and all the reforms he carried through were popular and beneficial, and the blind Postmaster came to be a character known and admired in every part of the kingdom. But all this belongs to his own life and is fully told by his biographer,[1] and it is only those parts of his new work which connect directly with his wife's activities which can be told in any detail here.

Henry Fawcett had, as we have seen, a great concern for the conditions of employment of women, and when he went to the Post Office he found that there were already a small number of women working there. The method of their appointment was not by examination, but by nomination and interview, and he was greatly troubled and distressed by the enormous number of applicants for each post, even when the salaries were exceedingly small. On one occasion he had to consider 900 applicants for 40 posts carrying a salary of £65 a year. Henry Fawcett realised that this was one of the many evil results of the very limited choice of occupations which was open to women, and he set himself at once to increase their employment and their prospects in the Government service. He instituted entry by competition, and appointed women supervisors for them, and in consultation with Mrs. Garrett Anderson he provided a woman doctor to look after them. He was anxious to safeguard their physical health, and was much interested in installing labour-saving and weight-lifting devices (from which, of course, the male employees also benefited), and he often enquired how the women were getting on. On one such

[1] *Life of Henry Fawcett*, by Leslie Stephen : Smith, Elder & Co., 1886.

occasion, their superintendent, Miss C. Smith, gave him an answer which greatly struck him. The girls, she said, improved markedly in health as soon as they got promotion, with its rise in salary, because then, in her own words, " they were able to dine more frequently." This answer, and the facts which underlay it, weighed greatly on Henry Fawcett's mind, and both he and his wife used frequently to quote it in their efforts to improve the position of women.

There was another direction, too, in which the position of the women under the Post Office was difficult, and that was with regard to marriage. No regulation requiring resignation on marriage was then in force, but a serious trouble arose in the case of " receivers " who combined the office of post-mistresses with the keeping of a village shop. After marriage, as the law then stood, the women were legally unable to enter into contracts, and in consequence of this it was customary to transfer the office, nominally at any rate, to their husbands, who were sometimes far from ideal for the post. Mr. Fawcett saw in this absurd state of affairs another argument for the Married Women's Property Bill, and after 1882, when that injustice had been corrected, he made arrangements for the post-mistresses to go on holding their own positions in their own right.

The Post Office work was in full swing, the Married Women's Property Act was just passed, and Millicent was in the full tide of literary and political activity when her dear cousin Rhoda Garrett, her " extra sister " as she used to call her, fell seriously ill, and died. Rhoda's death was a terrible grief to the whole family and particularly to Agnes, and of course Milly went at once to be with her dearest sister in her trouble. Just at that moment, however, Harry also fell ill, and she hurried back to find that he had both diphtheria and typhoid fever, and in a short time he was in serious danger. There followed two months of great anxiety, which was shared by thousands of people all over the country. The Queen telegraphed constantly, sometimes even twice a day, for news of his condition, and the greatest anxiety was felt by Post Office workers, and by working men and women of every kind for the recovery of the man whom they thought of as their best friend. At last, towards the end of December, he began to recover, and after a convalescence of three months he was able to go back to his official work again. He appeared to be fully restored, and was as gay and cheerful as before, and not only his wife but all his friends were profoundly thankful and relieved. Elizabeth, who had been one of the doctors attending him, expressed what they all of them thought. " I only feel," she said, " that you make too much of the small service I was able to give in December. It was in strictest truth a service of affection, and you rewarded us all quite enough by getting well at the end of it."

After Harry's illness the family life went on again as before, though Rhoda's death had left a great blank. But her younger brother, Edmund, whom they had seen much of when he was at Cambridge, became a close friend, and his charm and wit, which resembled Rhoda's own, made him very welcome everywhere. He had been what his cousins thought rather flighty at college, caring more for other outside work and interests than for his academic studies ; but he took all their scoldings very meekly, and was so lovable and so amusing that they could never be angry with him ; and he remained a close and really intimate friend of his cousins Milly and Agnes from then until his death.

During 1883 and the early part of 1884 the Women's Suffrage question, which had been quiescent in Parliament since 1870, came forward again. Gladstone was preparing for his Reform Bill, and even the most inexperienced of the Suffrage workers realised that unless women could be slipped into the Bill before it became law, the extension of the vote to fresh classes of men would make the inclusion of women harder than ever. There was therefore great activity among the Committees, and an attempt was made to collect the wildly ambitious sum of £5,000. Strenuous and successful efforts were made to get categorical promises of support from Liberal Members of Parliament, and the terms of possible amendments were discussed. There were differences of opinion about this, as about most things, inside the ranks of the movement itself, and the chief debatable point was whether or not the amendment should be so drafted as to enfranchise, or omit, properly qualified married women. In previous Bills and resolutions this point had hardly arisen, since the legal disability of married women to own property had prevented them from being qualified ; but after 1882 this state of affairs no longer existed, and it was therefore open to the suffragists to draw their amendment so as to include or exclude them. The matter was one of heated controversy, for although they were all agreed that married women ought ultimately to be enfranchised, some were afraid that it was too much to ask for at the outset, and believed that much more support could be secured for a really limited proposal which only included spinsters and widows.

Both Mr. and Mrs. Fawcett took a bolder view, and there is a letter from Mrs. Jacob Bright, dated February 1884, which calls up the echoes of this very dead controversy.

" Thank you *most heartily*," she writes, " for supporting the claim of qualified married women to the Suffrage at the Conference yesterday. We cannot exclude them without making ourselves and our cause ridiculous. What strength there is in consistency and courage, and how sadly we have been weakened by the timidity of our friends both in and out of Parliament. A true word from you will strengthen many weak knees, and I am thankful it has been spoken so opportunely.

" I am certain that women in their dealings with men

have nothing to fear and everything to gain by an evident truthfulness and straightforwardness. I never myself hesitate to tell men, when asked about my ' ulterior ends,' that I mean to have everything in the shape of a right or a privilege which they think worth having for themselves—no more and no less. No one is really frightened of a woman with a baby in her arms."

All the preparation and the trouble was, however, unavailing. When the Bill actually came on in the House, Gladstone turned his great guns against the women. He declared that their amendment would overweight the Bill, and that if it were passed he would abandon the whole thing and withdraw it ; and 104 of his followers, intimidated by this threat, incontinently broke the pledges which the women had so hopefully extracted, and defeated the amendment handsomely. And with this vote the political disillusionment of the Women's Suffrage Committees began.

Some of the friends of the movement stood firm, and Henry Fawcett was one of these. As a member of the Government he could not, of course, vote against the Party Whip, but as an honourable man he could not vote with it ; and accordingly he walked out of the House before the division, and Sir Charles Dilke, who was President of the Local Government Board, and Mr. Leonard Courtney, who was Secretary to the Treasury, went with him. The next day Fawcett received the following letter from Downing Street, written in Gladstone's own hand :

" *Confidential.*

June 16, '84.

" MY DEAR FAWCETT,—

" I have no doubt you bear in mind a correspondence which took place between us some time back on the personal voting of members of the Government, and the rules applicable to it, so that you will not be surprised at hearing from me after the recent division on Mr. Woodall's amendment. With this preface I beg you kindly to read the enclosed memorandum, which has received the sanction of the Cabinet.

" Believe me, sincerely yours,

" W. E. GLADSTONE."

The memorandum, which was no doubt also sent to the other two rebels, runs as follows :

" It has probably come to the notice of my colleagues that, in a division early this morning, which was known to be vital to the Franchise Bill and to the Government, three of its members abstained from voting.

" Preliminary intimation had been given to this effect, and some effort had been made to bring about a different intention. This change of mind was hoped for, but no question of surprise can be raised.

" It is, however, an elementary rule, necessary for the cohesion and character of Administrations, that on certain questions, and notably on questions vital to their existence, their members should vote together. In the event of their not doing so their intention to quit the Government is presumed, and in all ordinary circumstances ought to take effect.

" At the present moment, however, beside the charge of a great legislative measure, and an ever-increasing mass of other business, the Ministry is rapidly approaching a crisis on a question of foreign affairs which involves questions of deepest importance not only to the welfare of Egypt but to the character and honour of the country and to the law and concord and possibly even the peace of Europe.

" It would be most unfortunate were the minds of men at such a juncture to be disturbed by the resignation of a Cabinet Minister and of two other gentlemen holding offices of great importance on a question which, important as it is, relates mainly to the internal discipline and management of the official corps.

" I therefore propose to my colleagues that I be authorised to request the President of the Local Government Board, the Postmaster-General, and the Secretary to the Treasury that they will do us the favour to retain their respective offices.

" (Signed) W. E. GLADSTONE."

To this letter Henry Fawcett replied at once ; and the answer was in Milly's handwriting :

" *Confidential*.

June 17, '84.

" DEAR MR. GLADSTONE,—

" I beg to acknowledge the receipt of your letter of the 16th inst. and the accompanying memorandum. I was fully aware, after the correspondence which took place between us last year on the question raised in connection with the payment of the Indian troops employed in the military operations in Egypt, that any member of the Government who abstains from voting on a critical division virtually places his resignation in the hands of the Prime Minister ; and I can assure you that I did not decide to abstain from voting on Mr. Woodall's amendment until I had duly weighed in all its bearings the consequences which such a course of action might involve.

" With many thanks to you for the personal kindness of your communication, Believe me, dear Mr. Gladstone,

" Yours very truly,

" HENRY FAWCETT."

Mr. Gladstone's behaviour over this Reform Bill was a thing which Mrs. Fawcett never forgave or forgot. Until then she had disliked and somewhat distrusted the Prime Minister ; but from that day she felt much more strongly still ; and whenever, in later years, she found points which did not redound to his credit, she delighted in making them known. For, as she often said of herself, she was " not a forgiving person " ; and Gladstone, by his action, had outraged her whole sense of what a Liberal leader should be. There are some notes of a speech made at that time which express her opinions very exactly.

" Mr. G.," they run, " said W. S. would overweight the ship. The simile is unfortunate. The tradition of British seamanship in peril or disaster is ' Save the women first.' Mr. G.'s instinctive thought that rises unbidden to his lips is, ' Throw them overboard.' "

8

Millicent was, no doubt, upheld by her indignation when she delivered this speech ; but still she hated to do it. There is a letter from her to Miss Jane Cobden (Mrs. Cobden Unwin) dated earlier in this same year refusing a meeting at Birmingham, in which she openly confesses the fact. " No one knows how speaking takes it out of me," she says. " Before that last St. James's Hall meeting I was downright ill, but I know I don't show it, and I believe people think I rather like making speeches. Anyhow, invitations to speak flow in upon me in an unceasing stream, so I hope you will not think my refusal churlish. . . . Besides my own disinclination," she adds, " I do believe that it is very important to try and bring out fresh speakers. The debating societies of Girton and Newnham and other places ought to have brought out some new speakers if we could but find them ; and new people ought to try and speak. No one knows whether they can speak or not till they try. I believe everyone *can* speak who has got anything to say. Of course they don't like it, but no more do I."

Poor Millicent ! Neither her " disinclination " nor her refusals were of much avail against the " unceasing " calls of her conscience.

The Reform Bill debates and Mr. Gladstone's betrayal took place in the early summer of 1884 ; and that year the Fawcetts were kept late in London by some difficult negotiations which were going on between the Post Office and the private telephone companies, and Harry had no proper holiday. All seemed to be well, however. He was not as strong as he had been before his illness, but he was not at all ill, and felt fully equal to his work, even though it was more than normally arduous. In the autumn they moved as usual to Cambridge for his lectures, but he was obliged to travel to and fro a good deal because of the official work and the sitting of Parliament. There was nothing to show that he was feeling the strain too much, and they were all in their

usual good spirits, and living their happy lives, and eager
with schemes for future work, when the terrible calamity
of Harry's death came suddenly upon them.   Early in
November he caught a cold, which at first seemed to
be nothing more ; but it very quickly developed into
pneumonia, accompanied by heart trouble   In a
moment almost, from being in full work, he was in
serious danger ; and on November 6, after an illness
of less than a week, he died.

It is easy to realise the crushing effect upon Millicent
of this great and sudden bereavement.   She was thirty-
seven years old, in the midst of full activity and enjoyment, and all in a moment everything was altered, and
the companionship which had been the very centre of
her life was taken from her.   Harry, who had depended
on her, and on whom she had depended, was gone, and
the world was a different place.

" Left alone after seventeen years of happy active
married life," she said in her reminiscences, " I might
have fallen into a lethargic melancholy, if it had not
been for the help I received from many of my husband's
old friends, and also in a very high degree from all the
members of my own family—father, mother, sisters,
brothers, and also from my own daughter.   All these
stood by me and helped me at every turn."

Of course her family and her friends did help her, for
she loved them, and they her.   But it does not seem as
if this could have been the whole story of that time.
Lethargic melancholy could surely never have overcome a nature like Millicent's, even had she stood alone,
for she was neither selfish nor weak nor self-absorbed.

The first person to whom she turned when Harry
died was her own special sister Agnes.   Elizabeth, who
had been one of the doctors attending Harry, telegraphed
to her at once.   " We have lost our dear Harry," the
message ran, " Millicent asks for you."   And without
a moment's delay she came.

Henry Fawcett's funeral was at Trumpington, a

little village just outside Cambridge, and it was attended
by an immense concourse of people. Not only did his
friends come, and they were hundreds, but many of
those who had only seen him once, and many more who
had never met him, but only admired his life ; and
besides these, there were his colleagues, his Post Office
friends, and the University officials. The procession
grew and lengthened upon the road, and when it reached
the church many and many of the people could not
find room inside ; and even in the churchyard the
crowd was so great that it broke down the containing
wall and overflowed into the road beyond. Flowers
and letters and messages of sympathy poured in from
every part of the kingdom : the Queen wrote herself,
and there was but one feeling everywhere—we have
lost a great and a good man.

All this, of course, though it could not console, did
please Millicent. She knew, better than anyone else,
what it was that they had lost ; but it comforted her
to realise that her sorrow was shared in part by so many
friends, and that Harry's worth was understood and
Harry's influence felt so widely. At least he had not
lived in vain, and part of what he had hoped to do he
had done ; and as she dwelt on these thoughts she
found the way back to her own peace. She found that
it was possible to remember what she had had, and
what Harry had been, instead of only her own present
loss. And after the first misery and shock she was able
not to pity herself because he was dead, but instead to
rejoice because he had lived ; and in this way she met
her sorrow and overcame it.

Millicent did not often put her feelings into words,
and there is little direct record of how she brought herself to this position in the months after Harry died.

Sir Hubert Parry, who often went to see her and
Agnes at Rustington, "after the old fashion," noticed
how she "bore up bravely, and faced the world with
determined cheerfulness," but he added, " I know

there is a lot of tenderness and sentiment hidden behind the strong and determined front she shows to the world." Once, two years after her bereavement, he noted how when she had dined with them, she " often spoke of Harry. But once I saw her put her hand over her eyes, and her face looked as if she would break down. But she wrestled with it, and after a few tears won."

She was at all times exceedingly afraid of showing emotion, and almost passionately reticent, and the last thing which would occur to her would be to refer to her own sorrow. She could indeed hardly bear others to do so, and even twenty and thirty years later her friends could detect the desperate and rigid self-control with which she met any sudden mention of her husband's name.

Although there is no direct record of Millicent's feelings on Harry's death, there is much which is indirect, for her letters to friends who were in trouble were unconsciously self-revealing ; and it is from these more than from any other source that her attitude grows clear. Hundreds of these letters remain, for she forgot no one who was in trouble, and they are full of such deep sympathy and understanding, mingled always with such bracing and encouraging words, that her friends preserved them.

" Take up your work again," these letters say. " Remember what they would have wished for you in courage and power to face your life."

However bitter the grief, that was, she believed, always the way to meet it ; for it was the way she had known herself.

Perhaps the most personal and clear of all these is a letter which she wrote in 1887 to one of her friends among the Newnham students, Clotilda Bayne :

" I do not think constancy and fidelity to dead friends consists in any strain to keep up the great pain of the time when you first know you have lost them," she said, " but rather in trying to be and to do what they wished and what they thought you capable of doing and being.   One can't feel anything at first but a sort of numbness and then pain ; but later there comes a most blessed and even happy feeling about it all.   ' Blessed are they that mourn ' has a meaning in this sense too.   I do not know if I am quite clear, but what I mean is that the widow or widower who does not feel keen anguish is much more really to be pitied than the one who does ; because it shows that he has never had what the other is mourning the loss of."

Millicent did not often come as close as this to speaking of her own feelings ; but there was one aspect of the matter which she loved to talk of, and that was Harry's value and worth.   There is a letter to another of her student friends, Miss Barton, written in 1885, which reveals this point of view in very simple terms :

" What you say about my dear husband's example helping you to persevere with your work," she wrote, " and not give way to feelings of discouragement, helps me more than anything else.   The worst is when it seems as though people forgot him and that his great good influence is gone.   I do not really believe that it is so, but it is not easy always to keep alive a firm conviction of the reverse ; and it is a great help to be told, from the outside as it were, that courage and goodness have been made easier by his example."

It was this thought also which made Millicent very eager to see monuments erected to her husband, and which enabled her to take real pleasure in the Memorial in Westminster Abbey, the statues at Salisbury and Vauxhall, the drinking fountain on the Thames Embankment, the window at Trumpington and the tablet at Aldeburgh.   These and the scholarships and playing fields which bore his name were the outward symbols of what she herself clung to ; and it was comfort, not glory, which she drew from them.

The memory of her husband and the living value of his example were not the only things which helped

Millicent at this time. Thoughts of a future life, indeed, seem to have played little if any part in her adjustment to her bereavement, but her determination to live this life well was constant and stimulating. Like her husband, Millicent felt no certainty of personal survival after death, though, unlike him, she would have liked to believe it. She was more temperamentally religious, more definitely a theist, and much more sympathetic towards Christianity. About dogma, indeed, she always felt that there could be no certainty ; but about the goodness of God she felt very sure. Her grief, therefore, though it did not lead her to pray for the dead, did become transmuted into spiritual endeavour, and she soon found that work for others, and a courageous facing of her old tasks in the manner that Harry himself would have approved, was the best way to take up her new life.

By the time a year had passed she was able to write to Clotilda Bayne from a position to which she had attained :

" I think what we should all feel," she said, " who have been privileged to live in constant companionship with an exceptionally noble nature from which we are now removed, is not how wretched we are to have lost them, but how blessed we are to have had them to lift up our lives by their beautiful example."

This, indeed, was what Millicent came to feel in the first years of her widowhood, and what she continued to feel all her life long. She turned back, of course, to the interests and the work which occupied her life, and she regained her power of active enjoyment ; but instead of feeling that this was wrong, or any slight upon the happiness of the past, she knew that it was natural and right. She had had great happiness and a great inspiration ; it was right to be the better and the stronger for it, and to carry forward the principles in which they both believed with all her strength and all her power.

CHAPTER VI

THE " MAIDEN TRIBUTE "—THE LIBERAL UNIONISTS

W. T. Stead's articles and his imprisonment—Work with the Vigilance Association—Politics and morals—Party feeling—Agitation against Home Rule—The Liberal Unionist split—Visits to Ireland—The women's committee.

RHODA GARRETT had died in 1882, leaving Agnes very desolate and lonely in her London house, and when Henry Fawcett died, just two years later, it was the most natural thing in the world that Milly, her dearest sister, should come to live with her. The two houses in Cambridge and Vauxhall where there had been so much happiness and interest were given up, and Mrs. Fawcett and Philippa moved into No. 2 Gower Street, to share everything in future with Agnes. It was the greatest possible comfort and support to Millicent. Agnes had always been the dearest of all her well-loved sisters, and, as she wrote at the time to one of her friends, " she is a most loving companion, and we completely sympathise with one another in all the main things that go to make up life." Though her own personal life had received such a terrible blow, and though she was for the time being stunned with unhappiness, the main things were still unaltered—duty, work, steadfast courage, and the effort to realise some part of the unchangeable ideal ; even from the first Millicent remembered these things, and her sister helped her.

Before the end of the year 1884, indeed, another way of carrying on her work was offered to Mrs. Fawcett, when a suggestion was made that she should become Mistress of Girton. She did not consider it for a moment.

" I felt incapable," she wrote, " of thinking about

any subject but one " ; and in any case she knew that
it was not the work for her. Politics had been the
portion allotted to her by her sister Elizabeth and by
Emily Davies in her girlhood, and politics she knew
and understood. It was to this side of the movement
she must turn back, when she was able to work again ;
there were the things Harry had done to be continued,
and there was the suffrage still to be won. Nothing
else could be considered.

During the first winter after Harry's death Millicent
found some occupation and much comfort in the business
connected with the various memorials which were being
erected to his memory by public subscription. In all
the details of these she took the very deepest interest,
as she did also, of course, in the *Life* which she had
asked Leslie Stephen to write. To make Harry's worth
known to everyone, to spread his great influence as
widely as she could, these were the things Millicent
longed to do, and the things which it comforted her to
be concerned with ; and though she followed the course
of public events, and watched everything which had
a bearing on the women's cause, because she could not
help thinking as she had always thought, and behaving
as she had always behaved, nothing else had much
savour during that first unhappy winter.

In the summer of 1885, however, there came an
event which roused Millicent entirely, and which
brought back all her old fighting spirit with even more
intensity and strength than of old, and that was the
publication of Stead's " Maiden Tribute."

Until that time Millicent had not thought very deeply
about the subject of vice and prostitution. She had
indeed agreed with the objects of Josephine Butler's
Crusade, and had rejoiced in its success in checking
the operation of the Contagious Diseases Act in 1883,
but she had turned a little aside from the subject,
believing that it was wiser, if she was to do other things,
not to be too closely connected with this difficult and

terrible work. Her cousin Rhoda had thrown herself
into it vehemently, and Millicent had thought in a way
that she was right. But for herself she had held back,
and had not dared to let her thoughts dwell on the
horrors and the misery. She had not tried to make
Mrs. Butler's acquaintance, and although they had
many mutual friends and were both working in the
same causes, it had chanced that they had never met ;
and so, though Mrs. Fawcett had followed the whole
movement and was well acquainted with the Report
of the Commission on the White Slave Traffic of 1881,
and with the terms of the Criminal Law Amendment
Bill which had been making so little headway, she had
not let her imagination and her indignation flow out
into these channels. But now, in the summer of 1885,
it was no longer possible to turn away her thoughts.
Stead's articles in the *Pall Mall Gazette,* and the appalling
revelations they contained, were enough to fire the
soul ; and Millicent was roused as she had never been
roused before, and burnt and flamed with rage against
the evils he described.

The facts which had led to the publication were
indeed enough to rouse the whole country, though, as
the Commissioner of Police admitted, they did not, in
real life, even rouse the neighbours. As the law stood,
the age of consent was thirteen, to which age it had
been raised in 1880 ; and girl children of that age could
be, and were, bought and sold into prostitution with
absolute legality. The men and women who made a
living by this traffic, and the houses of ill fame where
the children were taken, were well known to the police,
but as the whole thing was not illegal, nothing whatever
could be done in the matter. The Royal Commission
had recommended a change in the law, but in the four
years which had passed since then nothing had happened,
and the reformers in the House of Commons saw their
Bill blocked time after time, and felt but little hope that
any change would be made. In the summer of this

year they saw the same obstruction prepared, and Mrs.
Butler and some of the others felt that they could not
endure any more delay.   They realised what the existing
system meant in ruin and terror and despair for young
children ; they saw what it involved in vice and degradation for men, and they felt they could not bear it.
They went therefore to Mr. Stead, the editor of the
Pall Mall Gazette, and begged him to give the whole
matter wide publicity, and, when he was satisfied of
the truth of their case, he took it up with enthusiasm.
With the help of the Salvation Army he arranged for
an actual *bona fide* sale of a child of thirteen to himself,
and had her taken to a brothel in London, carefully
guarded and protected, of course, but still really and
truly sold to him there for immoral purposes. And
the next day he began the publication of the story,
with all the other facts he had collected about the vile
traffic.   What followed can be told in Mrs. Fawcett's
own words, from an account which she sent ten days
later to her friend Emma Miller :

" With regard to the *Pall Mall*," she wrote, " the
series of articles began on Monday, July 6. The first
number gave a detailed account of the most horrible
outrages on children and traffic in children for immoral
purposes.   At first there was simply a yell to suppress
the paper ; its sale was stopped at all the bookstalls,
and newsvendors ceased to send it to their customers.
At first there was talk of prosecuting the editor ; by
degrees, however, the panic subsided a little, and people
began to say the right or wrong of publication depends
on THE TRUTH of the charges.   The *Pall Mall* went on
asseverating that they had stated nothing they could
not prove, and now the facts, at the instance of the
P.M.G., are being investigated by a small committee
consisting of the Archbishops of Canterbury and Westminster, the Bishop of London, the Lord Mayor and
Mr. Samuel Morley.   The first Parliamentary effect
of the affair has been that the Criminal Law Amendment Bill which has been regarded as one of the measures
doomed to drop through want of time is now nearly

certain to pass. All thought of a prosecution of the
P.M.G. has been formally renounced by the Government. People say that unheard-of efforts have been
made by the authorities to hush the matter up, and that
people of the highest rank are implicated in these
awful charges. The writer in the P.M.G. has taken
the line that if grown-up people of their own free will
choose to be immoral, the law must let them alone, but
that the law ought to protect helpless children from
the vile lust of wicked men. I think all the deep feeling
that has been aroused by a knowledge of the facts will
make a great many people understand for the first time
one of the reasons why women ought to have votes."

That was the outline : publication, shock, outcry,
panic, and then serious sustained indignation, accompanied by the protests and crowded meetings in St.
James's Hall, in Hyde Park and all over the country.
And the effect was immediate. Within five days the
moribund Bill, which had languished and loitered for
four years, had passed its second reading, and within
a month it had passed through all its stages. The
depth of the passionate feeling which was aroused
surpassed all ordinary political bounds ; men who had
closed their eyes to the evil, and women who had been
sheltered from the knowledge of it, were suddenly
forced to realise what horrors existed. They looked
at their own young daughters, and they could not
endure the thoughts which came to their minds. All
through July and the early days of August the storm
raged, and it was not until the Act was safely passed
that public opinion grew calmer ; and even then there
remained much anxiety and much watchfulness, so
that the old smothering blanket of silence could not be
pulled over the facts again.

Mrs. Fawcett's own course of action during this time
was exceedingly characteristic. Though she was fired
with an indignation as hot and burning as any, and
though she was immediately in the thick of the activity,
she kept a tight hold upon her sense of moderation.

Invective was not going to be very helpful, but truth and reason were ; and she wrote, accordingly, several quietly forcible letters to the papers, and made sure that no one whom she could reach should overlook the true moral to be drawn from all the revelations. An equal moral standard, and a share for women in the control of the laws, these were the remedies which a healthy public opinion must require ; and her intense indignation found expression in renewed work for these things.

It was a grief that Elizabeth did not see eye to eye with her about Mr. Stead's action. Millicent had at once written to him to thank him for what he had done, and to sympathise with him in the calumny and abuse which his articles brought down upon his head ; but Elizabeth had thought the whole thing ill-judged, sensational and harmful, and had told her sister so.

" It cannot be necessary," Elizabeth wrote, " to go through Stead's performance and to flood the world with sensational articles—disgusting and untrue. I myself believe that such things are done on some scale or other, having seen children about the streets—or creatures dressed up to represent children. But I cannot accept Stead's methods."

Elizabeth and Millicent were both very sure of their own minds, and they were both plain spoken ; but they respected each other profoundly, and loved each other dearly ; and over this, as over the C.D. Acts Crusade, they went their separate ways.

Before the House rose for the summer the Act was passed, and the victory of the reformers was won ; but in the autumn the price had to be paid. For the storm which Stead had roused, though it had awakened the conscience of the people, and forced the hand of the legislature, had also made him the bitterest enemies. If even Elizabeth could think him ill-judged and wrong, how much more those conventional people who thought open speech was wicked, and ignorance was virtue !

Mr. Stead's name was execrated even by many of those whom his revelations had awakened, and in addition he had made for himself a host of bitter foes among those deliberately wicked interests whose existence he had proclaimed. It was not therefore surprising that, after a few months had gone by, he was arrested and brought to trial on the charge of abducting the girl. The thing had been done repeatedly in the cause of vice, and no punishment had followed. It was done once in the cause of virtue, and all the subtleties of the law were invoked to discover some retribution ; and because the plan had been made with the child's mother (instead of with the father, who was the only legal parent) Stead was found guilty and sentenced to a considerable term of imprisonment. Stead, indeed, could have vindicated himself even from this technical offence, for the girl's parents were not, in fact, married ; and, as the law then stood, it was after all the mother and not the father who was the legal parent. But this fact had been carefully concealed by the family, and disreputable as they had been in many ways, Stead would not betray their secret. Rather than bring upon the girl a stigma which was no fault of hers he withheld this defence, and served a sentence which was neither legally nor morally his due.

Mrs. Fawcett was indignant at the prosecution, and threw herself into the efforts for Stead's defence, collecting money from her friends for his expenses, and doing whatever was possible to support him and his associates through the trial. When the verdict was given, she was deeply distressed, and wrote at once to Mr. Stead in his prison :

" I cannot find words to say how I honour and reverence you for what you have done for the weakest and most helpless among women. I always felt that by some legal quibble you might be tripped up, as it were ; but this is as nothing ; your work will stand. . . . I really envy you as much as I admire and honour you ;

very few people, even among heroes and martyrs, have had the happiness of seeing their faithful work so immediately crowned with good results. Everything I have written sounds so cold compared to what I feel ; but if gratitude and honour from myself and many hundreds and thousands of your countrymen can help you at this stress, I want you to have that help."

Stead needed all the comfort his friends could give him, for he was sent at once to Millbank and treated as a common prisoner ; but it was not in Mrs. Fawcett's nature to give nothing but verbal comfort. While there was any chance of doing anything real to help him, she was determined to do it, and she joined at once in the determined requests which were made to the Home Secretary asking to have him treated as a first-class misdemeanant.

In her own mind, too, she wondered whether more could not be done, and when on November 13 she received a letter from Miss Buss, she found she was not alone in the idea which had come to her.

" I can hardly write for shame and indignation," Miss Buss said. " Mr. Stead is being treated as a common convict-person, dress and diet, and condemned to pick oakum. Surely the country will not submit to such a disgraceful thing. . . . It never occurred to me as possible that the vengeance of his enemies could go so far. Is there neither law nor justice ? If Mr. Stead erred, surely the dignity of the law would be maintained by a quarter of an hour's imprisonment, or some such slight penalty. Mr. Stead's supporters will not allow this shameful thing to continue without a desperate effort. Is this to be done by monster petitions, by public meetings ? I do not know the way, I only know everything should be done to put an end to the imprison-ment as soon as possible. I am ashamed to be an Englishwoman. . . . Can appeal be made to the Queen, through some of the great ladies ? I do not know the procedure."

That was the way people were feeling and thinking ; and it was the way Mrs. Fawcett felt herself. But she *did* know the procedure, and even at the time Miss Buss was writing to her, she was putting the last suggestion into practice. She knew, of course, perfectly well that the Queen could not intervene, and that officially it was entirely a matter for the Secretary of State. But she also knew the Queen, and how things worked in the Palace. She wrote therefore to Sir Henry Ponsonby as follows :

" Your kindness to me and my late husband on more than one occasion emboldens me to ask your advice and assistance as to the propriety and possibility of bringing under Her Majesty's notice the fact that Mr. Stead is not being treated as a first-class misdemeanant. I yesterday saw the Rev. F. B. Waugh, after he had had an interview with Mr. Stead in prison. Mr. Stead was in the ordinary cotton prison dress, and appeared to be extremely cold ; his cell is very dark ; it contains a Bible, but the cell is so dark that it is impossible to read it. Mr. Stead therefore has to remain all day long doing absolutely nothing ; he was very cheerful when Mr. Waugh saw him, and complains of nothing, and desires his friends not to complain for him ; the warder treats him with respect and kindness. . . . Mr. Stead's friends, however, cannot help dreading the effect upon his health if he remains during the term of his imprisonment in cold and darkness on a lowering diet, without materials for writing and reading, and they venture to think that the fact that the Judge, both the Juries and the Attorney-General having drawn special attention to the purity of Mr. Stead's motives, gives him a claim to be treated during his imprisonment as a first-class misdemeanant. I have written as briefly as possible in order not to intrude too much on your time, begging your indulgence if there is any impropriety in my writing at all. Believe me, etc.

" I have written entirely on my own responsibility without consultation with any of Mr. Stead's friends. I have been prompted to write by the fact that I have heard so many people say, in speaking of Mr. Stead's treatment, ' I wonder if the Queen knows this,' or, ' I do not think the Queen would allow this if she knew it.' "

This letter was posted on November 12, and on the same day she received the following telegram from Sir Henry Ponsonby :

" Having no power to submit letters on public matters, I fear I could not lay yours before Her, but I have at once telegraphed substance to Home Secretary," was what he said.

But Mrs. Fawcett was not perturbed by this, nor surprised when, on the day following, the change she had asked for came about.   She at once wrote again :

" I am truly grateful," she said, " for the action taken in regard to Mr. Stead being made a first-class misdemeanant.   It proves how true was the instinctive reliance on Her Majesty, and the confidence that if the Queen knew the facts she would command the right thing to be done.   I do not wish in any way to intrude myself upon Her Majesty, but if you have occasion to mention the matter to Her again, I would desire to express with deepest respect my dutiful gratitude to Her Majesty.
" Mr. Stead is in prison for a legal blunder which he made in the course of a successful attack on the most horrible trade in the world, but that is bearable so long as his treatment in prison is such as not to endanger his health."

To this Sir Henry Ponsonby answered, as in duty bound :

" It would not be fair if I left you to suppose that it was in consequence of the Queen's intervention that the change was ordered in Mr. Stead's condition.   I telegraphed to the Home Secretary soon after I received your letter, at about five or six o'clock in the afternoon, but I think the Secretary of State had already issued his order on the subject that morning."

Whether this was just the official explanation, or whether it was actually so, did not much matter.   Mrs. Fawcett continued to believe that the Queen had intervened ; but in any case the chief thing was that the

9

wrong had been put right, and that Mr. Stead's imprisonment for his legal offence was made bearable and endur-
able to him, and no longer a disgrace to the country he
had served so well.   And with the completion of his
sentence the matter of the "Maiden Tribute" ended.

The scandal might be over, and the heat of the commotion died down, but something very serious and
valuable remained in an awakening of conscience upon
the question of public morals.   As Mrs. Fawcett said,
the stagnant waters had been troubled, and henceforward it was easier to speak openly of such questions,
and to get help when things were wrong.   The National
Vigilance Association, which was formed as the outcome
of all this disturbance, grew to be strong and powerful,
and for many years Mrs. Fawcett took an active part in
its work.

She now met Josephine Butler, and was deeply
impressed by her personality, and the saintliness which
seemed to radiate from her.   "Mrs. Butler was like a
flame," as she afterwards said.   "I never see *Parsifal*
without thinking of her—' durch mittleid wissend '—
taught by compassion to know all the horror and woe
of guilt, but by compassion also bringing back health
and purity.   She was one of the very great people of
the world."

Once she had made Mrs. Butler's acquaintance Mrs.
Fawcett missed no opportunity of seeing her when she
came to London, and though the two never became
very intimate, she followed with great admiration every
step of her work both in England and on the Continent.
Many years later, long after Mrs. Butler was dead,
Millicent was to write her life, and to tell the story of
her struggles to a new enfranchised generation.   But
in the 'eighties she did not think of this : she thought
only that she had seen a great woman, whom she felt
she loved ; and that she must do her part in the work
for which they both cared.

For some years after Mr. Stead's imprisonment,

therefore, Mrs. Fawcett took an actual personal part
in the affairs of the Vigilance Association, and interested
herself in some of the individuals whom they helped,
and followed the cases which came into Court of young
girls seduced or assaulted.

There was one episode in particular, of which she
wrote a full account to her friend Emma Miller, which
caused her a good deal of satisfaction. It took place
in December 1886, and is best told in her own words :

" I must tell you a most exciting experience which
I had the other day," she wrote. " Some intimate
friends of ours have a little servant aged seventeen to
eighteen whom they sent on a message one afternoon to
Bond Street. A beast of a man spoke to her at the
Circus and followed her, asking her to go with him to
Greenwich and so on. Fortunately, her mistress's
sister was waiting for her at the shop ; but the man
would not be shaken off, and followed her right into the
shop, and only decamped when he saw a lady in charge
of the girl. When the servant girl got home she seemed
very unsettled and said to her mistress, ' I can't bear
going out alone ; I'm so glad you never let me go out
at night by myself.' About nine o'clock the same
evening the girl received a letter from the beast signed
in full with his name and address. He is an Army
Surgeon. He told the girl to meet him on Saturday the
11th at one o'clock outside the British Museum. The
servant brought the letter at once to her mistress, her
mistress to me, and I to Mr. Coote, Secretary of the
Vigilance Association. No answer was sent to the
beast's letter. At 12.45 on the appointed day we
stationed the girl at the gate of the British Museum.
The mistress's sister waited out of sight just inside the
rails ; Mr. Coote and a ' rough friend ' lounged in a
doorway opposite, and the mistress and I walked up and
down. Punctually at one the Beast arrived, dressed
up to the nines, bowing and smiling, raising his hat and
extending his hand to shake hands with the little
servant. Before he could touch her Mr. Coote seized
him and bellowed ' Scoundrel ! ' and other appropriate
epithets. The rough friend seized him too and pinned

him to the spot. Instantly, a crowd of about fifty persons was on the spot. Mr. Coote shouted the Beast's name and explained his evil intents. I never saw a man so completely taken aback. Of course we should have liked to thrash him, but were anxious not to do anything illegal. Mr. Coote shouted, ' I demand this scoundrel's card,' and when a policeman arrived the scoundrel asked if he was to give up his card, and when the policeman answered in the affirmative Mr. Coote received it and gave his own in exchange. The worst of it is that this sort of thing is not illegal. It is illegal for a woman to solicit a man for immoral purposes but not for a man to solicit a woman. We tried hard to get the names published, but have failed so far. However, we shall make the man's name known at his club, but I don't suppose such things would count much against a man there. Publicity is what these villains dread."

There was another dramatic action which Mrs. Fawcett took somewhat later, which sprang from the same motives, and since it was at the time very well known, and involved many very important people, it cannot be omitted from her life.

Shortly before one of the general elections it came to Mrs. Fawcett's notice that the prospective candidate for a certain constituency was a young man to whose name a great deal of scandal was attached. He had seduced, but refused to marry, a young lady well known to all his friends. There was but one opinion among them, which was that he ought to marry her, and a great deal of the talk on this subject had reached Mrs. Fawcett. Independently of this, however, his candidature had been arranged, and she felt that it was an abominable proposal. She held the strongest views as to the importance of uprightness and good character in public life, and felt it incumbent upon her to prevent the election of a young man whose misdeeds were so notorious. She therefore let it be known that she intended to inform the leading people in the constituency what sort of a candidate they were adopting, and this of course immediately came to the ears of the young man and his friends.   One of the leaders of his party, who happened to be also one of his personal friends, took great exception to this proposed interference, the more so as he was doing his utmost to bring about the marriage. He felt that Mrs. Fawcett's action would be unjustified and uncalled for, and he did his best to make her hold her hand. He first sent a mutual friend to remonstrate with her upon the general question, but on this Mrs. Fawcett was adamant. Nothing anyone could say would shake her conviction that men whose private lives were not above reproach ought not to enter public life.   It was an opinion which, at that date, with the Parnell and Dilke cases fresh in people's minds, was very widely shared, and along this line all effort was unavailing. The emissary then reminded Mrs. Fawcett that she was the leader of a cause which had need of all its friends, and begged her to refrain from an action which would bring her the enmity of so many very important people in one particular party. But this argument had no weight either. What was right was right, Mrs. Fawcett thought ; and considerations of expediency could not affect it. She was as unyielding as a rock, and this had to be reported to the leader.

He then proceeded to try another means of dissuading her, and one which, if he had known her better, he would not have attempted. He sent one of his secretaries to call upon her, and gave this young man the difficult task of intimating that if she was so rash as to carry out her intention of going to the constituency in question, she would find herself involved in a libel action. The secretary had some difficulty in getting to the point, when actually seated in her drawing-room ; but at last he did manage to make his meaning clear, whereupon he was astonished to see Mrs. Fawcett begin to laugh. " How very fortunate it is," she said. " I thought I had lost £1,500 in an Australian bank, and only this very morning I heard that it was safe. That will go some way towards defraying the expenses of the action." It was her only comment upon the threat, and this emissary, too, had to return to his chief and report complete failure.

The immediate result of these two interviews was that Mrs. Fawcett at once packed her bag and set out for the constituency, where she already knew the leaders of local opinion. And the result of this was that the prospective candidate was obliged to withdraw from the field. No libel action followed ; but the affair was not forgotten, and for many years it made more difficult the dealings between Mrs. Fawcett and the party leader, who never, indeed, entirely forgave her.

This incident, which was inspired by Mrs. Fawcett's strong moral indignation, was the only one of the kind in her life. The whole tendency of her mind was away from individual cases. What seemed to her important was the effort to improve the attitude of the general public. It was dreadful when an individual suffered or was led astray ; but the more far-reaching wrong was " the utter rottenness of the whole of public opinion on morals."

" You prosecute the street walker with one hand," she wrote, " and with the other elevate to the place of chief magistrate in the town a man who is living in adultery. Nothing good can come of this sort of hypocrisy."

It was even more important to deal with that than it was to save the fallen or comfort the outcasts of the world. Little by little, therefore, she began to attend less to the details of the rescue work, and more and more to the great political remedies. In 1887 she was writing to a friend about one of the local societies for the Protection of Public Morals as follows :

" I don't think you show anything like sufficient activity in proceeding against the people who TRADE

in vice in the town.   If you analyse the accounts you
will see that during the year the great sum of £1 9s. 2d.
represents the expenses of the Society in its proper work.
According to Mr. H.'s first letter to me, the town is
swarming with houses (the report speaks of one having
been closed).   Who keeps them up ?   Who runs them ?
Who are the customers ?   Get at these facts and make
them public, and you will have done something to
attack the evil at its source.   Prosecuting victims,
children who are the products of the evil rather than
its causes, does absolutely nothing but obscure the real
issues."

But even this, clearsighted as it was, came to seem
to Mrs. Fawcett too small a thing to put first.   The
rottenness of public opinion, which was behind the evil,
came from the low position of women generally.   As
she watched the divorce and separation cases she became
more and more sharply aware of the helpless and unpro-
tected state of unhappily married women.   She saw
husbands again and again using their sole power over
the children as a means of taking revenge upon their
wives, and she felt that it was intolerable.   But it was
no use to attack the problem piecemeal.   You must
strike at a wrong as near its roots as you could, she felt,
and she knew therefore that she must turn back to her
chosen work.   All these causes were indeed tied up
and connected together, but for her the suffrage was
obviously the most important, and it was the task which
lay to her hand.

The years after the Reform Bill disappointment were,
however, difficult and discouraging for the suffragists,
for not only had their cause gone out again into the
darkness, but they had become divided in counsel themselves.   Many of them had lost their faith in the Liberal
Party altogether : Gladstone had betrayed them, their
friends had broken their promises, and there was no
more hope from that quarter.   Mrs. Fawcett was herself
tempted to take this view, though she was not quite so
embittered.   In 1886, when she was asked to become

a Vice-President of the Liberal Alliance, she refused emphatically :

" While I am thoroughly in sympathy with Liberal principles," she wrote, " I not infrequently find myself out of sympathy with the conduct of the Liberal Party. To give two instances, I would refer (1) to the conduct of the Party as soon as they came into power in 1880 with regard to the Transvaal and to the policy which led to the long series of disastrous events in Egypt ; and (2) to the strenuous efforts made by the managers of the Liberal Party to exclude women householders from the benefits of the Reform Bill of 1884. In both these cases it appears in my judgment that the Liberal Party acted in direct opposition to the principles of Liberalism, and as that, whether rightly or wrongly, is my conviction, I do not feel that I can with propriety identify myself with a purely party organisation."

This was direct and straight enough, but a year later, when she was urged by the Bristol Society to accept nomination to the Executive Council of the newly formed Women's Liberal Federation, she went even farther. Her full reply is lost, but the summary she made upon the back of the invitation is clear and cogent. It runs as follows :

" No. Can best serve the various political movements in which I am interested by keeping clear of party associations. Not at all condemn others, but for me questions, e.g. on women and morality, come first and party second —a long way second. Mrs. Gladstone's meeting was ' party—nothing but party.' I dissent from this so absolutely that it would be waste of strength for me to join."

The lesson she had learnt from the Reform Bill time was not so much distrust of the Liberals as distrust of the party system, at any rate in so far as voteless people were concerned. Her great hope was that the women's cause might be recognised as greater than party, and so her effort all through the troubles of the 'eighties was to keep the movement upon a straight non-party course.

It was not an easy course to follow just at that moment, for all the women who were interested in politics at all were being vehemently urged to join their own party associations. The passage in 1883 of a Corrupt Practices Act, which made paid canvassing at elections illegal, had led to the discovery that women might be a useful political asset, and both the Liberals and the Conservatives had suddenly become eager to organise them. While paid men canvassers had done the work it was easy to believe that the rough and tumble of elections was no place for women ; but when it had to be done by voluntary effort, there was a remarkable change in this attitude. It was no longer the rough and tumble which was bad for women, only the heavy responsibility of deciding on policy ; and the Primrose League, which was formed in 1883, and the Women's Liberal Federation, which followed shortly after, sought to enrol all the women they could find. The suffragists were, of course, deeply interested in politics, but they were not all of them ready to join these new organisations. Many of the leading Liberal women were bitterly disillusioned, and others felt, like Mrs. Fawcett, that they must wait till they were enfranchised before they came into a party fold. But there were others still who obeyed the call, and it was these who made the difficulty within the suffrage societies. They were more than a little aggressive and positive in their orthodoxy, perhaps because of the bitterness and distrust of some of the others, so that the committee meetings of the suffrage societies became the scenes of elaborate battles, very polite and circumspect, but very fierce and unrelenting.

The ladies who waged these battles were novices in the political game, and brought to it not only their fierce and inexperienced political convictions, and their ardent idealism, but also the ladylike traditions in which they had been brought up. They made their most damaging accusations in the most circuitous way, and the records of their disagreements are to the last degree

obscure and muffled. They were dilatory, too, even in
the heat of controversy, and were always being called
away from their quarrel by the emergencies of family
life. They were scrupulous to a fault, and very touchy,
and the disagreements among them were accomplished
in agitated tea-parties and prolonged personal interviews, and accompanied by a swarm of confidential
correspondence. Amidst all these turmoils, Mrs. Fawcett came out more and more clearly as the leader of the
forces. She always saw plainly what it was all about,
and could explain it so that the essential points came
clear. She it was who could always be reasonable and
not angry, and could always keep her head. Her facts
were always accurate, her resolutions always explicit,
and she was always at hand when she was wanted.
She had had much more experience of the real world of
politics than most of the others, and she had profited
by it. She had her eyes clearly fixed upon the cause,
and not upon the temporary troubles, and even those
who did not agree with her came to feel that she was
the most trustworthy and the most reliable and, in some
way, the most important of them all.

But for all that she did not wholly get her way in
this crisis of the suffrage societies. The struggle went
on for three years, each side trying to get control of the
organisation, and neither quite succeeding. At last a
real formal split took place, and after a terrific meeting
at which passions rose to fever heights, Mrs. Fawcett
found herself the leader of a minority, possessed of the
old rules and the old affiliated societies, but deprived
of the office, the funds and the name. It was a tangled
technical matter upon which they had finally divided,
but the substance of it was the party question ; and
Mrs. Fawcett, with Miss Becker and most of the older
workers, stuck firmly to the non-party way.

This split occurred in 1887 ; and in the previous year
the Liberal Party had taken a course which had entirely
alienated Mrs. Fawcett from them, when they had

supported Mr. Gladstone in his sudden conversion to Home Rule.

Mrs. Fawcett was, and always had been, a strong opponent of this measure. She had wholeheartedly agreed with Harry, when he had said, years before, that he would rather the Liberal Party should remain out of office until its youngest member had grown grey-headed than be intimidated into supporting Home Rule ; and everything which had happened since had served to strengthen her conviction. The outrages, the murders, the cattle maiming and the boycotting in Ireland, and the proceedings of the Irish Nationalists in Parliament, while they had done nothing to alter what she believed to be the fundamental rights and wrongs of the situation, had greatly intensified in her eyes the importance of standing firm. To give in to violence seemed to her a base thing, and to betray the Irish loyalists would be to do injustice because of timidity. As she saw it, the Liberal leader had done just this ; and, moreover, he had done it from motives of political expediency, changing his view only because he was faced with a small Parliamentary majority and an Irish vote which could turn the scales. She held that Gladstone's course was lacking in ordinary political integrity, and that he was betraying Liberal principles and the honour of Great Britain itself, merely to catch the illiterate Irish vote. Feeling this she had, of course, no choice but to break away from her husband's old colleagues, and stand in with the other dissentient Liberals, Lord Hartington, Leonard Courtney, Lady Stanley, Lady Frances Balfour, and the rest in their new Liberal Unionist group.

The whole business, of course, created a tremendous storm in the political world. It meant the breaking of old ties, and the forming of new ones, and much shifting not only of party allegiance but of private friendship. People felt so strongly about the question that not only in Dublin, but in London drawing-rooms, the opposing

sides kept far apart.   Argument was almost impossible,
and in the country at large, as well as in the centre of
things, agitation ran very high.   Crowded and enthusiastic meetings were held on both sides, and all other
political questions were temporarily submerged in the
uproar.

The dissentient Liberals, when they came out of the
party fold, did not intend to join the Conservatives.
They still held all their old convictions, so that in the
first years of the new movement there was much talk
of its non-party character.   This, of course, was congenial to Mrs. Fawcett, whose distrust of the party
system was already profound, and it gave her an
additional inducement to throw herself into the business
of organisation, in which she at once began to play a
leading and important part.

Two Associations of Liberal Unionists were formed,
for men and for women, and curiously enough it was
the women's which came first, and which was the more
energetic and successful.   During the years of its prime
it was a most active body.   It got into immediate touch
with a number of very able and energetic women in
Ireland, at one time bringing over as many as 800 to
take part in an Albert Hall Demonstration ;   and
speaking tours and conferences, and all the concomitants
of political agitation were carried on with vigour and
enthusiasm.   There were grand formal receptions and
garden-parties, long business gatherings, stirring propaganda meetings, demonstrations, publications, protests,
election campaigns and all the rest, with the terrible
tales of persecution and boycotting in Southern Ireland
to keep it all at fever height, and to colour the outline
of constitutional faith with burning resentment.

All this continued with unabated strength during the
years between the defeat of the first Home Rule Bill in
1886 and the inclusion of Liberal Unionists in Lord
Salisbury's Government in 1895.   The ups and downs
of these years, the elections of 1888 and of 1892, the

change of Prime Minister and the repercussion of other political happenings upon the Home Rule cause were all of the deepest interest to Millicent. Her training, her knowledge, and her strong political sense enabled her to appreciate very justly all that was going on, and from the first she stood out as a real political leader.

She herself visited Ireland repeatedly, and made many firm and lifelong friends there, and she did a great deal of very effective speaking against the Home Rule proposals. Her care in making certain of the facts, and her natural inclination to base conclusions upon definite principles, attracted a good deal of attention, and her help was most highly appreciated by the men who were leading the revolt in the Liberal Party. Lord Derby, who was not as a rule inclined to look favourably upon the political activities of women, went so far as to say that the best speech he had ever heard in his life was one of hers, and she came to be thought of among the statesmen of the 'eighties as a force to be reckoned with, and not just a member of a ladies' committee to be used in getting up bazaars and finding hospitality for delegates. At the first great public meeting which the new movement held, when Lord Hartington brought forward the Liberal revolt in set terms, Mrs. Fawcett was invited to speak with him ; and though there was much criticism of the fact that a woman should be invited to speak on such an occasion, the effect of her speech drove all such nonsense away. Mrs. Fawcett herself was glad to appear on this platform, both because of her wholehearted opposition to Home Rule, and because it gave her the opportunity of recalling Harry's views on the matter, and so bringing his influence once more into the political field. And she was glad, too, that the new movement should recognise women so publicly and honourably as comrades ; though for herself it was terribly agitating, and she suffered such agonies of nervousness as to be physically ill before the meeting.

The women's committee was much encouraged by this recognition, and they were extremely enthusiastic, so that Mrs. Fawcett was for a time involved in a mass of work which was straight politics, and had little obvious connection with the women's cause. But, of course, she could not leave this out of her thoughts or her speeches, and every time she took part in the deliberations of the Liberal Unionists she implicitly and explicitly rubbed in the fact that the help of women, which was so strongly welcomed, would be ten times more valuable if they were enfranchised.

Lady Stanley of Alderley was the chairman of the women's committee, and in '88 Mrs. Fawcett was asked to become its secretary; but this she refused. She was willing and eager to work, but resolved not to take up any official positions save those in her own movement; and though she probably saved herself little by the refusal, since everyone consulted her about everything, she held firmly to her decision.

There were many amusing moments in the course of this campaign which Mrs. Fawcett enjoyed to the full. The Irish ladies were full of unexpectedness, and always ready to laugh, and even the English committee had its humours. Lady Salisbury's proposal, that the speakers should be sent out in couples, one a good speaker and one good-looking, was very much appreciated (though not acted upon), and old Lady Stanley, who was the Chairman, made things very exciting by her love of a good fight. "Somebody must contradict me quickly, or I can't get going at all," she would say; but when they took her at her word there was a great turmoil. Her daughter, Lady Carlisle, who remained an ardent Gladstonian, used to provide her with plenty of opposition, and there were times when she was with the utmost difficulty kept out from the conferences of her mother's friends. On one such occasion, when an important gathering was being held at Lady Stanley's house, and when great precautions had been taken to keep Lady

Carlisle away, she revenged herself upon her mother. The butler had been instructed to lay out in the hall a table for the display of the " literature " of the anti-Home Rule movement, and once the gathering had assembled Lady Carlisle swept down upon him and removed it all, putting in its place a lot of pamphlets on burial reform, which the assembled delegates innocently carried home.

All this was very entertaining ; but there were aspects of the campaign which were not so comic, though it was possible and even necessary to laugh at them too. The women's committee was so much more energetic and efficient than the men's committee, and took so much more trouble over the details of their work, that they were conscious of an undercurrent of jealousy. This gave them a good deal of pleasure, of course, but they needed it to set off against the constant snubs which came to them on the score of their sex.

" I have been getting very indignant," wrote Mrs. Fawcett in '88, " with the aristocrats who are patronising the Women's Liberal Unionist Association for saying that it is a very undesirable thing for women to take part in politics, but because the other side have done it we must too. If it *is* undesirable, I say we ought not to do it, if fifty thousand other sides have done it. It does enrage me, this kind of feebleness. At the meeting at Lady Stanley's, Mr. T. W. Russell, M.P., who keeps a Temperance Hotel in Dublin, made a capital speech in which he put the whole thing on its real ground—work to be done and workers wanted to do it—no matter whether men or women. ' Let's have done with this nonsense about women's sphere,' he said. I felt very glad I belonged to the middle classes. The Duke of Argyll was very funny. He said he had never had the honour and pleasure of addressing a company consisting mainly of ladies ; and a little while after, having occasion to use the expression *ad nauseam*, he kindly added in a parenthesis the meaning of the learned expression,' to the sickness.' "

Ad nauseam indeed the work seemed at times, in spite of all the excitement and success ; but Mrs. Fawcett was not one to turn back for that reason. Through the years of great interest, when the Home Rule Bills were before the country, and afterwards through the quieter 'nineties, when there was only a watching brief to hold, she remained a leading figure among the Liberal Unionists, growing steadily better known and more respected from year to year.

Mrs. Fawcett's connection with the Liberal Unionists sprang from her political beliefs and convictions, and had no other motive. But it was, in fact, very useful to the whole of her career. Her own movement was at that time completely outside the stream of " real politics," but this work kept her in the centre of things, in close touch with the leading figures of the day, by whom she was well known and deeply respected. She won her standing as an independent politician in the 'eighties and the early years of the 'nineties, and the prestige which this gave her she carried back to the unpopular and disregarded movement which was her chief concern. Anything which she said or wrote was sure to command serious attention, and although the feminist case was still considered absurd and ridiculous, it gained stability from her growing political reputation. Nor was it only among the great and important that Mrs. Fawcett began to be well known. With every year that passed she was more truly respected by her colleagues and by the public at large. Every time she spoke, whether it was on Home Rule, on Women's Suffrage, or on the other topics which touched on the women's movement, she increased her reputation ; for what she said was always solid, and left behind matter for thought and a lasting impression. She took, indeed, a great deal of pains over her speaking, and would prepare what she was to say with great thoroughness ; and she always found a way to bring into her speeches things which were recent and relevant to the matter in hand. She would read the papers and the speeches of leading men, and extract anything which could be turned to her purpose, and she collected quotations from her general reading, and illustrative jokes, and made all these things serve her turn.

She hated public speaking, both for the " cold spasms," as she called them, which always preceded a speech, and for the strain and effort which it called out ; but no sign of this was apparent when she stood on the platform. She was not eloquent, and made no appeal to the emotions, but she moved people none the less. For she would speak as directly to any audience as to her own friends, she would assume the same power of understanding plain truths, and the same impersonal desire for honesty and good sense as animated herself. There was no elaboration in her speeches, but no great simplification. Her argument was thoughtful, and sometimes difficult, but always fully worked out ; and, repressed and hidden though it was, the strong feeling which lay in her own heart could be detected. People came away from her meetings knowing that they had been in contact with a woman who possessed fixity of purpose, strength of mind and calmness of soul ; and the impression deepened with every successive hearing. And so, as the years went on, and Mrs. Fawcett journeyed about the country on her speaking tours, and met with the leading people of town after town and group after group, her fame and reputation grew. She might not always convince everybody ; but she could not fail to impress them ; and Cabinet Ministers and working men alike began to know her name.

CHAPTER VII

ABOVE THE SENIOR WRANGLER, 1890

Family, friends and relaxations—Philippa at Cambridge—The Tripos results.

THE main outlines of Mrs. Fawcett's life after her husband's death were determined by her political interests, and by the speaking, writing and organising which she did for the women's movement and the Liberal Unionists. But, of course, with a person of such unflagging energy, such strong interests and so many friends, there was much which fell outside the main pattern, and which formed, so to speak, the embroidery of her life.

In a general way her enjoyments and relaxations were the same as they had been before Harry's death—travel, reading, music, and intercourse with her family and friends ; but, of course, there was a difference. The blind husband who had been the centre of the household left a dreadful blank. There were no more books to be read to him, no more problems of political conduct to talk over, no more walks and rides. The dining out, and the parties at home which had so much delighted him were over, and the happy winters at Cambridge were at an end. These changes could not but mean a great break in Millicent's life, though of course it was the loss of Harry himself which mattered most ; and her instinctive reaction to the change was to take on more and more work, and to keep her hands and her time very full.

The first people to whom she turned were, as she said, her own family, and throughout the rest of her life they remained her nearest friends. With Agnes she now shared her daily life, and Sam, who had become a solicitor, lived near at hand, and helped them with all business affairs. For him, she said, she saved up all her jokes ; and he was the closest and the dearest of her men friends. Edmund Garrett, too, lived near by, in rooms with his friend, J. J. (now Sir John) Withers, and these two young men came often to the house in Gower Street, and by their high spirits and their jokes brought much gaiety with them. Her sister, Alice Cowell, who had come back from India with her young children, was a very close friend, though she did not live in London ; and Elizabeth, of course, had a very special position. All the others, too, the brothers and sisters and cousins, and the young families which were growing up in the next generation, had their place in Millicent's thoughts and affections, and she saw them all very often. Her father and mother were still living at Aldeburgh, and there were great family reunions there at Christmas and other holiday times, when sometimes as many as forty of the clan would gather there to talk, argue, discuss and laugh together and to compare notes about the changing world. " Aunt Milly " was a very important figure on these occasions, and her advice was very much sought after. She was, perhaps, a little formidable to the young ones, for she never let things slip by, or tried to hide a disapproval she felt ; yet she was endlessly kind, and always willing to take trouble for them, and so truly sympathetic that even her reproofs were welcomed, and her approbation valued more than that of anyone else. In these family meetings she herself was happy, resting from the strain of her heavy political life, and refreshed by the sympathy, the congeniality and the love of her own kindred.

Among Harry's relations at Salisbury there was relaxation, too, though of a rather different kind. The old people there had been terribly shaken by the tragedy of his death, and Millicent paid many visits to them in the following years, when she would try to talk of him as fully and freely as her desperate reticence would

allow. Mr. Fawcett died in 1887, and Millicent then
stayed on several weeks with Maria and the old lady,
" as I find there are so many little things I can do for
them." Her friendship with Maria, which had been
strong and genuine while Harry lived, grew even closer
now, and between these two it depended not merely on
living back over the past, as with his father and mother,
but also on a congeniality of outlook on the things of
the day. Maria Fawcett worked in her own town for
the things which her sister-in-law promoted on a
national scale. She was secretary to the local society
for the education of girls, and associated with local
government, and she was able to show Millicent in detail
both the need for, and the effects of, women's public
work.

Besides the friends in her own family, Mrs. Fawcett
had an increasing number of new outside acquaintances,
who turned into friends almost too fast. As she went
about on her speaking tours, and in Ireland, she was
given hospitality in every part of the country, and the
people she stayed with liked and admired her, and sought
her friendship. It was not only her public virtues
which made her popular. There was a steadiness in
all her ways which made people admire and trust her,
and an evident kindness which, in spite of all her
reserve, drew them towards her. And then, too, there
was a spice in her talk which was very refreshing. She
had an immense store of good stories, which she told
with evident enjoyment and used with an appropriate-
ness which was in itself entertaining, and the mixture of
the homely and the comic with the difficult and serious
was always evident in her talk.

But everyone, of course, did not like her. Some
people said that she was harsh and stern, compounded
only of " thrift, industry and self-control without any
of the gentler virtues." They missed altogether the
real Millicent, who loved goodness so much for its own
sake, and followed it as a matter of course, and they saw

only the fixed principles, the unswerving judgments, the undeviating purposes which governed her life. And she on her side saw no reason to make uncongenial acquaintances aware of the stores of kindness and the deep feeling which her friends and fellow-workers knew. She had plenty of people to love, and plenty of work to do, without wasting time, and she left such people severely alone. To the others, however, she was very ready to be a friend. She did, indeed, seem to keep a clear distinction between the private territory of her own feelings and emotions, which few might enter, and the region which she shared with the majority of her friends. She would speak freely to them of her thoughts and opinions, and of the daily affairs of life, and she would discuss their interests, and even, though rarely, their emotions. But what she chiefly expected from human intercourse, and what she seemed to prefer, was practical friendship—the doing of kindnesses, the sharing of occupations and interests, and, above all, work. Among the hundreds of people whom she met in these active years there were remarkable men and women of all kinds, and there were unhappy and unfortunate ones, as well as those who were strong and successful. Mrs. Fawcett was ready to be interested in them all, and certainly did an immense amount of kindness to an extraordinary number of people. She said nothing about it, and hardly let her left hand know what her right was doing ; but she sent boys to school and girls to college, she helped widows to earn a living, rescued young men's businesses times without number. Nor did she confine herself to these considerable charities. She followed and remembered the affairs of everyone, wrote to them when they were ill or unhappy, sent them flowers or books or little presents, remembered if their children collected stamps and post cards, and showed her practical friendship in every conceivable way. She answered every letter by return of post, never missed or was late for an engagement, never seemed hurried or fussed, never failed to write what she promised, and never neglected the calls of politeness or the expression of gratitude. The volume of it all grew rapidly, but her methods and her competence did not change. And in this astonishing industry she found her contentment.

Music was one of the relaxations she enjoyed most, and she became a very regular attendant at all the main London concerts and at the opera whenever she had the chance. She had a special seat for the Saturday " Pops," and never failed to occupy it when she was in London ; and there is an amusing little correspondence concerning concert-going which reveals both her love of music and her unwillingness to let a thing she disapproved of pass in silence. The first letter is addressed to the occupant of seat 6, row 3, dated June 8, 1885 :

" MADAM," it begins, " I feel sure you cannot be aware that the constant conversation which you kept up with a friend during the performance of the Pastoral Symphony at the Richter concert last Monday very seriously interfered with the enjoyment not only of myself but of many others who sat near you in the balcony. I am confident that if you realised how very much the enjoyment of others depends on the audience being quiet while the music is being performed, you would not talk so much as you have done at each of the Richter concerts this season, at which I have been in your immediate neighbourhood. I might apologise for taking the unusual step of writing to an entire stranger ; I can honestly say I should not have addressed this letter to you if I did not feel that you yourself would be the first to regret it, if those who sat near you had the whole series of concerts spoiled to them because of your conversation."

Mrs. Fawcett did not know when she wrote this letter who the occupant of seat 6, row 3, might be. But the answer reveals that it was Laura Tennant, who had just married Alfred Lyttelton, and that the people she was talking to were her husband, her sister Margot Tennant, and Mary Gladstone.

Miss Gladstone replied at once, enclosing a penitent letter from Laura ; and these are as characteristic in their way as Mrs. Fawcett's own remonstrance.

" DEAR MRS. FAWCETT," Miss Gladstone wrote, " I think I must send you this letter from my little cousin. I am so very sorry ; I did not know it was you who was sitting in No. 6.   Not that that would have made much difference, for whoever is near one no talking during the music should be allowed.   I did try, and so did Alfred, but it is very difficult, she is brimming over with life and fun, and the remarks she shoots out whether on the music or on the concert-goers are so unique that it is difficult to quench.   I am afraid I sometimes err in exclaiming about the music, particular passages, or particular instrumentation while it is going on, which of course is wrong.   But Laura really has a musical soul, though it may be difficult to believe ; only she is carried away by impulse.   I hope you will forgive.   She is very young and almost the whole world is at her feet, which is so spoiling.   Please forgive us."

Laura's letter was enclosed.

" DEAREST MARY," it runs, " isn't it dreadful ? Look at this letter from Mrs. Fawcett ; I am very unhappy about it, because I shall never be able to say how it happened or to accuse myself more in her eyes by excusing myself.   How can she know I did all I could to prevent Margot talking that fatal honeymoon wane. But I am very sorry.   I cannot imagine doing a thing more against my best intentions.   I want everyone to enjoy the Richters ; and it is a wretched punishment to the little outburst of reseeing Margot to think I have spoiled Mrs. Fawcett's concert.   Please, darling, if you see her, tell her I am sorry, and that I hope all her life she may sit next someone who in the future will be as quiet as I should be were that my fate."

Mrs. Fawcett was not one to look indulgently upon people because they were young and had the whole world at their feet.   In her view youth and good fortune were but added reasons for considerate behaviour ; and though, of course, the correspondence ended

there (and possibly the chattering also) Mrs. Fawcett
never forgot the incident.

The pursuit of music led Mrs. Fawcett abroad a great
many times in her life ; but sometimes she went for
other things, for scenery and sightseeing, or just for
the fun of going off with her friends away from all the
steady work at home. Philippa was often, of course,
the companion of these travels, and sometimes she
brought her own friends with her ; and there are
many tales of the adventures they met with, and the
odd people they encountered at table d'hôte. Sometimes, of course, Mrs. Fawcett's identity would leak
out, and her connection with the women's movement
would set the guests talking on that subject, with
curious results. There was one time in '87 when she
found herself sitting next an American lady who informed her that " a woman who steps upon the rostrum
unsexes herself entirely," and this tactful opening
was followed up by her neighbour on the other side,
who asked her if she knew of any woman doctor
at whose hands she would be willing to undergo an
operation. Mrs. Fawcett was amused rather than
annoyed, and answered, in the most matter-of-fact way,
" Yes, there is one woman doctor by whom I would
rather have my head cut off than by anyone else,"
leaving her neighbours to make what they could of this
remark. On another occasion she encountered a party
of Germans who stared at her so persistently that it
became a nuisance. She was not able to say anything
very crushing herself, since she could not speak their
language, but turned to one of her party who could,
and said, in a clear voice so that everyone else in the
room could hear, " Do tell them, Clotilda, that if they
think we are waxworks they ought to pay."

In all her travels Mrs. Fawcett remained very English,
and much as she loved going abroad, and keenly as she
felt the importance of international movements, she
cherished her own sense of nationality very strongly.

To her, from her childhood, loyalty to one's own country had seemed the first of virtues, and though she believed that other peoples should have the same feelings towards their own lands, she did not attempt to deny that she thought her own the best and most wonderful.

There is a letter from her to one of her young Newn-ham friends who had gone to teach in Germany, which shows her attitude on this point. It was written in May 1888 :

" I am grieved to hear that the feeling against the poor Empress remains so vehement," she wrote. " She has been a most devoted wife, and has been foremost in promoting all kinds of good womanly activity among women, and I cannot help feeling it is mean and narrow-minded of the Germans to hate her in the way they do. There was a good deal of the same contemptible sort of feeling in England against the Prince Consort, partly because he was a German and partly because of the stand he and the Queen made against the loose morals of the previous reigns and against the waste and extravagance of the Royal households. I think the Empress is probably very like her father in character, and that her son is inferior to her in almost every way, and has consequently the sort of resentment a mean-natured man often feels against superiority in a woman. I think all the squabbling of the doctors and others over the Emperor's deathbed is most indecent. Pray don't get into any sort of despair about England. Of course there is a great deal to mourn for in many ways, but I believe that in many ways too England is leading the world. I mean particularly on some branches of moral questions where the deep feeling which first awakened in England has caused a revival of moral sense in almost every other country, and has led to efforts towards a higher moral life that formerly was looked upon as a hopeless dream. Within this generation England has produced such men and women as Darwin, Gordon, the Lawrences, Octavia Hill, Florence Nightingale, George Eliot and Sister Dora, so I do not think we need look upon ourselves as ' played out.' With regard to Art, no one can have seen the English pictures of the last fifty years at the Manchester

Exhibition without wondering at the immense variety, originality and power displayed. I could not help feeling, when I saw that exhibition, ' We are a very great people.' "

Mrs. Fawcett never missed an opportunity of going to a picture show if she could help it, and tried to ensure that her friends saw and appreciated what she did. In '88, for example, she wrote to Mr. Dryhurst to " be sure and go to see the Holman Hunts at the Fine Art Gallery in Bond Street. The Light of the World," she added, " is one of the most wonderful pictures I have ever seen. It does one good to be a contemporary of the man who painted it. I saw it twenty-five years ago, but it surpasses what I remembered of it, though it impressed me very much even then." In pictures, as in books, she was still looking for the meaning, heightened by the form, just as in her early youth. It seemed to her, indeed, that there lay the essence and the value of art ; so that it was not merely pleasure and relaxation she drew from it, but much more, an outlet, as it were, to her emotion, which in all the rest of her life she kept so severely hidden and controlled.

Religion still remained a little remote from her. She cared intensely for goodness, and for the promoting of what would make for it in the world, but creeds and beliefs seemed very unimportant. " You must not think," she wrote in '89, " that because X is High Church I therefore cannot sympathise with his aims and work. I care so very little about people's beliefs in comparison with what they *are* ; and all goodness helps what is good, though the people who are seeking it may be as diverse as the poles." In the course of her work, of course, Mrs. Fawcett met the most different people, seeking for goodness in the most varied ways ; but she never saw cause to change this opinion, and to the end of her life she believed that " goodness helps what is good," wherever and whenever and however it appeared.

But although Mrs. Fawcett was tolerant in this way,

she was not, and did not really try to be, tolerant of opinion. Some things seemed to her so demonstrably true and just that she could not excuse those who would not see them so. The black mark which might be acquired in her judgment was not at all easy to wipe out, and it is safe to say that no one who held the old-fashioned view of women could ever stand well in her eyes. They might be amiable and worthy in other ways, she would admit ; but they were fundamentally wrong-headed ; and as such were put out of her life. And if, added to their wrongheadedness, they were active in retarding or injuring the causes which she upheld, then they were entirely beyond the pale. She used to say herself that she was " an unforgiving person," though it was only towards the public enemies that it was apparent. But towards them it was true ; and, after affixing the black mark against them in her mind, she would wholly disregard them.

Mrs. Fawcett's life was full enough without such people, and it was lived among those who were congenial to her, and in the last years of the 'eighties it was still further enriched by a renewal of her ties with Cambridge. She was still on the Council of Newnham, and often had occasion to go there, and in 1887, after Philippa became a student, these visits were even more frequent and enjoyable.

Philippa went to Newnham with the Gilchrist scholar-ship won on the results of the Higher Local examination, and this in itself was a great pleasure to her mother. " We heard the good news when we were at Bayreuth for the Wagner festival," Mrs. Fawcett wrote to a friend, and added, with a brevity which did not conceal her pride, "she was first class with distinction in Latin, first class with distinction in Algebra and Euclid, and third class with distinction in Logic."

This was a good beginning, and as term after term went by it became clear that there was going to be a good ending too. Philippa worked neither too much nor

too little, and because she was interested rather than
for any other reason ; but, of course, those who were
watching her could not help having ulterior thoughts in
their minds.   It would be so wonderfully suitable and
satisfactory if she, of all girls, could bring distinction to
the college.   And as her mathematical gifts developed,
and her tutors spoke more and more certainly of her
prospects of doing very well, there was a good deal of
suppressed excitement around her.   There was some
anxious correspondence between her mother and the
Principal as to how Philippa was standing the strain, but
she was working so steadily and behaving so sensibly
that anxiety had little to feed on.   They didn't want
to disturb her, but what a thing it would be if she could
be among the first two or three !   And as the Tripos year
came round, and the actual date drew near, they thought
even more daringly still.   Her tutors were so sure, she
herself was so steady ; and, as Edmund Garrett wrote
to her mother, the chance of her being Senior Wrangler
seemed " almost too good *not* to be true."

Mrs. Fawcett tried hard not to let her expectations rise
too high.   " I am going to Cambridge to-morrow week,"
she wrote to Clotilda Marson in May, " and I shall have
my last sight of P. G. F. till after the exam.   I have made
up my mind not to be too anxious about it.   There are
a great many better things in the world than beating
other people in examinations."   But all the same, she
could not help being anxious when the critical days
arrived.   They came, and they passed, and all the reports
which reached Mrs. Fawcett were encouraging.   Philippa
had done the papers without any fuss or disturbance, and
she had done them as everyone had expected ;   and
before long it was pretty well known in Cambridge what
place she would take.   The official results did not come
out, of course, until the ceremony of the reading of the
lists, but the Newnham contingent went down to the
Senate House that day in a state of joyful anticipation,
and the undergraduates packed the floor till there was

PHILIPPA FAWCETT (*seated left*) AND NEWNHAM STUDENTS, 1890.

not room for a single one more. Mrs. Fawcett admitted that she " felt too keenly about what was going to happen to dare to be present," but old Mr. Garrett came over from Aldeburgh with two of his other granddaughters, and one of these sent home to her mother a graphic description of the proceedings :

" It was a most exciting scene in the Senate this morning. Christina and I got seats in the gallery, and Grandpapa remained below. The gallery was crowded with girls and a few men, and the floor of the building was thronged by undergraduates as tightly packed as they could be. The lists were read from the gallery and we heard splendidly. All the men's names were read first ; the Senior Wrangler was much cheered. There was a good deal of shouting and cheering throughout ; at last the man who had been reading shouted ' Women.' The undergraduates yelled ' Ladies,' and for some minutes there was a great uproar. A fearfully agitating moment for Philippa it must have been ; the examiner, of course, could not attempt to read the names until there was a lull. Again and again he raised his cap, but would not say ' ladies ' instead of ' women,' and quite right, I think. He signalled with his hands for the men to keep quiet, but he had to wait some time. At last he read Philippa's name, and announced that she was ' above the Senior Wrangler.' There was a great and prolonged cheering ; many of the men turned towards Philippa, who was sitting in the gallery with Miss Clough, and waved their hats. When the examiner went on with the other names, there were cries of ' Read Miss Fawcett's name again,' but no attention was paid to this. I don't think any other women's names were heard, for the men were making such a tremendous noise. We made our way round to Philippa to congratulate her, and then I went over to Grandpapa. Miss Gladstone was with him. She was, of course, tremendously delighted. A great many people were there to cheer and congratulate Philippa when she came down into the hall. The Master of Trinity and Mrs. Butler went up into the gallery to speak to her. Grandpapa was standing at the bottom of the stairs waiting for Philippa. He was a good bit upset. I entreated him not to upset Philippa, and he

said he wouldn't. He pressed something into her hand
—a cheque, I fancy. [It was really a ring.] She was
very composed. A great many of the Dons came to
shake hands with her. The undergraduates made way
for her to pass through the hall, and then they all followed her, cheering, and I saw her no more. Grandpapa
called the servant girl of our lodgings up as soon as we
got in, gave her ten shillings, telling her first that his
granddaughter was Senior Wrangler. He said, ' You are
the landlady's daughter, aren't you ? ' She, not wishing
to lose the ten shillings, and yet wishing to keep to the
truth as far as possible, said, ' Not quite.' He replied,
' Very nearly,' and gave her the tip. Grandpapa is now
lying down."

A telegram, of course, went off instantly to Gower
Street, and Mrs. Fawcett came down at once—and was
in time to take part in the rejoicings at Newnham to
which the rest of the day and night were devoted. She
was still very much afraid of her own emotion, and one
of those who met her on her arrival in the college remembered very vividly the curious effect of her formal
greeting, the abrupt " How do you do ? " with which she
tried to keep a hold upon her feelings, and the shy pause
which followed. But even Mrs. Fawcett's reserve could
not withstand the enthusiasm of the students, or the
unfeigned delight of Miss Clough. The college dinner
that night was the occasion for very heartfelt toasts and
speeches, and the bonfire which followed in the garden
was a great relief to young ladies who could no longer
go on being ladylike. They chaired Philippa all over
the place, and the undergraduates from Selwyn came in
and joined them in making a really satisfactory noise,
and only the head parlourmaid was able to feel at all
shocked. It was simply the most perfect thing that
ever happened ; and the only regret which anyone
had—and everyone had it—was that Philippa's father
was not there to share the joy.

The next day, of course, the news had got out to the
world. *The Times* and many other papers had leading

articles, in which the advancement which this triumph had made for the cause was apparent ; and congratulations began to pour in upon Philippa and her mother. Telegrams came to Gower Street " like snowflakes in a storm," until even the telegraph boy was driven to ask what was going on in the house, and suggested that it might be a wedding. " Oh no ! " was the housekeeper's answer ; " it's a great deal better than that."

Everyone, certainly, did regard this achievement as much more than a personal event, for it was a triumphant vindication of the women's colleges, and one of those startling sensational things which travel all over the world, and do more than years of unanswerable argument to promote a good cause. Even genuine opponents told Mrs. Fawcett that her daughter's success weakened their disapproval of women's suffrage, and though she well knew that this was but " a passing phase of emotionalism," it was agreeable hearing. To her friends, of course, the event was unmixed satisfaction. It was so eminently right and glorious, so perfect, that words were sometimes quite inadequate to express their feelings. The first time that Mrs. Fawcett appeared at a Women's Liberal Unionist Committee after the Tripos results were known, Lady Stanley " arose and enfolded her in an embrace, as generous and prolonged as the battle had been agelong." And it was some time before any of the Committee were in a condition to settle to their business. On the Suffrage Committees the joy was even greater, and the little note of thanks which Mrs. Fawcett sent out to the hundreds of her fellow-workers who wrote to her expressed the feeling which they all shared :

" The news on Saturday made me very happy," she wrote. " You will know that I care for it mainly for the sake of women ; but of course I also feel especially blessed in the fact that the thing I care most of all for has been helped on in this way by my own dear child. She is perfectly well, and has taken all the work as well as all the excitement of the last day or two as quietly as possible."

This last remark, which was included because it was one of the things all their friends were glad to know, was one which it was rather necessary to make. For all the enemies of the cause, and the people who hated to relinquish their belief in the unalterable superficiality of women, began busily to spread the report that Philippa had ruined her health by overwork, and to assert that they knew for a fact that she had completely broken down under the unnatural strain. There was nothing even remotely approaching truth in the suggestion, but it was popular in some circles, and hard to kill. Indeed, it never was quite killed, and a year later, after Philippa had taken her brilliant first in the second part of the Tripos, it showed its head once more.

" A friend of mine at Manchester," wrote Mrs. Fawcett in 1891, " wrote that she had heard a doctor telling people at a party that Bennett (the official Senior Wrangler of 1890) had beaten Philippa in the second part of the Tripos, and that P. was so chagrined that she took to her bed from disappointment, and that her health had quite broken down, and that he had no hesitation, etc., as a medical man, etc., etc., in saying ' no wonder.' This is quite a lovely complication of inventions. First, Bennett did not beat her. Second, she would have taken it quite calmly if he had. Third, she has been in splendidly vigorous health all along."

This deliberate belittling of the great achievement was tiresome, but after all it was relatively unimportant. What counted most was that it was now proved that a college girl could give a good account of herself even in the regions of abstract theory, and that all the world was aware of the fact. That was an achievement safely completed, and nothing could ever thereafter disprove it.

The enormous publicity which followed Philippa's success had, of course, its reactions upon her mother,

who now became even better known to the general
public than she had been before. She gained, indeed,
in popularity both by her husband and her daughter,
and their fame kept adding to her the element of publicity which her own quiet ways might perhaps have kept
at bay. While Henry Fawcett had been alive he had
been very well known indeed among the working people
of the country, both because of his heroic blindness and
because of the stand he made for the liberties of the
people ; and his popularity at the Post Office had given
him, as it were, agents all over the country to sing his
praise. The tall blind man and his gentle wife were
romantic figures in the public mind, and on his death
the romance stayed and clung to his widow. And now
their daughter had distinguished herself in this very
sensational fashion, and the papers were full of her
triumph, and the legend revived again. By 1890,
therefore, Mrs. Henry Fawcett's name was known far
more widely even than her work extended. And then,
to add to this vicarious fame, there came, bit by bit,
her own personal reputation. Everyone who had heard
of her—as nearly everyone had—was anxious to see
her ; and everyone who met her or heard her speak,
or who read her letters to the papers or her articles in
the reviews, was struck by the quality of her mind. Her
reputation grew with every year that passed, not only
with politicians and the learned world, but in the slums
and in the villages ; and every action which she took,
increased it. In details, as in essentials, she was
courageous, wise and true as steel ; and no one failed
to see it.

CHAPTER VIII

WOMEN'S SUFFRAGE IN THE 'NINETIES

The election of 1892—Difficulties of suffrage work—Mr. Labouchere—
Dr. Jane Walker—Visit to Athens—Second Reading victory in 1897—
Attitude of the Liberals.

IN 1890 and the immediately following years the Liberal
Unionist work was very important in Mrs. Fawcett's
life, although even in the midst of it the suffrage movement, and its kindred agitations, still held the place
nearest to her heart. Everything went on simultane-
ously ; now one thing and now another came, as it
were, to the surface ; but they all blended together to
fill her days with steady political effort.

The position of the loyalists in Southern Ireland
was very serious at this time, when " boycotting " was
at its height, and this was one of the things which
occupied the Liberal Unionist ladies in England. Mrs.
Fawcett was very active in trying to help these people
and in raising money for their relief. The work involved
constant and detailed communication with Ireland, and
her correspondence in the 'nineties shows a regular
interchange of news and opinions among a group of
intelligent women in both countries who not only fully
trusted each other, but found real relief and comfort
in the opportunities which the Association gave for
sharing the humours and the labours of their campaign.
Some of the Irish ladies were exceedingly witty correspondents, and they by no means overlooked the absurdities which accompanied their own enthusiasm.

They told Mrs. Fawcett about Mrs. D., " who talked
about her husband instead of her point " ; Mrs. L.,
whose speech was " nothing but I, I, I's " ; poor Miss
H., " who got the most horrid inward pains from

nervousness " ; and Lady B., " who has the family peculiarity of speaking against a proposal which she subsequently votes for." They told her all the ins and outs in the certain knowledge that she would appreciate all the fun there was to be had, but they also turned to her whenever they needed help.

In 1891, for example, there was a good deal of anxiety about a proposed new Local Government Bill for Ireland. It seemed to these ladies more than likely that the matter of including women in the electorate would be overlooked amidst the great controversies connected with the subject ; and yet it was a point they must not fail to press at the right moment.

" There is one matter I want to ask your earnest help about," wrote Miss Fanny Currie to Mrs. Fawcett in January of this year. " I frightened our poor females out of their lives by assuring them that in the Local Government Bill it was almost certain they would have votes like Englishwomen for County Councils. Will you watch the matter ? Never, never will these poor women be any better if such an opportunity of developing their energies is lost. They are really doing their little political work pretty well, and it would be awful if for want of some watching and warning at headquarters the women were forgotten in the Bill. The R.C.'s who call themselves L.U.'s, and who earwig the Government, being deadly foes at heart to women's progress, will do nothing. And if the Council does not look after our interests no one else will. As for our getting up petitions, etc., it would be impossible. Not five women in the South here know what County Councils are ; not more than twenty understand that a new Local Government Bill for Ireland is preparing."

It was quite safe to write so to Mrs. Fawcett. There was no fear that she would think these ignorant women did not deserve enfranchisement ; no fear that she would be slack or dilatory in acting ; and, having sent off her letter, Miss Currie felt safe.

In 1902 another similar appeal reached Mrs. Fawcett

on the question of the admission of women to degrees at
Dublin. She went over to see what could be done,
only to hear the same tedious old arguments over and
over again ; and even the attempt to get " a little less
needlework and a little more mind into the elementary
schools " seemed hopeless. Yet perhaps some good was
done ; for it was Dublin which a dozen years later
opened its degrees to the women of Oxford and Cambridge, and gave them a recognition which their own
Universities refused.

Besides the work in Ireland, and the various problems
of organisation and tactics in the Liberal Unionist
camp, the propaganda meetings against Home Rule
went steadily on in England. In February 1892 Mrs.
Fawcett held one of these meetings in Cambridge, glad
to do so because it was a place where Harry had been
so well known, and where she always loved to stay.
But the meeting was not a success. It was crowded
to the doors, indeed, but with a hostile crowd. The
Liberal working men of the town felt it to be dreadful
that she, of all people, should come and speak to them
against Gladstone and his proposals, and they refused to
allow her to proceed, so that the meeting broke up in
disorder. Such an occurrence was most unusual for a
woman speaker to encounter in the 'nineties. Mrs.
Fawcett herself thought little of it, but the prominent
men and the local associations of the town felt it to be a
terrible disgrace to Cambridge. There was a great deal
of talk and discussion as to what could be done to wipe
out this affront, and finally an elaborate address was
prepared, signed by all the leading Conservatives and
Liberal Unionists, and presented to her at a grand and
formal Guildhall meeting. Mrs. Fawcett's letter accepting the invitation to this meeting was characteristic.
After using the correct phrases about the honour they
were doing her, and their over-estimation of her
" small efforts in the service of the Unionist cause,"
she added :

" I do not attach any importance to the fact that a considerable number of Gladstonians made noisy interruptions at a meeting which I addressed in Cambridge last February. This was merely an object lesson in the methods of political controversy which commend themselves to them ; I hope that the meeting on the 28th of June may have no reference to this trifling incident, but that it may serve to some degree to reinforce and stimulate the enthusiasm all Unionists must feel in the face of the great electoral struggle which is now approaching. For Ireland the issue of the struggle will involve the maintenance or the destruction of civil and religious liberty; not for the loyal minority only, but for the whole country. For England the issue of the struggle involves the destruction and violation of her greatness and honour ; whether she shall capitulate to those who boast their hatred of her, or defy them and stand true and steadfast to those loyal Irish men and women who know that all they value most in life depends on their remaining under the protection of the Parliament of the United Kingdom."

That was the way in which Mrs. Fawcett and the Liberal Unionists looked at the election of 1892, and it explains why they threw themselves so vigorously into the fight, and why they cared so tremendously for the result.

When the election returns came in, it was evident that the Liberals had secured only a very narrow majority, and neither Mrs. Fawcett nor any of her colleagues were at all discouraged.

" I don't feel that we have done so badly," she wrote to Emma Miller in July. " Remember all the Gladstonian press and people were saying before the election that their majority was going to be 100. The very utmost it can possibly be now is 48, and it may be only 44. Thus Great Britain, taken by itself, is still against Home Rule. The anti H.R. majority is turned into a minority by the 80 Irish H.R. votes ; but it is quite likely that the majority thus formed will burst up on the details of the H.R. Bill. They (the majority) are composed of the most discordant elements. . . . They will be a queer lot to drive. ' A queer thing to drive, for one man, when there's many of 'em, is a pig.' There will be a lively time in Parliament, and I believe we shall see Gladstone's majority melt away before he has had time to do much harm. The strong stand they made in Ulster, and the grand orderly demonstration has done and will continue to do much good. . . .

" We have immensely enjoyed the German operas in London. They have really been splendid, and have upheld me through the work and worries of the election. They (the Ring series) have a wonderful bearing on the woman question. I often think that the only real political and social seers are the poets."

Mrs. Fawcett's work with the Liberal Unionists continued until 1903. In that year Mr. Chamberlain conducted his " raging tearing campaign for Protection," and Mrs. Fawcett, being a staunch and ardent Free Trader, was unable to follow the official view. She did her best to stop the drift towards the Protectionist doctrine which was apparent among the Liberal Unionist women, and she called special meetings, and issued circulars in the hope that she could prevent the Association from " unfairly lending the prestige of the words ' Liberal ' and ' Unionist ' to a policy which has no claim to either designation." She tried, but she failed. The Liberal Unionists became almost indistinguishably merged into the Conservative Party, and Mrs. Fawcett left them, and was never again associated with any political party at all.

The whole of her connection with this Liberal Unionist work had had an interest for Mrs. Fawcett over and above its intrinsic meaning and importance. For it had been real political work, similar to that which she had done with her husband, and carried out in the genuine political atmosphere. The men with whom she had to deal were prominent within their parties, they commanded public attention, and their decisions resulted in immediate and tangible action. But her other work, the women's suffrage work, political though it was, was in a very different position. There there was very little political reality, but only a sort of impenetrable fog. Not only did progress appear to be at a standstill, but every attempt to move was enveloped in the baffling sensation of powerlessness which came from being political outsiders. Most of the women by whom this cause was advocated were completely innocent of political experience ; and their judgments of chances and expedients were of little value. And not only were they ignorant and easily deceived, but the people they were dealing with were anxious that they should remain so. There was a sort of tolerant condescension on the part of all but a few of the men with whom they came in contact which greatly impeded their progress, and the half-disguised joke with which they were usually greeted made serious discussion very difficult indeed.

Mrs. Fawcett herself, of course, knew very well what was real and what was sham in the support which they secured, and during the early 'nineties she became in consequence more than ever the leader of the political activities. She it was who had to compose all the political letters, and to make the opportunities to see the right people at the right times. She had to catch them when they were likely to be both disengaged and good tempered, and to put the necessary points before them shortly and persuasively. Miss Lydia Becker, who had been the Parliamentary agent of the suffrage societies, had died in 1887 and there was no one who was able to give help to that side of the work at this time. Mrs. Fawcett was the Honorary Secretary of the society whose headquarters was in Great College Street, and many a long afternoon she spent there, attending the committee meetings, writing the letters and advising her colleagues how to steer the best course through the obstructions which surrounded them. There were constant rumours of Redistribution Bills and of sudden Parliamentary crises which had to be watched. There was the ever-lasting question of who was to lead the forces in the

House, and how the friendly M.P.'s were to be induced to follow him ; there was a recurring difficulty when their best friends accepted minor office, and then became frigidly official, and there was constant trouble in keeping the separate and very independent country societies upon the same tactical lines. And all the time they were hampered by their position as sheer political outsiders. They could not get easily into the precincts of the House, they could not informally meet the Members they wanted to see, and their go-betweens, the friendly Members, were terribly apt to forget all about them, and needed constant jogging to make them bestir themselves in a cause which was so very unpopular and so obviously outside the main stream of Parliamentary business. Even Mrs. Fawcett, with her long experience, her individual standing and her political reputation, found most Members of Parliament elusive, and their attitude baffling. It was possible sometimes to get them to agree in general terms to what she wanted ; but it was incredibly difficult to get anyone to *do* anything at all, and for years and years the main Parliamentary effort was to secure time for any discussion whatever in the House. " If we had votes," Mrs. Fawcett used to say, " it would be easy to get votes." But as things were, the task was appallingly hard.

The vagueness and muddle were not all on the side of the political people. Mrs. Fawcett saw clearly enough how amateurish many of the proceedings of the suffragists were, but she felt that this was a diminishing trouble. There is a letter of hers to Clotilda Marson which expresses her outlook on this point. It concerns an organisation formed to improve the working conditions of dressmakers, and not the methods of the suffragists, but her attitude was the same for both.

" I do not take a desponding view of the Association's chances of success," she wrote. " Of course it has very often happened that philanthropic schemes of this kind

have only ended in failure, because they were not
managed by people with business experience ; but on
the other hand a great many have succeeded splendidly
and have done a great deal of good.   Even if this and
fifty others fail, I believe it is better to try and try, and
so learn by degrees the conditions of success in these
efforts to make the condition of the workers better than
it is now.   I mean that anything is better than placid
contentment with a state of things in which a woman
has to work sixteen hours a day to earn a shilling and
to find her own needles and thread."

For all her tolerance of amateurish efforts, Mrs.
Fawcett had by this time a very clear notion of what
political organisation ought to be, and she and her
associates were gradually improving their technique.
It was in 1892 that she first drew up the outline of an
election policy in a letter which she sent to all those with
whom the suffrage societies were in touch.   The phrases
she used read curiously now : " Our political influence,"
she said, " is apt to be neutralised by well-known ladies
speaking on opposite sides in the same constituency ;
but if we are careful never to work against the friends
of women, and only to work for those who are our friends,
our political influence is not neutralised but acquires
additional value."   It was such a small thing, that
political influence, in any case ; all women put together
did not count for much, and the number of those who
would put their allegiance to women's suffrage before
party was infinitesimal.   But even so, Mrs. Fawcett
believed that something could be done, if they were
consistent and stood by each other ; and the event
proved that she was right.   Five or six years later the
Women's Liberal Federation was split in two by this
very question of election policy, and the possibility of
securing or alienating the women's organisations began
to be considered in the choice of candidates.   But it was
a long, slow business ; and at first it appeared to make
little progress.

There were, indeed, some moments of encouragement, but they never lasted long.

" I am in a flutter of REAL HOPE about the W.S. Bill," Mrs. Fawcett wrote to Emma Miller in April 1891. " We went on a deputation to W. H. Smith on Monday about it, and he promised that the House should not rise before May 13, the day on which the Bill is down as 1st Order. My impression is that the Government mean to help us ; but we must not let this out to Gladstonians, who are very timid of W.S. as it approaches practical realisation. Mr. Penrose Fitzgerald is one of our staunch friends, so we need not trouble about him, but I think the Cambridge W.S. Society ought to be called together and serious consideration given to what they can do to make Cambridgeshire Members on both sides of the House of Commons vote for W.S."

By the 28th of the same month, however, the " flutter of real hope " was over.

" I would certainly try to arrange to come down and meet Sir G. Stokes if it could be arranged," Mrs. Fawcett wrote to the same correspondent, " but I am in a state of considerable anxiety and perplexity just now in consequence of disquieting rumours that have reached me from an apparently well-informed source that the Government mean, after all, to filch our day from us. The report is that Labouchere has bargained with them that, if they will defeat or shelve the women, he will let the Land Bill through without much more delay. If they have sacrificed us in this corrupt way, I feel inclined to have nothing more to do with politicians any more for the rest of my life."

A month later it was clear that the bargain had been struck ; but of course Mrs. Fawcett was still having plenty to do with politicians, and was even then urging Mr. Balfour and other members of the Government to give them another day of Parliamentary time.

" The poor dear W.S. Bill has been murdered," she wrote, " and there is no more hurt it can receive this session. It is rather dispiriting to find the same stupid old coarseness trotted out by the enemy in the place of anything to the point. . . . Try not to let yourself get too depressed. One way of rousing yourself is to be convinced that it is this beastly weather which makes all the world look black, and not one's own particular misfortunes. The only addition I have thought it necessary to make to my wardrobe this summer is a waterproof cloak."

After all, as Mrs. Fawcett knew, Parliamentary opportunities were not the only important matters in the suffrage movement, and she gave much of her time to strengthening the provincial societies, to propaganda meetings, to money-raising, and to the newspaper sides of the campaign. It was in the early 'nineties that she had to make a rule not to speak more than once a day, nor more than four times a week, but she found it impossible to keep to it. So many appeals came, and so many emergencies took on the appearance of special cases, and seemed to need her more than anyone else !

It is difficult to recapture the rush and hurry of those outwardly uneventful years, the glow of hope, the fever of excitement, the anxieties, the worries, the prayers, the small triumphs, the heavy despairs, the jokes, the personalities, the tears and the humours of this period. Some of the early workers were already gone. John Stuart Mill had died long since, and Mrs. Peter Taylor was now very ill. She wrote to Millicent again and again in her trembling hand, and always in the same strain : " I grieve that I cannot work any more. My life is nearly over. It would have been pleasant to know our cause triumphant, but it will be before long under your guidance." That was what everyone felt, but it was slow in coming.

While they waited they all turned more and more to their leader, and letters poured in to No. 2 Gower Street in an unceasing stream, expressing the anxiety or the impatience of her fellow-workers. " I should not be at all surprised," wrote Mrs. Hallett in '92, " if

Stansfeld or some other Gladstonian were to pretend to take our Bill for the express purpose of getting it shelved." Of course Mr. Stansfeld would do no such thing, as Mrs. Fawcett told her ; but the suspicion showed the depths of disillusionment into which they sank at times. And indeed, disillusionment apart, there was a great deal to discourage them. In the same year Mrs. Hallett wrote again :

" Your letter to-day fills me with trouble at the thought of you alone struggling with difficulties. I read all the Borthwick correspondence. It impressed me deeply with the difficulties of getting men to ballot. It is evident that a tremendous effort will be necessary to get together twenty. Only think that out of that bundle of letters only three men were secured. It is a critical moment for us, especially trying and painful to me when I can only sit at home and pray. You have done splendidly, and at least will have the consolation of feeling that you have done what you could."

It was the only consolation there was, very often ; for things were most confusing and disheartening. In '95, for example, a good deal of trouble was made by a lady who suddenly began to lobby single-handed in the House of Commons, without reference to the existing societies. Miss Frances Power Cobbe wrote anxiously to Mrs. Fawcett to enquire about this, adding at the end of her long letter, " It is not fair to give you the trouble of writing in answer to all these questions, but there is no one whose opinion can be of any guidance to me but you."

On receiving Mrs. Fawcett's prompt and explicit answer, she wrote again : " This is certainly a justifiable case for blasphemy. Miss C. must be scraped to death with oyster shells." But, of course, the scraping was left to Mrs. Fawcett.

It was an occupation in which, when necessity arose, she could be very expert, for when she wished she was able to make remarks of great severity, or jokes with a

(her uncle) for a room in the H. of L. He said, when she spoke to him about it, ' Why don't you have Westminster Hall ? ' and told her who to apply to and how to get it, and she promptly went and did. It is such a fine snub to the Speaker to be able to go one better than any room in the H. of C."

Ups and downs like these, together with the endless details of the petition work and the country propaganda, went on day after day and year after year ; but it was not only the reverses and triumphs of the cause itself about which the workers of the 'nineties corresponded so copiously. There were minor matters too, which sometimes became very difficult to handle, disagreements among themselves, rash actions of local committees, and the everlasting question of appearances. This last was a very important matter from the propaganda point of view, though some suffragists could not bring themselves to admit it. The movement naturally attracted women who were in revolt against the various conventions of the time, and the result was that Mrs. Fawcett passed through some awkward moments.

" Something will have to be done about Miss X being made more presentable," Mrs. Hallett wrote in anxiety. " If I were in London I would insist on this, and I spoke very clearly last time to her about her appearance. We must have a clever smart person in the office to help to keep Miss X tidy if she remains our secretary. I also entirely agree with you about her not taking up other things. Of course other things to a large extent enlarge her circle of friends among the workers and so help our cause in indirect ways. But she is a hopeless person in drawing lines, and cannot keep shape, so to speak. There is great value in her, of course, and the absence of all petty-mindedness covers a multitude of things. . . . Of course, you are always there to feel and to be troubled."

That was very true. The brunt of everything, whether great or small, fell to Millicent's share, and in this particular matter she was helpless. Plain speaking or tactful suggestion, or even presents of new bonnets were all alike unavailing, and Miss X remained what Mrs. Fawcett described as " an uncouth old dear " to the end.

Besides these domestic difficulties, there were always distinguished outsiders to be adequately handled ; and Mrs. Fawcett's tact was called upon again and again to get from the great men of the time a pronouncement which could be used. There was something about the question of women's suffrage which seemed to let loose all the cantankerousness of such people. Whether it was that they did not take it quite seriously, or that, unknown to themselves, they really hated what they thought they approved of, cannot now be known. But it is certain that people who were capable of being practical enough on other questions felt free to indulge in all sorts of fine-spun qualifications and hair-splitting, so that it was difficult to get really quotable or comprehensible support from them.

Dr. James Martineau was such an one, and though he was counted as a supporter, Mrs. Fawcett had to bear patiently with such impractical suggestions as the following :

" Married life would be quite unworkable were it a mere dual partnership without a casting vote. I do not care a fig whether the man or the woman gives the vote. The presumption is in favour of the former, as usually the breadwinner ; but on proof of his unworthiness I would have it transferred to the latter."

Mrs. Fawcett was neither annoyed nor worried by suggestions such as these. For her the important thing was that he declared he did not believe a member of the female sex was necessarily unfitted for responsibility. The rest, she knew, would settle itself in the light of ordinary life, if once that principle were accepted. And so she got what she could where she could, and was thankful for every scrap.

All sorts of extraneous matters mixed themselves up with the straight suffrage work of these years. Mrs. Fawcett was asked to help and advise about the prospects of women in the Post Office and their possible employment on similar work in Calcutta ; she corresponded with Mrs. Peachey Phipson about women doctors for India, and with all sorts of people at home about the inclusion of women on Hospital Boards. With her usual thoroughness, indeed, she not only got some women appointed, but continued to encourage them in their subsequent trials.

" You have done a very good bit of work," she wrote to one of these ladies in '92, " to insist on the hospital people seeking the real cause of their repeated fires. Don't be vexed because people prefer those who prophesy smooth things. It is always so, and has nothing to do with your being a woman. Don't you remember too what the old waiting maid in *Felix Holt* says : ' It mayn't be good luck to be a woman. But one begins with it from a baby ; one gets used to it. And I shouldn't like to be a man—to cough so loud, and stand straddling about on a wet day, and be so wasteful with meat and drink.' "

One minute Mrs. Fawcett would be writing this, and the next she would be helping to start Swanley Horticultural College, and from that she would turn to the task of collecting material for the Chicago Exhibition. She had been asked to produce something to show the value of University education for women, and among other exhibits she decided to send " a frame full of photographs of prize babies whose mothers are graduates. Some of the mothers I have asked to give me photographs of their babies," she added in writing to a friend of this enterprise, " are too plaguey genteel to let their babies appear in an exhibition ; but I am beginning to get a nice collection." It was a job which pleased her, for she took a genuine interest in the children of her friends, and especially of the Newnham

students, and felt a sort of personal pride in their charms.
The letters she wrote to their mothers when a new one
was born were full of exultation, especially, perhaps,
when the baby was a girl. To Mrs. Merrifield, for
instance, she wrote in great delight when her granddaughter Helen Verrall was born. The baby's mother
was that same May whose Tripos Mrs. Fawcett had
secured for her, and this no doubt added to the delight.

" The 4th of July," Mrs. Fawcett wrote, " is a beautiful day for a birthday. I hope the baby's declaration
of independence will date from it, and that she will be a
worthy descendant of those who have gone before her."

To Clotilda Marson when her daughter Mary was born
she wrote in the same strain :

" We were made very happy by the joyful telegram
' Strong daughter both well.' Strong daughter sounds
so nice, it is what we all hope for her all through her life ;
it made us think at once of the beautiful bit in the
Baptism service, ' Manfully to fight under His banner
against sin, the world and the devil, and to continue
Christ's faithful soldier and servant unto her life's end.'
She will need to be a strong daughter for that, as well
as for many other good and beautiful things."

But there were sad and terrible things to be attended
to also, and Millicent did not shirk them. The work
of the Vigilance Society still interested her deeply, and
in 1893 she embarked upon a campaign of letters to the
Press against the exclusion of women from the courts
when cases of assaults on children were to be tried.
One of the letters she wrote will serve to show the spirit
in which she carried on the attack.

" It appears to be a universal custom in the police and
law courts," the letter runs, " to exclude every woman
from the court when charges of outrage upon little
children or cases of a similar nature are heard. In a
particular case which was heard a fortnight ago at
Marlboro' Street, and then at Middlesex Sessions at Clerk-
enwell, the child was only eight years old. Both in the

police court and in the law court an order was given for
the exclusion of every woman, including the child's
mother and a lady who attended to support the mother
in the performance of a public duty.   The little child
was thus left to give her evidence and be examined and
cross-examined in the presence of the lawyers and of
a miscellaneous crowd of idle men who frequent law
courts to pass the time.   The little thing was not
allowed the support of the presence of a single creature
of her own sex.

No doubt the judges and magistrates act in the interests
of what they believe to be public morality.   But I think
further reflection, especially from those who look at
these cases from the social and domestic rather than
from the legal point of view, would show that while
the interests of public morality are served by the exclusion of young persons of both sexes from the hearing
of these cases, public morality is injured by anything
which is likely to add to the reluctance of the parents
of an injured child to prosecute the offender.   This
reluctance is already very strong, and, on purely selfish
grounds, it is very natural.   The best thing for the
child herself of course is that she should, if possible,
forget the whole affair as speedily as possible.   The
prosecution is frequently undertaken in the purest
public spirit, in order that offences of this kind may not
be committed with impunity.   The order of the magistrates to exclude women places an additional penalty
on public-spirited prosecution.   For the child to have
to tell her pitiful story in a court of justice is a sufficient
ordeal ; to have to tell it quite alone without the presence
of the friendly face of a mother or other near kinswoman
might probably break down the self-command of a
nervous excitable child and render her evidence almost
worthless.   Even if this is not so, and the child has the
courage to tell her story calmly and succinctly, as in
the case I refer to, it seems an unnecessary cruelty to
permit the presence of as many strange men as the
space set apart for the public will accommodate, and to
exclude every woman. . . ."

The Press campaign had no visible results.   It was
continued more or less for a great many years, and taken

up again whenever a particularly flagrant case was reported, but the judges and magistrates took no heed. And Mrs. Fawcett grew surer and surer as time went on that this and all the countless things like it would not be remedied until after the suffrage had been won.

This fact, while it drove her back with renewed ardour to her own particular work, did not prevent her from still doing what she could for the other evils which she saw ; and one of the foremost of them was the condition of the sweated women workers.   Mrs. Fawcett did not, indeed, join actively in the Trade Union movement, for she felt little confidence that women's interests would be properly cared for within it ; but this did not mean that she did not care deeply about the needs and troubles of working women.   In every problem connected with work and wages and the conditions of work she still held undeviatingly to the individualist doctrine which she had accepted in the 'seventies, and she therefore distrusted and opposed almost all forms of legislative intervention.

In 1887 she had taken a vigorous part in the agitation which the women chain-makers of Cradley Heath were making against the imposition of rules forbidding them to do any but the light work, and she had herself taken a deputation of " pit brow lassies " to the Home Secretary, and had greatly enjoyed the outspoken comments which they made upon the proceedings.   As they left the room where they had been interviewed, one of them remarked, in a commiserating tone, " It's very 'ard on the pore gentleman to 'ave to make the laws, and not know nothing about it."   This comment chimed in so exactly with the whole of the suffrage propaganda that the saying became a favourite with Mrs. Fawcett, and was often repeated in other connections.

Besides these matters, and a hundred more, the progress of the women's colleges needed a good deal of time and thought.   In 1896 the possibility of giving degrees to women at Cambridge began to be canvassed again, and Mrs. Fawcett gave much help in securing the memorials necessary to get the question raised. As always, she thought and spoke hopefully.

" Fret not thyself about the ungodly," she wrote. " I am disappointed about little B., because he has the making of better stuff in him ; but on the whole I am VERY much encouraged by the response to both the memorials. More than 2,000 members of the Senate have signed the memorial to the Council, and as far as I can judge, a very large proportion are YOUNG men who have grown up therefore in a more wholesome atmosphere. In former times it was only a few men of first-class intellects and hearts, like your father and my husband, who were uniformly just in all their ways and thoughts about women ; but now the ordinary young man who is so is no miracle. I rejoice over the fight too, because it is an education to the younger generation of women, who don't realise what an uphill task their elders had to gain what the younger ones are now enjoying. So cheer up."

It was all very well to say this, but when all the elaborate formalities of University machinery had been gone through, and the vote actually came to be taken, it was overwhelmingly adverse. Mrs. Fawcett was really disappointed, and for once she admitted it.

" I am dreadfully cast down about Cambridge," she wrote. " It is the worst throwback we have had for a very long time. From the virulence of the opposition and the immense size of the majority I felt that they could if they liked deprive women of the right of examination, so that our best plan at present, I believe, is to lie low and say nothing till ' this tyranny be overpast.' The most disappointing thing is the opposition of the young men, especially the younger dons—not all, of course, but a very large proportion. The undergraduates I do not so much care about : they are boys who were led on and excited by their elders."

But if Cambridge was still a backwater, there were other Universities which were more enlightened. When

Holloway College was being started, though the same old difficulties appeared, things went better. Mrs. Fawcett described the negotiations with amusement.

" The Conference about Holloway last Saturday was a weight on my mind till it was over and well over," she wrote. " The enemy are trying to drive us on to the rocks of a separate University for women. Fortunately, each individual among the enemy has a different plan of his own : there is no unity in their plan of campaign, whereas our side are solidly united. At the Conference it was really almost ridiculous, we were so completely of one mind."

And so the work went on, week after week, month after month, and year after year ; and even Millicent admitted that she grew rather tired of it, rather weary of saying the same thing again and again, and of meeting the same silly objections, and the same shifty political tricks. " I could not have done it," she said in her reminiscences, " without long holidays " ; nor without the music and the books and the other non-political interests which gave her change of thought.

There are a few characteristic sentences scattered through her letters of this period which show how much she depended upon these things for the balance and serenity of her life. In '96, for example, she wrote to Clotilda Marson :

" Do not fret yourself about Bernard Shaw's nonsense about Shakespeare. The subjects of conversation and writing would be unduly limited if people confined themselves to sense ; and G. B. S. would not be G. B. S. unless he tried to slap people's faces as it were with ridiculous paradoxes. He is very good fun very often. I have been tremendously impressed this week by *Little Eyolf*. It is quite wonderful—a very great tragedy that we can only think of along with the very greatest, such as *Macbeth* and *Lear* ; and all made up of ordinary every-day elements, love and jealousy and passion, and without the aids of stately verse and antiquity and a dramatis personæ of kings and queens ; it is just ordinary everyday villadom, and its tragedies are as great as the greatest."

It was this same idea, doubtless, which caused her to write to Thomas Hardy on the subject of Tess. Her letter does not survive, but his answer, dated April 14, from Max Gate, is of interest :

" I am most gratified," he wrote, " to learn that so good a critic as yourself has found interest in Tess—a book which, like so many books, comes far short in its execution of what I had hoped beforehand to make it. With regard to your idea of a short story showing how the trifling with the physical element in love leads to corruption : I do not see that much more can be done by fiction in that direction than has been done already. You may say the treatment hitherto has been vague and general only, which is quite true. Possibly on that account nobody has profited greatly by such works. To do the thing well there should be no mincing of matters, and all details should be clear and directly given. This I fear the British public would not stand just now ; though, to be sure, we are educating it by degrees. The other day I read a story entitled *The Wages of Sin*, by Lucas Malet, expecting to find something of the sort therein. But the wages are that the young man falls over a cliff, and the young woman dies of consumption— not very consequent, as I told the author.

I shall be in town soon, and if you are likely to be at home any afternoon, I will if possible give myself the pleasure of calling. Believe me, Yours sincerely, THOMAS HARDY."

It was not only from books and ideas, however, that Millicent drew her pleasures. Though her life was spent so much in towns and in public work, she kept the keen delight in the countryside which had been part of her childhood. She still rode whenever she was at Alde-burgh, and learned to bicycle, and even on her railway journeys she caught up what she could. In '95 she wrote to a friend about one of her speaking expeditions :

" A little south of Doncaster I saw three wild swans flying high up in the air. I had never seen swans flying before, but I feel sure they must have been swans ; they looked immense, their long necks stretched out. It was quite a little excitement for me, nicer than Creighton's book ! ! "

There are not many such passages in her letters. Millicent had to write so much in connection with her work, and she had so many things to do every day, that the record of these little bits of refreshment was excluded. But everyone who met her was aware of her quick eager interest and of the full appreciation with which she looked at the physical world.

There was another thing which no one who met Mrs. Fawcett in these years could miss, and that was her vitality and joy in life. It was seldom that she said any-thing self-revealing, but a friend who often saw her at this time remembers travelling with her on the top of an omnibus, talking of work and projects for the future, and how suddenly Millicent exclaimed, a propos of nothing in particular, " Oh, I do enjoy myself so much ! " And it was obvious that she did.

The greatest of her private pleasures was still her friendships, and the large family circle in which so many of the dearest of them were made. The cottage at Rustington, where Rhoda and Agnes had spent many happy holidays, was still kept on, and there was also a small house at Aldeburgh to which they sometimes went. More often, however, they stayed at Alde House, to be with their father, who was in failing health ; and even after his death in 1893 their mother still lived there, so that it remained a centre for the big family reunions.

One of Millicent's nephews, Philip Cowell (the son of Alice, who had been so abnormally clever at arith-metic at the Blackheath school), rivalled his cousin Philippa by being Senior Wrangler in 1892, and this success caused great rejoicing in the family. Old Mr. Garrett was immensely proud of his two brilliant grand-children, and they all felt that sex equality was being properly demonstrated by the event.

Besides Millicent's friends in her own family there were many more, and in 1890 a new and most important one was added to them, namely, Dr. Jane Walker. Although they were neighbours in Gower Street, their first meeting was accidental ; but acquaintance soon grew into close friendship, and from that time onwards they shared a great deal of work, and a great many jokes, meeting very frequently when they were in London, and corresponding freely when apart. Of the many projects which they both supported, the most important, and the one which took up the largest share of their time and thoughts, was the East Anglian Sanatorium at Nayland. This institution was created by Dr. Walker, and the funds were raised and the business conducted by a Board of which Mrs. Fawcett was the active chairman for over thirty years. The first buildings were opened in 1898, and the project prospered so greatly, and was of such incalculable benefit, that its size was extended again and again. It was to Naylands that Edmund Garrett came, when the German cure failed to restore him. For more than a year he lived there, recruiting the strength which was to give him his last six years of life ; and until his death in 1907, Dr. Walker, as well as his cousins Agnes and Millie, remained among his dearest friends. To love Edmund Garrett was a heartbreaking thing in those years, for he was all too plainly dying ; but no one could know him and not love him. As Millicent said, the impression that he left upon those who saw him " was simply one of gay courage " ; that, and " a bright flame of life," which would burn clearly while it could burn at all.

The care for Edmund, and the planning and working for the Sanatorium were interests which united Mrs. Fawcett and her friend ; but they had many others also. Several times they took their Continental holidays together, and it was in 1896 that Mrs. Fawcett set out with Dr. Walker on the first of her more distant travels, when they went to Egypt, and on, in the spring of '97, to Constantinople and Athens.

" Our delight," she wrote on reaching this latter place, " has only been tempered by our ignorance, and we have felt dreadfully sorry not to be able to understand a syllable of Greek and not to know more about the great time of Athens. It is very delightful all the same, ignorance and all, walking about on the Acropolis and looking across the blue sea to Ægina and Salamis."

The ignorance, of course, stimulated Mrs. Fawcett to exertion, and she diligently read whatever her classically instructed friends recommended to her, and did her best to submerge herself in it all. But even in Athens she was not allowed any peace ; for it was while she was there that letters came giving details of an unexpected crisis in the suffrage work.

What had happened was that the Parliamentary friends of the cause had suddenly secured the promise of a day to bring in their Bill, and early in February it was not only debated, but passed through its Second Reading in the House of Commons. The letters telling of this surprising news, and describing all the ins and outs which preceded and followed the great day, must have interrupted Millicent's classical studies very severely, but of course she was glad of every one.

" It was an anxious time in many ways," wrote Lady Frances Balfour on February 14. " I always thought that Arthur would not take the day from us, and that our safety lay in his having had to do just that before, but he was pretty strongly urged to do so by Chamberlain and others. . . . Though I carried my head high, I was anxious.

" We had no idea how the Division would go. The Secretaries (who did splendid work) all thought it would be a defeat. The debate was the very poorest we have ever had, Courtney's fighting speech at the end the best, and the opponents were really *indescribably* bad. It was a full House throughout, though not an

excited or much interested one. The Division list will
reveal to you many new friends and several rats. I was
very bad with severe fever and bronchitis, and could
hardly hold myself together for shivering, but when at
length the Division came it nearly cured me. It was a
great moment. I was between Alice Balfour and Mrs.
Courtney. Mrs. Hallett we had to look carefully after,
we could not restrain her shouts and snorts. She said,
' I have waited for this for thirty years,' and embraced
me, while her sister melted into sobs. Faithfull Begg's
voice as he gave me the figures was simply breathless
with excitement, and it *was* a great day for him, as well
as for us. Salisbury was delighted with our success, and
once more much was due to him. By his advice, at the
last minute, I wrote to Wyndham, urging him not to
say we did not intend to carry it beyond the Second
Reading if we secured a favourable division. He and
Faithfull Begg had intended to do this to secure certain
votes, but Salisbury said it was a wrong policy, and
Wyndham took his advice. The moment the Bill was
passed Faithfull Begg went to Paris and Wyndham to
Dover, and we had some difficulty in communicating
with them ; and the women got into a wild fuss about
the Committee stage. I did not understand it all, and
much wished for you. . . . The Press as a whole has
gone crazy with rage, *The Times* simply made people
laugh. . . . A week after I met Asquith, and demanded
his congratulations ; all he would say was that it con-
firmed the view he held, that this was the stupidest
Parliament he had ever sat in !

" Altogether, my hair is a little greyer, but I am a
happier and a better woman."

On the same day Mrs. Hallett sent off her account :

" The whole suffrage position seems to have changed
by magic," she said, " and we none of us yet fully
realise how we stand. Wyndham and Faithfull Begg have
done splendidly. They appear to have been in constant
touch with the Government Whips and wire-pullers. Miss
L. Stevenson, Roper, Baxter, Palliser and myself lived
much in the lobby those anxious days. . . . Lady Frances
was much in evidence. . . . It was most dreadful to

have you away and poor Miss Blackburn. . . . I am
very thankful I have been able to be up each week to
give help and stability to Miss Palliser, who nearly got
beside herself with anxiety and also want of help at the
office. Miss Torrence was also away just at the top of
the pressure. As soon as the London work was over
the country secretaries rushed back to their respective
Committees in order to get out the whips, etc., etc.
That this was wonderfully well done is shown in the
Division lists. Our dear good Mr. Courtney has helped
us through the Committee stage. Lady Frances saw
the Bill through this stage at twelve o'clock, and describes Courtney as pulling Faithfull Begg up and pulling
him down to dodge the Moment ! I believe from his
manner Courtney thinks we shall get the Bill through. He
will stick to us and advise us, and we can't be in safer
hands. The letter to M.P.'s, signed by so many great
names of ladies, must have been a power, and yesterday
another went out of thanks which Miss Balfour herself
drew up. It is now proposed to get petitions to Parliament from every constituency as a means of keeping
our M.P.'s up to the mark. It is also proposed to have
a big meeting with a mixed platform, both London
Committees uniting. I am not myself quite clear as to
the wisdom of this meeting, but the Victoria Street
people are quite wild about it. I believe Cozens and
Mrs. Elmy and all those ' outside ' people have all been
so much to the good. They have got hold of men we
can't influence, and I'm sure Lady Carlisle must have
been worth at least 20 votes in the Division. Once
when the Irish benches cheered, she flung her arms up
in the air and turned exclaiming, ' Listen to the dear
Irish cheering.' Finding the unfamiliar faces of Edith
Palliser and me behind her, she subsided. We nearly
exploded, but we realise how she had been nobbling these
men, and Laura McLaren informed us that Lady
Carlisle had been romping round Harcourt, Asquith and
Bryce, cajoling and threatening by turns."

All this made incongruous reading on the Acropolis,
but Millicent naturally longed for every detail and
could not hear enough. She could see it all so well in
her imagination.

" We were at the Duchess of Devonshire's reception,"
Mrs. Hallett goes on. " Jesse Collings came up to me
in great fuss, saying we must not send so many letters of
thanks to M.P.'s, for they were complaining. ' Indeed,'
I said, ' let them, for I cannot control the forces which
are behind this Bill, neither can our Suffrage Committees.' Then Mr. Hallett joined in and told him,
' You have called women out to help you win your
election, and you must respect the power they have
become.' He had to climb down before our sneers, and
I told him the wisest course was for them all to let the
Bill go through before worse trouble came upon them.
He tried to soothe me by saying, ' Chamberlain refrained
from speaking against you ' ; ' And so he had better do,'
said I, ' and let him now assist the question.' He went
off looking and feeling smaller.

" They are all crying out at our office for you to
return, but I don't see any need for you to cut short
your holiday. The work is now all being arranged, and
therefore the need for you ought not to be acute until
April or May."

That was true, and Millicent very sensibly acted upon
it ; but it was difficult not to boil with rage over the
newspaper comments, and not to long to be on the spot
to answer them. *The Times* was very crushing.

" Apart from a mere handful of ladies of masculine
ambitions," its leading article announced, " the experience of every man is that the overwhelming majority
of the best women of his acquaintance are perfectly
content with the influence they wield in feminine ways,
and have no wish whatever to mix themselves up in
the dirty business of politics."

Certainly, it seemed a dirty business, when Millicent
got back from her holiday, for she perceived that there
were influences at work against the further progress of
the Bill which it was almost impossible to meet in open
argument. Mr. Asquith was an unremitting opponent,
and so was Mr. Chamberlain. That was plain sailing—
but what was so difficult was the atmosphere which
prevailed in the Liberal Party. The majority of its

Members had voted for the Bill, and were pledged over
and over again in its support, and yet they seemed to be
feeling that they had done all that was required by
voting for the principle, and that now the thing might
drop, and all the awkwardness of going against their
leader be avoided. The *Daily Chronicle*—then one of
the leading party organs—actually expressed this
attitude :

" While our political machinery is so imperfect," it
said, " while hundreds of thousands of adult men are
still outside the pale of the franchise, are taxed and
rated without being represented, it would be wise on
the part of Liberal leaders to concern themselves first
with these pressing grievances. So many special
women's grievances have been dealt with since the time
when the suffrage was demanded for the sex mainly on
their account that there is no violent hurry for settling
this question off-hand, while there is known to be such a
difference of opinion inside the party on the subject."

No violent hurry indeed ! It was already thirty
years that Mrs. Fawcett had been working, and twenty-
seven since the House had first endorsed the principle ;
but the political machinery was imperfect indeed, and
so the Bill was safely destroyed. The actual method by
which the calamity of really carrying out their pledges
was staved off from the Liberals was, in a literal as well
as in a metaphorical sense, a dirty business. On the
day when the Third Reading was due, Mr. Labouchere
was put up to talk upon the measure standing just
before it on the Order Paper until the available time was
all spent ; and the subject happened to be Verminous
Persons. Upon this fertile subject—in which he had no
faintest genuine interest—he managed to produce a flow
of wit which lasted for three hours and which was much
appreciated in the House. Outside, indeed, it was less
well received, and many people thought and said that
the women had been robbed of their share of justice and
fair play.

Mrs. Fawcett came out with a broadside, the notes for which are characteristic :

" That the H. of C.," they run, " should have preferred to spend last Wed. afternoon in useless talk on a disgusting subject rather than be obliged to say aye or no to the question of making further progress in the W.S. Bill is a new illustration of the difficulty, under a representative Govt., of getting anything done for the unrepresented. We have not the franchise, and therefore we can safely be neglected and treated with contempt.

Those that ask shan't have, and those that don't ask don't want.

But it is not wholly evidence of weakness. Why do the opponents of W.S. dread a direct vote upon it ?

Ask respectable opponents if they approve of these methods."

It is easy to imagine the speech she made from these notes, and the strong indignation which she felt and expressed. But privately she tried hard not to be disheartened. She wrote to Clotilda Marson a week after the " verminous " debate as follows :

" I don't wonder at your feeling discouraged. We have had so many bad blows lately ; still, I think it is only a backwater, and that the main stream is going on undisturbed. The H. of C. really disgraced itself on the 7th. It was all a prearranged thing ; the forms of the House allow a few unscrupulous opponents to prevent progress in this way ; but I feel that our friends were mean in not making a protest. Moral courage is very scarce ; there is not too much among women and next door to none among men. The root of the opposition to W.S. is not a party matter at all. Labouchere was mainly responsible on the 7th. I do not think it has done us any real harm ; so many people have said to me, ' I don't care much for W.S., but I hate these mean ways of burking discussion upon it.' Many newspapers have had articles in the same sense."

But still, the evil had been done, and the whole dreary business had to begin again—the effort to persuade

Members to ballot, the pressure to secure time, the constituency petitions, the weary meetings and all the rest. It was an uphill task.

The suffragists, however, under Mrs. Fawcett's leadership, braced themselves afresh after this fiasco. The two divided central societies, which had flown apart in the stress of party feelings in '85, were now reunited, and a scheme for the organisation of all the local societies into one National Union, under the Presidency of Mrs. Fawcett, was drawn up and adopted.

If the struggle was to go on—as of course it must until victory was won—they would try to make their machine as efficient as possible, and therefore they tightened all the connecting links. They realised that it was worth their while to make a good sound democratic scheme, capable of expansion, and they put time and brains into the business of political organisation.

Mrs. Lynn Linton had recently dedicated one of her books to " Those sweet girls who are willing to remain dutiful, sheltered and innocent " ; but the suffragists were not of that type. They had grasped the fact that, as their leader told them, " those who take part in politics must expect to have lies told about them," and they had shed some of their Victorian illusions. Enfranchisement would imply taking the rough with the smooth. They meant to use it, when they got it, to clean and purify politics as far as they could, and they meant to run a straight course themselves ; but they faced the realities of their situation, and prepared for a long hard fight.

CHAPTER IX

THE SOUTH AFRICAN WAR

Mrs. Fawcett's books—Hon. LL.D. at St. Andrews—Sir William Moles-worth—South African War—The Concentration Camps—The Ladies' Commission—Miss Hobhouse—Visit to South Africa.

ALL through the 'nineties Mrs. Fawcett's life was, as we have seen, filled with work and political activity, with travel and meetings, and business correspondence. In spite of all this, however, she managed to do a good deal of literary work as well, and though much of this was merely controversy and propaganda, some was of a more permanent kind. Millicent did not dislike writing as she disliked speaking. She rather enjoyed it, in fact, though how she found time to do it in the rush of all the other things is not easy to see. Find time she did, however, not only for the crushing replies to antifeminist journalists, and for the serious articles for the quarterlies, and for all the topical letters to the daily papers which the exigencies of the cause required, but also for real books. In 1889 she wrote a volume of short biographies called *Some Eminent Women of our Time*,[1] which, although largely made up from the lectures she had for many years given on famous women, never-theless must have required a good deal of work in its preparation. It is, of course, a book with a moral ; but it is an eminently readable book all the same ; and, like everything to which she put her hand, it gives the impression of being the simple straightforward truth. Besides this book she also wrote *Five Famous Frenchwomen*[2] some years later, and in this her very

[1] *Some Eminent Women of our Time*, by M. G. Fawcett. Macmillan, 1889.
[2] *Five Famous Frenchwomen*, by M. G. Fawcett. Cassells, 1908.

great enthusiasm for Joan of Arc is evident ; and this book, involving as it did some historical research, must have taken longer to write than the other.   In 1895, undeterred by all that was piling up around her to be done, Mrs. Fawcett embarked upon an even more difficult undertaking, namely, a life of Queen Victoria. This was in some ways a labour of love ; for though, of course, she knew that the Queen disapproved most heartily of all the evidences of the women's movement, she believed that Victoria was in herself a living proof of its justification.   The Queen might say what she liked about women's sphere being the home and only the home ; yet so long as she ruled the country in the efficient and business-like way she did, she remained a wonderful feminist argument ;   and Mrs. Fawcett determined to make this so plain in her book that no one could miss the moral.

The book was published in '97, the year of the Diamond Jubilee.   It was deservedly popular, and was reported to have given great pleasure to Her Majesty, notwithstanding its feminist touches.   Like all Mrs. Fawcett's writings it is very readable, and although it seems perhaps a little over-enthusiastic about the Queen, it is full of shrewd observations, and exceedingly clear and coherent.   Some of its author's deep love of England appears in this book, and much of her under-standing of the English character ;   and, although perhaps the historical outline is a little too simplified to be quite convincing now, the book is still well worth attention.

Its appearance and its favourable reviews naturally gratified Mrs. Fawcett ;   but they did nothing to alter or modify her way of life.   The same occupations absorbed her, month after month, and the same interests held her attention.   The Home Rule controversy was for the time quiescent, but other Irish problems re-mained, and Mrs. Fawcett twice went to Dublin in 1898.

It is difficult, and perhaps unnecessary, to disentangle the threads of Mrs. Fawcett's activities year after year. Some of the more notable things stand out, as, for example, a fine speech she made in this same year, '98, upon the continuance of the C.D. Acts for the Army in India. This speech was bare of adjectives, clear and calm and moderate, while at the same time it was firm and definite, and it created a deep impression. But such things were her daily work. Some were more immediately effective than others ; but all were part of the same continuous effort which inspired and occupied her life.

One very tragic and terrible experience befell her at this time during the holidays of 1898. Millicent and Agnes went to Switzerland with a party of friends, which included Professor John Hopkinson and his wife and children. They were at Arolla, very much enjoying themselves, and the Professor, who was an experienced mountaineer, made a number of short expeditions. In September he set out upon another of these, accompanied by one of his sons and two of his daughters. Through some inexplicable accident the whole party fell, and all were killed. There followed for those they had left many dreadful hours of anxiety and fear before the certainty of the tragedy was known. To Mrs. Fawcett and to Miss Garrett fell the task of helping Mrs. Hopkinson and her remaining daughter in all the funeral arrangements and of bringing them back to England. The tragedy, indeed, brought out all Mrs. Fawcett's stores of kindness. Nothing could, of course, make much difference in circumstances such as these ; but whatever was in the power of quiet tact and steady sympathy was at the service of her friends.

The winter which followed was like the preceding winters, packed with work, and with diverse interests. But in January it was diversified by a public recognition, which was both personally and impersonally delightful. Professor James Stuart, Millicent's old friend and colleague of the early Cambridge days, was appointed Rector of St. Andrews University, and among those whom he recommended for a Degree *honoris causa* upon his installation was Mrs. Henry Fawcett. He asked that the degree should be given in recognition of her work for the higher education of women ; and this was the first time that such an honour had been offered to any woman for any cause at all.

Millicent was really delighted. As she said, in writing to express her appreciation, she felt that she was " reaping in a field where many have sown." " But," she added, and it was strictly true, " I am happy in believing that all the men and women who have worked on behalf of improved education for women will derive encouragement from the action of the University, and will feel that it is their cause which has received honour at your hands."

The actual ceremony was described in a letter to Philippa written by Dr. Jane Walker :

" We took Millie to the robing room of the Volunteer Hall, where the ceremony was to take place, and put on her gown for her," she wrote. " She carried her hood (scarlet and white) on her left arm. The gown is black, rather like an old-fashioned waterproof in shape, relieved by large red buttons. We left her with the other honoured individuals, and went to our allotted seats in the gallery.

" The men and women students, all dressed in bright scarlet woollen gowns, sat in the front of the body of the hall, the Professors' wives and grandees at the sides, and the townspeople behind. Friends of the recipients were in the front row of the gallery. The students kept us more or less amused by songs and snatches and cheers or groans when anyone they knew came in. Then all the dignitaries of the University came first, followed by the Lord Rector and the recipients of the Hon. Degree : Buckle, Broadbent, the Chief Rabbi and others, and our dear Millie, who looked very nice. The colour of her hair showed up to perfection in the bright sunny day. She soon recognised Agnes and me in the gallery and nodded to us.

"The first part of the ceremony was the installation of Stuart as Lord Rector; after a Latin prayer, read by Principal Donaldson, he put on a gorgeous gown of crimson and purple and took off his Cambridge one. The students cheered vociferously (they had elected him unanimously) and sang, ' For he's a jolly good fellow.' Then came his address, which was extremely good. After the address Prof. Burnett got up and read a very nice description of each of the recipients written by himself—nothing could have been better done, and I was delighted to see that *The Times* of Tuesday put in the whole bit verbatim that he said about Millie, and about no one else was there even a mention.

" After this came the capping, and here came a variation which was for a moment disturbing. In the description they were taken alphabetically, but when the capping came they left Millie to the last. The ceremony is as follows : each recipient goes up to the Lord Rector, and as he says the words conferring the LL.D. upon them, the usher more or less throws the hood over their heads. No cap is put on the recipients' heads, but they are rubbed on the forehead with John Knox's cap ! When Millie's turn came the students all got up and cheered tremendously and waved their caps in the air, and the rest of the audience got up and cheered. Both Agnes and I had big lumps in our throats, we felt so proud and happy and so glad to be there really to see it for ourselves."

That was in January 1899 ; and it then seemed that the regular course of Mrs. Fawcett's life would go on without interruption, through committees, meetings and all the rest. But within a few months her activities were changed and interrupted by the outbreak of the South African War.

For many years South African affairs had been of absorbing interest to Agnes and Millicent. In 1895 their cousin, Edmund Garrett, who had worked on the staffs of the *Pall Mall* and the *Westminster* after leaving Cambridge, had been appointed editor of *The Cape Times*, and through his letters, and the detailed information which he eagerly sent home, they had been able to follow the course of events very closely. Their sympathies, of course, were very strongly with the disfranchised British settlers in the South African Republics, and as time went on, and the tangle of South African politics grew worse and worse, they came to think that fighting would be the inevitable outcome. Millicent was no lover of war ; she hoped for peaceful negotiation, and tried to believe that it would lead to settlement ; but she was not prepared to see her country abandon its rights rather than fight for them. It seemed to her inevitable that if the Dutch would not live in harmomy with their neighbours they should be forced to submit to them ; and she indignantly repudiated the contention that the English were working up war merely in order to capture a profitable territory. People who said such things were, she thought, both ignorant of the facts and disloyal to their own country, and she had no patience with them. When, therefore, the war actually broke out, and a large section of English people began to criticise and decry it, she sprang into the opposite camp. War was terrible, of course ; but there were things which were even worse ; and for a time she devoted the greater part of her energies to making known what she believed to be the justifications for England's action.

Edmund had broken down in health and been obliged to leave Cape Town just before the outbreak of war, and he was sent to a sanatorium in Germany. There, of course, he encountered the full strength of continental opposition to England, and his cousins thus realised, in a direct and personal manner, the criticisms and misinformation current abroad, and the sufferings of patriotic English people who lived there. This realisation troubled Mrs. Fawcett very seriously. After reading one of Edmund's letters she lay awake grieving over it, and wondering what could be done, and by seven o'clock the next morning she had worked out a scheme to bring at least some comfort and support to

British exiles. By eight o'clock she was consulting
the other members of the Women's Liberal Unionist
Committee, and before nine she was at the office of *The
Times*, trying to see the Editor. At that point in her
lightning campaign she was forced to pause ; but
before midday the whole thing was well started, and
the support of *The Times* assured. The plan which
she carried through so impetuously was to provide a
number of special pamphlets, written by men of international standing, professors, scientists and authors,
setting out the British case in such a way as could best
be understood abroad. These pamphlets were to be
sent to all exiles who could be reached, to British
doctors and clergymen, to Consuls and business people,
so that they might be armed with facts, and encouraged
in their patriotism in the midst of critical communities.
No one supposed that this would check pro-Boer
sympathies in Holland or Germany ; but at least the
other side would be clearly and intelligently put, and
the British people who had to live amidst the storms
of hostility would be given help and support.

The carrying out of this scheme naturally involved
an immense amount of correspondence, which Mrs.
Fawcett and the Women's Liberal Unionist Committee
cheerfully undertook, and for many months, until the
ground had been extensively covered, they toiled at it
early and late.

In political circles, and indeed all through the country,
feelings were running very high. There was a considerable group of Liberals and Radicals to whom the war was
anathema, and they attacked not only the Government,
but everyone who supported it, and were attacked in
return with surprising bitterness. Among the pro-
Boers were many of Mrs. Fawcett's old friends, many
of her fellow workers in the women's cause and some of
her husband's old colleagues. To these people her attitude towards the war seemed monstrously wrong, and
her activities harmful and pernicious. They attacked

her unsparingly, and the rumour spread that she was a violent Jingo, exceedingly bloodthirsty, and with a mind quite closed to reason or argument. It was far from the truth, of course ; but in the excited feelings of the time there were no shades of feeling. Those who upheld the war at all were Jingoes, those who criticised it were pro-Boers, and the two could not meet.

Mrs. Fawcett paid little attention to the abuse which was directed towards her, and continued to hold the moderate opinions which were natural to her. Though she believed that the war must be fought and won she was already looking towards a just settlement afterwards. In December 1899 she wrote to a friend on the subject. " I don't think much," she wrote, " of the suggestion to disfranchise the Boers of Cape Colony. I expect the settlement after the war, even if everything goes on as we most wish, will offer tremendous difficulties, but I hope we are too deeply pledged to the principle of equal political privileges for all white races to abandon it."

The war, as she saw it, was a fight for freedom ; and it was inconceivable that it should be followed by tyranny.

It was in part this feeling which made Mrs. Fawcett select this moment for the writing of a book she had long had in mind, namely, the life of Sir William Molesworth.[1] She felt that an account of his work for colonial reform, and of the principles which had guided his political thinking, might be helpful in the existing crisis, and might tend to reinforce those who believed in a generous settlement for South Africa when the war should be over. It was the right moment for such a book to appear ; and Millicent was rather freer than usual to undertake it, since nearly all the regular work for the women's movement was at a standstill, and for once the dreary succession of suffrage meetings was

[1] *Life of the Right Hon. Sir William Molesworth, Bart, M.P., F.R.S.,* by Mrs. Fawcett, LL.D. Macmillan & Co., Ltd., 1901.

interrupted. Accordingly, she threw herself energetically into the task, and wrote at top speed what is one of the most interesting of all her books.

Mrs. Fawcett had not known Sir William Molesworth, who died in 1855, while she was still a child ; but she had known many of the Philosophical Radicals, of whom he had been one of the early leaders. He had been just such a man as she most truly admired ; " a thorough English statesman," with " singleness of mind, honesty of purpose, clearness of judgment, faithfulness of conduct, courage in difficulties and equanimity in success " ; and she took pleasure in writing his life. There was another link with the subject, too, which pleased her, and which she referred to in the Preface. " Almost exactly forty-one years ago (October 1860)," she wrote, " Henry Fawcett, young and unknown, offered himself as a parliamentary candidate for the Borough of Southwark, the constituency which had been represented by Sir William Molesworth at the time of his death five years earlier. Henry Fawcett stood as an Independent Radical in opposition to the official Liberal candidate, and he described himself as a political follower of Sir William Molesworth. Needless to say, he was unsuccessful, but it was his introduction to practical political life, and it is a source of some interest that the younger man associated himself with the views and aims of the elder."

Sir William Molesworth had been a strong advocate of Colonial reform, and indeed almost the originator of the idea of British co-operation with Colonies which should be independently governed. He had championed this cause for years in the House of Commons, had fought for and won step after step towards their self-government, and had destroyed, almost unaided, the shameful system of transportation. He had vehemently opposed the belief of the Manchester School that Colonies were a burden which should be cast off, and, although Mrs. Fawcett thought he had been wrong in his policy in regard to South Africa, she felt that his general outlook was both right and practical, and she wrote of him with great understanding.

There are many passages in this book which reveal the thoughts and even the feelings of its author. The subject was one entirely unconnected with the women's movement, and therefore an unusual one for her to treat ; and the book includes a number of comments and reflections to which she did not elsewhere give expression.

There are, for example, interesting passages upon Molesworth's religious beliefs. He was generally considered an " infidel and an unbeliever," but Mrs. Fawcett was concerned to prove that a man could be both good and humane without the spur of dogmatic belief, and quoted in this book, as she often did in her own life, Matthew Arnold's sonnet, *The Better Part :* " Hath man no second life ? Pitch this one high."

With the casualty lists which came so regularly from South Africa, many people were thinking of survival after death, but it is clear that at this time, as at the time when Harry died, Mrs. Fawcett felt no certainty about personal immortality, and no great anxiety upon the subject. Speaking of an outburst against the Burial Service, which Molesworth had addressed to Mrs. Grote after the death of his sister, she wrote, " It is one thing to bear calamity with courage, and another to pretend that bad is good, and that bitter anguish is a source of thankfulness " ; and this was undoubtedly an expression of her own thoughts, as well as an interpretation of his.

In another direction, too, Mrs. Fawcett allowed her own opinions to be apparent in this book, for she did not prune, after she had written them, sentences which criticised the pacifist party.

" Why," she wrote, " do those who profess peace principles so often apply them only to the region of

physical conflict ? It not infrequently appears that the
peace-at-any-price man is even below the average fighting animal in power of bringing the qualities of gentleness
and generosity to aid the judgment in those regions
where the conflict must have some outlet, and that those
who are, for conscience' sake, debarred from taking part
even vicariously in physical conflict import ten times
more bitterness into the controversial battle. ''

This was the feeling which the talk and the tactics of
the pro-Boer party inspired in most of the people who
did not agree with them. Mrs. Fawcett was very
conscious of it, even before the events of the next year,
which were to bring her into such close touch and such
sharp conflict with their methods. It was only a small
matter, indeed, as she knew. The justifications or
condemnations of the war rested upon deep considerations of patriotism, national honour, ideals of government and acceptance of responsibility ; but it was a
matter much upon the surface, and constantly coming
to her attention ; and although as a rule she was sparing
of criticism, she did allow herself this small outburst.

The book appeared early in 1901 ; and during the
months while it was being written, things had been going
badly with the British Army in South Africa. The
continual British reverses were making people very
gloomy indeed ; the conduct of the war was being
sharply attacked on all sides, and the actual details of
military operations were widely discussed.

Mrs. Fawcett was deeply concerned over the mismanagement of the war, but she could not resist a gibe
against its critics. A paragraph appeared in *The
Times* giving an account of a Referendum in Australia
(where women voted) showing a very high proportion of
informal votes due to spoilt papers, and adding the
characteristic comment, '' the informal votes are attri-
buted mainly to women.'' Mrs. Fawcett's observations
upon this paragraph were as follows : '' Adam ought
never to be deprived of his Eve, ' the woman Thou

gavest to be with me.' What a splendid thing it would be for men now if they were able to say that the military blunders made in the conduct of the South African War were due to women."

These military blunders, however, were soon seen to be very serious indeed, and early in September 1899, a further cause of complaint was given to the critics in England. At that time the military operations were making necessary the provision of camps for refugees. At first these refugees consisted only of civilians anxious to surrender, and so escape from the guerilla warfare in which most of the Dutch farmers were engaged ; but as time went on their number was enormously increased. In June and July, 1900—the midwinter months of South Africa—the British authorities began to burn and destroy Boer farms, in order to clear the country behind them of enemy strongholds, and to hinder and thwart the small bands of enemy commandoes which were perpetually harassing their lines of communication.

This policy, which was considered a military necessity, was, like all military necessities, cruel and savage. The inhabitants of the Boer farms had to see the work of years ruthlessly destroyed, and without warning they found themselves starving and homeless. The only thing which the British could do for them was to gather them together into camps, just as they had gathered the surrendered Boers, and to clothe and feed them as best they could. During the last six months of 1900 and the first six months of 1901, 105,000 such refugees were assembled, and thirty-four Concentration Camps were improvised for their accommodation. Amid the exigencies of the war the arrangement of these camps was not efficiently conducted. Unsuitable places were selected, overcrowding was great, and all the necessities of life were scarce and inadequate. There was but one line of railway to carry supplies to the army, and its capacities were strained to the utmost, so that food trucks for the camps were slow and difficult to secure.

Firewood was almost unobtainable, and medical supplies scarce; moreover, there was a great difficulty in finding efficient administrators for the camps. There was incompetence enough in the British Army, yet all the best men were there, and the organisation of the camps suffered accordingly. The numbers, too, increased much more rapidly than was anticipated, and the unfortunate people who came in were not only hostile and indignant at what had been done to them, but were also alarmingly ignorant of what was necessary for the hygiene of camp life. Instead of co-operating in the arrangements of the camps, they were for the most part idle and complaining; they opposed all sanitary measures, and disputed with each other, so that the discomfort and squalor of their surroundings were intensified. To make matters worse, severe epidemics broke out, and the limited hospital staffs, with their inadequate stores, were unable to cope with them. The mortality, especially among the small children, became very high, and the whole matter was without question deplorably mismanaged.

News of this state of affairs began to reach England in the summer of 1900, and the matter was taken up with violence by the people who were opposed to the war. They very naturally seized upon the hardships and cruelties inflicted upon civilians as additional evidence of the monstrosity of the war, and they made a violent attack upon the whole policy of farm burning and concentration camps. Relief funds were raised in England for the Boer women and children, and in December, 1900, Miss Emily Hobhouse went out on their behalf to South Africa to enquire into the situation and to distribute the gifts.

Mrs. Fawcett's old friend, Leonard Courtney, was among those who supported this mission, and on Miss Hobhouse's arrival in Cape Town she was met by the following message from him: " Be prudent, be calm." It was, however, useless advice, for she found herself incapable of either prudence or calmness in the face of the dreadful situation which prevailed.

Emily Hobhouse was, of course, a violent pro-Boer. To her the war appeared to be the unscrupulous attempt of a great power to devour and destroy a small independent nation ; and even if its cause had seemed less unrighteous, she would still, as a pacifist, have denounced it. She went out, therefore, in a spirit of hostility to the military authorities, and she was animated by an overflowing sympathy for their foes. She was, moreover, of an enthusiastic and imaginative temperament, and quite lacking in patience or restraint. She was easily deceived by agitators and impostors, and since she was ready to believe all good of one side and all evil of the other, many false or exaggerated stories lodged in her mind.

There would indeed have been much for the most impartial observer to condemn in the organisation of the camps, and much to stir the pity of the most hard-hearted. The mortality rates were shocking, and the sufferings of the people were severe. Even granted the necessity for the existence of the camps (which neither Miss Hobhouse nor her friends would allow), there was a truly terrible amount of avoidable hardship, and heavy responsibility for carelessness and delay rested upon the British authorities.

The accounts which Emily Hobhouse sent home were little short of blood-curdling, and they naturally caused the greatest distress to everyone who heard them. Unfortunately, the demonstrable untruth of some of her statements and the excessive bias of others went far to discount the whole indictment in the official mind ; and her warm friendship for the families of most of the Boer leaders led her to be regarded almost as a traitor to her own country.

Emily Hobhouse returned herself to England at the end of May 1901, and her first step was to visit the Secretary of State for War, to lay before him the things

she had observed in the camps.   From him she received
assurances that improvements would be made, but,
failing to be satisfied with this, she and her friends
decided to circulate to the Members of the House of
Commons all the reports which she had written on the
spot.   This action, naturally, brought the whole matter
into the most lurid limelight.   The pro-Boer party seized
upon and made great capital from the alleged atrocities
for which the Army was responsible, and Sir Henry
Campbell-Bannerman, the leader of the Liberals, made
a resounding speech denouncing the " Methods of
Barbarism " which were being employed.   The Government, equally naturally, denounced Miss Hobhouse's
reports as exaggerated, and defended the action of the
military authorities as best they could ; and the storm
raged with the utmost fierceness all through the Press
and the country.   Meanwhile, the publicity in England
had its effect in South Africa, and the camps received
much more attention and were in many ways substantially improved.   But the mortality continued to be
alarmingly high, and the clamour at home refused to
be stilled, so that early in July a decision was taken to
send out a Commission from home to investigate the
camps on the spot, and to recommend immediate
practical improvements.

The Commission selected consisted of six ladies, two
of whom were doctors, and one a nurse ; and the person
selected to be the leader of the party was Mrs. Henry
Fawcett.   In 1901 it was an unprecedented thing for
an official commission on whatever subject to consist
only of women, and though naturally Mrs. Fawcett was
proud to be asked to serve her country in such an
important capacity, this fact added yet another argument to persuade her to accept.   She had no hesitation
whatever, and although the invitation did not reach
her until the middle of July, she was ready in ten days,
and sailed in a troopship, reaching Cape Town before
the middle of August.

The appointment of this Commission gave no comfort to Miss Hobhouse and the pro-Boer critics of the camps. They instantly dubbed it " The Whitewashing Commission," and without enquiring into the spirit in which it was approaching its work, they began to attack it with violence. Letters of abuse reached Mrs. Fawcett from total strangers, as, for example, the following, which arrived on a post card from Switzerland:

" How can you expect the Boer women to make you their confidante when they know perfectly well (as we know too) that you have been sent to South Africa for the express purpose of whitewashing the administration of the Concentration Camps ? You have been well paid for your dirty work, and that ought to be a sufficient reward to you."

Miss Hobhouse herself felt the same, and before Mrs. Fawcett's party had been in South Africa three weeks she addressed an open letter to the Secretary of State for War, and to the Press, in which the following indictment is made:

" Will nothing be done ? Will no prompt measures be taken to deal with this terrible evil ? Three months ago I tried to place the matter strongly before you, and begged permission to organise immediate alleviatory measures. . . . My request was refused. . . . The repulse to myself would have mattered nothing, had only a large band of kindly workers been instantly despatched with full powers to deal with each individual camp as its needs required. The necessity was instant if innocent human lives were to be saved. Instead we had to wait a month while six ladies were chosen. During that month 576 children died. The preparation and journey of these ladies occupied another month, and in that interval 1,124 more children succumbed. In place of at once proceeding to the great centres of high mortality, the bulk of yet a third month seems to have been spent in their long journey to Mafeking, and in passing a few days at some of the healthier camps. Meanwhile, 1,545 more children died. This is not immediate action ; it was very deliberate enquiry, and that too at a time when death, which is unanswerable, was at work ; nay, when the demands of death, instead of diminishing, were increasing. Will you not now, with the thought before you of those 3,245 children who have closed their eyes for ever since I last saw you on their behalf, will you not now take instant action, and endeavour thus to avert the evil results of facts patent to all, and suspend further enquiry into the truth of what the whole world knows ? "

The suggestions that the Commission was one of enquiry only, and that it was dilatory in approaching its work were both false ; but the statement that the condition of the camps was in desperate need of improvement was all too true. Miss Hobhouse's proposal that " a large band of kindly workers " with independent authority to do as they pleased should be sent into a country under military occupation was a very wild one ; but the passionate protest against the sufferings and deaths of little children which underlay her bitterness was one which everyone could respect.

There was another side from which the members of the Commission were attacked, and that was the political. Miss Hobhouse considered it a monstrous thing that two at least of the ladies who were chosen for the Commission were known to be in favour of the policy of the concentration camps.

" My opinions were discounted and barely tolerated," she wrote, " because I was known to feel sorry for the sickly children, and to have shown PERSONAL sympathy to broken, destitute Boer women in their PERSONAL troubles. Sympathy shown to any of Dutch blood is the one unpardonable sin in South Africa."

Arguing in this fashion, she assumed that the Commission must be harsh and hostile, and useless to the population of the camps, and as Mrs. Fawcett said later, the members of the Commission and everyone who did not condemn the camp system were spoken

14

of almost as if they were " Herod, presiding and gloating over a deliberately planned massacre of the innocents."

There was, however, another way of looking at the camp system, which was based on the realisation of what would have happened if it had not been established. The epidemics which attacked the camps were rampant in the country outside, and many people believed that the plight of the refugees and of the Boer women and children would have been far worse if they had been left to wander at large over a devastated country. In the camps they were fed, clothed and housed at the expense of the British Government, and regular supplies were brought to them from the coast. Nothing was fully sufficient, and much was incompetent and ill organised, but had the policy of the camps not been adopted matters would, Mrs. Fawcett believed, have been far worse. In this sense she did approve of the camp system ; but it was a sense which included accept- ance of a state of war, and of the actions dictated by " military necessity " ; and this, of course, neither Miss Hobhouse nor her Committee were willing to do. That really was the crux of the difference ; and it was fundamental.

The Ladies' Commission spent four months in South Africa, and visited practically all the camps. They did not wait for their final report to make suggestions and alterations, but, being armed with authority, they exercised it at once. They recommended the removal of some of the camp superintendents and doctors, and an increase in the nursing staff, and their suggestions were at once accepted and acted upon. They advised also upon a host of concrete matters—boilers, ovens and sanitary arrangements ; and finally, an increase in the quantity and an alteration in the kind of rations distributed. Their final report was a severely practical document, with nothing in the nature of palliation or " whitewash " from the first page to the last. It contained a detailed account of existing conditions, including the difficulties created by the camp inmates themselves, and it recommended none but remedies feasible in the prevailing situation of the country.

The pro-Boers, of course, denounced it roundly. " In the whole of their report," as one article put it, " there is not a word of pity for the misery they witnessed. . . . No one would dream of charging Mrs. Fawcett or any of the ladies forming her Committee with ' hysteria ' or ' sentimentality.' "

Miss Hobhouse herself criticised their unsympathetic attitude very strongly, and denounced the speed of their operations which, as she said, " precluded them from entering at all into the life of the camps as felt by the people, for the Boers are not a race inclined to open their hearts to strangers of a day's acquaintance." But, after all, they had not been sent out to express sympathy or compassion, but to remedy the mismanagement of the camps ; and this they did. Even Miss Hobhouse herself admitted that substantial improvements resulted from their labours, and that they had not turned out to be purely a whitewashing body.

" The Commission in the various camps," she says in her book, *The Brunt of the War*, " make admissions and conduct sweeping reforms which are the more significant considering the spirit in which they write about the women. They do not shrink from condemning ill-chosen sites, dismissing incompetent superintendents, reforming entire hospitals, urging various improvements in food, fuel, water, recommending beds and ameliorating sanitation."

These recommendations, coming as they did from an accredited Government Commission, were promptly adopted, with the result that after the date of their visit the condition of the camps rapidly improved, and no further serious complaints were received.

The actual work of the Commission was both hard and

tedious. For nearly four months they lived in a railway carriage.

" We each have a little hole of our own," Mrs. Fawcett wrote home in describing her progress, " but it is a very small one, and the saloon in which we eat and have our meetings is of such dimensions that each must go to her place in turn ; there is no passing one another in the saloon. An equable temper is of primary importance for getting on in such a life. We had an abominably bad-tempered man-servant for the first two months, and the intense relief it was to get rid of him was a thing to be imagined rather than described. If he had been one of the Commission his temper would have been still more oppressive, and it would have been simply imposs-ible to get rid of him."

This fate, however, the Commission escaped, and its members got on very happily together. Mrs. Fawcett was the Chairman, and her colleagues were Lady Knox, Dr. Jane Waterston, Dr. Ella Scarlet, Miss Katherine Brereton and Miss Lucy Deane. Besides these Lady Knox took with her a maid, Miss Deane her sister, and Mrs. Fawcett her daughter, who, she wrote, "sets a noble example to the other ' maids ' in the energy with which she airs our blankets and turns out our sleeping cabin."

Their work was urgent and laborious, and they had little time for relaxation ; but from time to time their train was held up, and they took advantage of the delays to see what they could of the country. Mrs. Fawcett's letters from South Africa were very unim-formative. " We have sworn an oath not to chat in our home letters about the camps," she wrote, and there was little else which occupied them. But one descrip-tion of their time in Mafeking in August 1901 is of interest.

" We started in Cape carts each drawn by three pairs of wild mules," she wrote, " driven by black boys of prodigious ugliness who wielded enormous whips and

bumped along over sand and boulders which serve for
roads here.   We went to Canon Kopje and saw the fort
there and then went on to the site of the Boer laager and
the place where their Long Tom was placed.   Our guns
most of the time were outranged, so the Boers could
disport themselves at ease.   Cronje first and then
Snyman made his headquarters in a nice little farmhouse. . . .   We went in ;   the best parlour is now
decorated with shells and bullets.   Some members of
our Committee have a passion for things like this and
wish to buy them, they sell for quite big prices.   I am
so glad I don't want them in the least.   Then we went
on past the racecourse to the women's laager and the
place where Eloff was taken.   The women's laager is a
most extraordinary hole in the ground not roofed or
made habitable in any way.   I cannot imagine how the
women stood it.   A lot of them didn't, but just went
about their business as usual."

"Business as usual" is never easy to achieve in war-
time, and even in communities which were far from the
seat of war everything was in an uproar.   On their
arrival in Cape Town the Commissioners had found that
the heat of feeling prevailing in England, furious as it
seemed, was as nothing to the tension on the spot.

"We found Cape Town riven into hostile sections,"
Mrs. Fawcett wrote, "full of gossip, of inventions and
unfounded suspicions and fears. . . . Rages and feuds
were then tearing the social world in Cape Town into
violently hostile factions.   We discovered then and later
that in a war the people who have not fought are much
more vindictive than those who have."

Moreover, Mrs. Fawcett and her companions were
very soon convinced that much of the savage criticism
of the camps was induced by race and party feeling, and
by propaganda, and that it was divorced altogether
from a knowledge of the facts, or even a real desire to
help the sufferers.   Thus, for example, she tells in her
reminiscences of the Committee of the pro-Boer ladies

whom the Commission interviewed in Cape Town before
they set off for the camps.

" We told them we had at our disposal a moderate
sum of money from private sources which we wanted to
spend in a manner most calculated to be of service to
the people in the camps ; could they, with their experience, tell us how best it could be employed ? They
immediately replied, ' Send them calico to wrap their
corpses in.' This startled us. We had, while on the ship,
prepared a list of twenty-one questions bearing on what is
now called Welfare Work, but we never thought of this.
. . . We now added a twenty-second. . . . In the ensuing
months we visited thirty-three camps, some of them
twice, and in each we made special enquiries. . . . It is
almost unnecessary to say that we did not in this, nor
in any other of our enquiries, content ourselves with
asking questions solely of the officials. We did this as a
matter of course, but we also went, either singly or two
of us together, to visit the women in their tents, and
endeavoured, by friendly talk, to encourage them to
tell us whatever was uppermost in their minds. We
had many interesting conversations in this way, and
never once did a single human being utter a word which
justified the Cape Town ladies' insinuation that what
these poor people wanted most was calico to wrap their
corpses in. They naturally wanted a great many things,
but not this."

This and similar experiences, as she said, " showed up
the methods of the set. . . . The whole Committee
are to blame," she added, speaking of one of the London
groups ; " they knew that I was seeking information
about what was needed in the camps, and they withheld it from me. Nothing could have been easier than
to have told me what they were sending and what was
most wanted. BUT THEY WERE MORE ANXIOUS TO
HAVE A STICK TO BEAT THE GOVERNMENT WITH THAN TO
HELP THE CAMPS."

Mrs. Fawcett felt the profoundest contempt for this
spirit, and when it was combined, as in this case she
believed it to be, with questionable accuracy, and with

that perverted form of patriotism which extols every country but its own, she lost all patience. " The O lot," as she called them, seemed to her worth nothing but scorn ; and she gave them nothing else.

With the British authorities, on the other hand, she was exceedingly firm ; and though her methods were neither tactless nor unfriendly, she yielded nothing which she thought essential. There remains a correspondence between her and Sir Alfred (later Lord) Milner, then High Commissioner at Johannesburg, which throws a good deal of light both on her methods and on the actual situation. It is dated November 19, 1901.

" Miss Deane and I," Mrs. Fawcett's letter runs, " thank you sincerely for allowing us to see the draft of your letter to Bloemfontein and Pretoria on the subject of the camps ; and we venture to offer the following suggestions upon it. On page 2 we think the passages marked with pencil are expressed with too little qualification. We feel that in certain camps bad blunders have been made, for example, the removal of measles patients from Kroonstad to Heilbron, the long-continued sanitary conditions at Mafeking and the disorganisation of the hospital at Brandfort. In every camp where there has been an exceptionally bad outbreak of disease, we think we see causes which more foresight and better organisation might have avoided. We feel that while it is only just to acknowledge the honest wish of the two head officers to do all that should be done, it is not accurate to say that ' nothing which you or the officers working under you could do with the means at your disposal was left undone.' "

The letter goes on to recommend certain practical changes, including a better diet allowance, and it was answered the same day by the High Commissioner.

" Dear Mrs. Fawcett," he wrote, " Many thanks for your letter. I will modify the passage you refer to. I did not mean to express my approval of everything that had been done, but rather, as regards the two administrations, my feeling that they had done the best

with the existing material—including *human* material.
That the Doctors, Superintendents, Nurses, etc., etc.,
have not been of the best is, I think, admitted. Enough
good ones DID NOT EXIST HERE to deal with such thousands of people, and as you see for yourself to-day, it is
very difficult to find any man fit to fill in the Transvaal
the same position as Col. Bowen holds in the Orange
River Colony. . . . I feel rather for A. and M. that they
have had to make bricks without straw. The policy was
not theirs. They were never even asked about it, or
warned that the people were coming, or whether
hundreds or thousands would be thrown on their hands
at any given spot on any given day. They just had to
pick up whom they could to struggle with this disor-
ganised mass of humanity.

" Thank you very much for your other notes also.
I feel it is very important that your recommendations
about increase of rations in the Transvaal—with which
I entirely agree—and also about B., since on further
consideration you still attach so much importance as
to his immediate appointment, should be formally
addressed to Maxwell without delay. I will communicate with him about both of them."

Milner was a friend of Edmund's, and an easy man to
work with ; but Kitchener was notoriously abrupt and
difficult and, moreover, was said to have the very lowest
opinion of the female sex. He was Commander-in-
Chief, and the decision whether or not extra food trucks
could be allocated to the camps rested with him, so the
Commission were obliged to seek an interview at
Pretoria.

As Mrs. Fawcett said, they " rather smiled " when
they read his answer, for " he expressed a wish that of
the six of us only two should come on the deputation to
see him." " I think," she added in a private letter,
" he was very much alarmed. We heard him say in an
awestruck voice to General Maxwell just as we were
coming into the room, ' How many are there of them ? ' "
But the interview which followed was " most satisfactory and businesslike. . . . Not an unnecessary

word had been spoken, and therefore no time had been wasted. I liked him," she added, " far better than any of the politicians I had gone to on deputations in London. I always say that Lady Knox and I, after this interview with Lord Kitchener, received the compliment of our lives, for, after sampling two of us, he invited the whole six to dinner ! We did not all go."

By December the work of the Commission was over, and its members scattered. Those who were going home sailed by way of Mozambique, Zanzibar and Aden, and greatly enjoyed the strange scenery and the exotic vegetation of the East Coast. They felt, no doubt, that they had a hard and good piece of work behind them, and that they had deserved a rest.

On their arrival in England, however, Mrs. Fawcett quickly realised that the consciousness of work honestly done, and the achievement of solid results, were not enough to clear her from abuse. Some of her pro-Boer friends, of course, remained on good terms with her, but " the O lot " attacked her more than ever. She received sincere and official thanks from His Majesty's Government for " the very zealous and able way in which the Commission's arduous work was brought to a conclusion," and the Report was alluded to with high praise in the House of Commons, but all this only added to the suspicion with which some people regarded her.

" Several pro-Boer people who used to be quite good friends of mine now cut me dead," she wrote to Dr. Jane Walker, " and turn their backs if I am coming towards them. I don't exactly like it ; but I try to bear it with patience. It takes a many people to make a world."

With the end of the war in May 1902, of course, both the praise and the abuse quickly began to be forgotten. Hatred and evil feelings died down, and animosities gradually weakened ; and before long nothing but a faint echo of the controversy remained alive. As far as

Mrs. Fawcett was concerned, however, this echo took a
very definite and curiously untrue form. It became
generally believed by people who knew nothing about
her that she was a real diehard Conservative, an ardent
Imperialist, and a militarist ; and there were many to
add that she was a hard and wicked woman, willing to
support authority whether it was right or wrong, and to
lend her service unscrupulously to the Conservative
Government.

But Millicent was not perturbed by such reports.
She dropped back at once into her old place and her
old work. Ignorant people could think and say what
they pleased about her ; she was much too busy to care.

Mrs. Fawcett's connection with South Africa did not
end with the return of the Commission. There had
been one part of the organisation of the camps which
they had been able to praise wholeheartedly, and that
was the educational work. The schools which had been
improvised for the refugees were not only good in themselves but were very eagerly welcomed by the people,
and in this direction Mrs. Fawcett believed that there
lay a hope of easing the settlement after the war. The
establishment of elementary education in the Transvaal
was one of the things for which Edmund had longed ;
it was part of the benefits which the British people
could bring to the country, and in the eagerness with
which the camp population seized upon what they could
get there seemed to be encouragement for the future.

Philippa shared her mother's interest in this subject,
and as soon as she reached England she sought and
obtained permission to return to South Africa to take
part in setting up a permanent educational machinery.
This undertaking had Mrs. Fawcett's full support.
Philippa was the most eminently satisfactory of
daughters, but ever since the Tripos success her career
had nevertheless caused her mother a good deal of
perplexity. It seemed to Mrs. Fawcett that she ought
to follow up her academic distinction by adopting some

very striking career, and so carry still farther the good
work she had already done for the cause. She had
wanted her to become in turn an astronomer, a physicist,
a lighthouse designer or an engineer ; or at any rate
something which no woman had ever been before.
When Philippa rejected these plans, her mother suggested that she should train as a solicitor, or an actuary,
and so force open a new calling to women ; and when,
instead of doing any of these things, her daughter went
back to Newnham to teach Mathematics, she refused
to look on this as a permanent choice, and continued
to hunt for some more adventurous opening. Now the
South African work, though it had no connection with
the women's movement, was real pioneer work, of
incalculable importance, and Mrs. Fawcett was proud
that her daughter should play her part in it. She
therefore sent Philippa off with her full approval, and
in 1903 she went out to visit her, and to renew acquaintance with the friends she had made on her former visit.

Not long after her return from this visit another
opportunity offered of finding work for Philippa which
was at once useful in itself and new to women. The
London County Council advertised for an assistant to
the Director of Education, and Mrs. Fawcett ascer-
tained that, although there had been no previous
intention of appointing a woman, applications from
them might be considered. She at once cabled to South
Africa for permission to apply in her daughter's name,
and did so, with the result that Philippa received an
appointment, at the same pay which would have been
given to a man, in the administration of education ;
and that post she continues to hold. She came back
from South Africa to take it up in 1905, and thereafter
lived with her mother and aunt in Gower Street, and
shared with them the interests and the vicissitudes of
the great suffrage struggle.

CHAPTER X

THE SUFFRAGE REVIVAL AND THE MILITANTS

New recruits—First militant demonstration—Outcry of Press—The affair in the Lobby—Visit to Holloway—Banquet to released prisoners—N.U. protest against militancy—Mrs. Garrett Anderson—Lady Constance Lytton—The £1,000 gifts—Daily work—Open-air demonstrations—Violent disturbances—The Antis.

THE England in which Mrs. Fawcett took up her work again after the South African War seemed on the surface to be the same as that she had known all through the 'eighties and 'nineties ; but it was on the verge of change. Motors-cars and telephones were coming into general use, to distract and hasten the machinery of life and government, and in less material ways also development was at hand. The Victorian era was definitely at an end ; the political Labour Party, though still in its infancy, was becoming a real force, and new and revolutionary ideas were beginning to permeate the public mind. Education was more and more widespread, and was extended to women ; social insurance was under discussion ; death duties and graduated income taxes were growing important, and every economic and political theory was being questioned and examined anew.

Mrs. Fawcett herself was now fifty-seven years old. She had been working continuously for forty years, largely in the same movement, and in the same surroundings. She knew her cause in every aspect save that which was now approaching. She had seen it despised and laughed at, had watched through the weary years when it was apparently forgotten and unnoticed, and she had been one of a small band of supporters persevering without external sympathy in a hostile world. But now popularity and enthusiasm were coming, and thousands of new recruits. Opposition was to be violent, but no longer contemptuous, and support was to increase from hour to hour. The young women who had profited by the higher education won for them ten and twenty years before were at last ready to come into the ranks, and in the women's movement, even more than in the rest of the world, a great ferment was at hand.

It might well have happened, in these circumstances, that the leader who had been adequate in the old days would have proved a failure in the new. Mrs. Fawcett might easily have been unable to adjust her outlook to the new conditions, and instead of being the chief helper she might have become a stumbling-block to her followers, to be considered and honoured, but tactfully set aside by the rising generation.

But no such fate was before her. On the contrary, as the scope of the work widened, and as its magnitude increased, she stood out more and more clearly as the architect of its progress, not, indeed, originating new plans, but taking everything that came and welding it into a coherent whole. She it was who could always be trusted to shape the argument according to the firm lines of known principles, to prune off the inessential, and the inessential only, and to infuse into the turmoil that element of political realism which the work required. Neither sex antagonism nor hysteria were possible to her nature, and she was neither lifted up with false hopes nor cast down by sudden despairs. No matter what was going on, she still saw her cause steadily and as a whole ; and as time went on, and thousands came to follow her, she built up an organisation in which enthusiasm was tempered by humour and conviction by common sense.

Mrs. Fawcett believed that the new activity which so soon became manifest in the suffrage ranks was in part the result of the South African War. In the little history of Women's Suffrage which she wrote in 1911 she expressed this very clearly.

" The war," she wrote, " in the first instance originated from the refusal of the vote to Englishmen and other ' Uitlanders ' long settled in the Transvaal. The newspapers therefore both in this country and in South Africa constantly dwelt on the value and significance of the vote. *The Spectator* once put the point with great brevity and force when it wrote, ' We dwell so strongly on the franchise because it includes all other rights, and is the one essential thing.' Now this is either true or untrue ; if it is true it applies to women as well as to ' Uitlanders.' After thinking of the war and its causes the first thing in the morning and the last thing at night for nearly three years, there were many thousands of Englishwomen who asked themselves why, if the vote to Englishmen in the Transvaal was worth £200,000,000 of money and some 30,000 lives, it was not also of great value and significance to women at home. Why, they said to themselves and to others, are we to be treated as perpetual ' Uitlanders ' in the country of our birth, which we love as well as any other of its citizens ?

" Therefore in the long run the war, though it temporarily caused a suspension of the suffrage agitation, nourished it at its source, and very shortly after the declaration of peace it became more active than it had ever been before."

This was the sort of argument which had weight with Mrs. Fawcett's own mind, and the sort of consideration which moulded her own opinions ; whether it had in fact much effect upon the ordinary mass of non-political English people is open to question. But in any case, whatever the cause, it is certainly true that a revival of interest in women's suffrage was apparent in the early years of the nineteenth century.

When the South African War broke out there were but sixteen societies united to form the National Union of Women's Suffrage Societies. These sixteen were of course in the big towns, London, Edinburgh, Manchester,

Birmingham, Bristol and so on, and although they were strong and of old standing, their methods of work were quiet and uninteresting. Decorous public meetings once or twice a year—large and sympathetic, indeed, but unnoticed in the Press ; petitions from women (which Members of Parliament consigned, without a glance, to their wastepaper baskets) and private letters to candidates at election times were the main lines of their activities. At the London headquarters, indeed, Mrs. Fawcett infused rather more energy and reality, but even there there was no thought of public advertisement. The movement was confined very largely to people of the professional and political worlds ; it proceeded by reasoned argument, and it would have been incorrect to describe it as in any sense a popular movement.

Now, however, this began to change. In the North of England, particularly in and around Manchester, open-air meetings for factory hands were organised. The stimulus which the formation of the Labour Party was giving to working men was spreading to working women, and they were beginning to ask why they had not the vote. In the South, at the same time, new recruits began to drift into the societies. Young women, who were not very much afraid of being unconventional, began to ask whether there were not fresh things to try, and the click of typewriters was heard in the offices. New societies were formed in fresh districts, preparations were made for more thorough election work, and new members were elected on to committees. The Press still ignored the whole subject, and the average man accorded it only a laugh ; but Mrs. Fawcett, the President of the Union, was aware that developments were at hand.

It was not until 1905 that the ferment in the suffrage world began to become evident to the public ; and then it was through the actions of a group of people not included in the National Union, and not recognising

Mrs. Fawcett's leadership. In that year the first of the " militant " demonstrations took place, when Christabel Pankhurst and Annie Kenney were thrown out from the Free Trade Hall, Manchester, for asking straightforward questions on Women's Suffrage at a Liberal meeting. After their forcible ejection they held a protest meeting outside, and were promptly arrested for causing a disturbance, and both of them chose imprisonment rather than pay the fine which was subsequently inflicted. This action suddenly set fire to the smouldering interest in Women's Suffrage. The newspapers rang with shocked horror, and all in a moment the subject sprang from being one of academic interest to the sensational headline rank.

Mrs. Fawcett knew nothing of this demonstration until she saw the newspaper reports, and the series of events which immediately followed from it was in no way connected with her ; and yet it is necessary in considering her life to pay considerable attention to the militant movement. It is true that she did not join it, and that many of its manifestations were repugnant to her taste and judgment ; yet for many years it was an acute and almost constant preoccupation to her, and its effect upon the cause she was leading was startling and profound.

When militancy first began there was nothing unconstitutional about it. The " suffragettes," as they were called, confined themselves to asking unwelcome questions at Liberal meetings, to going on importunate deputations to public men, and to marching in small bands to Westminster Hall to try and present petitions. In themselves none of these things were unlawful, but the rough behaviour of the Liberal stewards, the commotion made in the Press, and the vehement language which the suffragettes used contributed to draw crowds around them on every such occasion. The police had very great difficulty in keeping order, and the responsibility was thrown upon the women. They were arrested again and again for " obstruction," and before long were actually imprisoned for this crime. Nothing, of course, could have suited them better. Notoriety for their cause was what they aimed at, and their sensational behaviour very quickly roused and agitated the whole country. For a time, indeed, the result of the new advertisement appeared to be unfavourable. As Mrs. Fawcett said in describing these days :

" The anti-suffrage papers came out day after day with columns of hysterical verbiage directed against our movement. At the outset the directors of these papers made the mistake of supposing that the suffrage movement was capable of being killed by the batteries which were opened against it. If abuse and misrepresentation could have killed it, it most assuredly would have died in the early years of the twentieth century."

This adverse comment was met with everywhere, and not only in the anti-suffrage Press. Many members of the old suffrage societies characterised the new development as " childish folly " and " hysterical violence," and scores of Members of Parliament and public men who had hitherto been considered friendly announced that they could no longer support a cause which was so disgracefully advocated. Mrs. Fawcett's account of these days continues :

" It is difficult now to realise the tremendous sensation caused by the doings of the suffragettes. Wherever one went nothing else was talked of ; intense hatred and contempt being frequently expressed and answered by equally violent approval. An old friend of mine called out to me across the table at a dinner-party that after the outrageous conduct of the militants he would never again do anything in support of Women's Suffrage. I retorted by asking him what he had done up to that moment, but got no answer."

This quick retort did indeed represent Mrs. Fawcett's general feeling at the time when the militant movement began. If people could be turned away from the cause

15

because of the behaviour of a handful of its other supporters, they were not worth keeping. " No reformer is fit for his task who suffers himself to be frightened off by the excesses of an extreme wing." This sentence Mrs. Fawcett culled from Morley's *Life of Gladstone*, and she turned it over and over in her mind.

" Personally," she wrote long afterwards, " it was to myself the most difficult time of my forty years of suffrage work. I was helped a good deal by recalling a saying of my husband's about the Irish situation in the 'eighties, when he was heard saying to himself, ' Just keep on and do what is right.' I am far from claiming that we actually accomplished the difficult feat of doing what was right, but I believe we tried to."

During the year 1906 it almost seemed for a time that the question of methods was obscuring the issue of Women's Suffrage itself. The Parliamentary situation was unpromising ; the Liberals, who had come into power with a huge majority, were as favourable in word and as unfriendly in action as ever, and a huge joint deputation to Sir Henry Campbell-Bannerman had produced nothing more useful than the advice to " go on pestering." The country was roused to keen interest in the struggle, but it was mainly an amused interest, mixed with disapproval, and prospects looked rather dark. However, there were some significant developments. Liberal women, at last losing hope in their party, were coming out into the National Union by scores, never, as it turned out, to return ; and all over the country the sensational deeds of the militants were turning passive supporters into active enthusiasts. Though the general public was as yet unconverted, the converted themselves were roused ; and Mrs. Fawcett's societies grew apace.

In October 1906 a militant " outrage " took place in the Central Lobby of the House of Commons which troubled Mrs. Fawcett profoundly. In itself the action was unimportant. Four ladies, one of whom was Mrs.

Cobden Sanderson (a daughter of Richard Cobden), entered the Lobby, mounted the padded seats, produced small flags and began to make speeches in favour of votes for women. They were, of course, promptly removed, and there, had the matter been an ordinary political question, it would have ended. But it was not an ordinary political question ; and consequently the four ladies were taken to the police court and sentenced to two months' imprisonment, and the newspapers came out with flaming headlines describing how they had scratched and screamed and bitten the police.

Mrs. Fawcett had known Janie Cobden from a child, and she was certain that these stories could not be true ; she knew also that the offence was a purely technical one, and she decided that she must take steps to express her disapproval of the way the militants were being treated. She therefore at once obtained an interview with Mrs. Cobden Sanderson in Holloway Prison, and she gave a full account of the visit in her reminiscences :

" I was put in charge of a wardress, who had orders to show me everything in the prison. I was first taken to a cell exactly resembling the one in which my friend was shut up—a long narrow slip of a room ; the bed and bedding were rolled up in a tight bundle and placed perpendicularly against the wall, so that the bed could not be used as a couch ; the window was small and very high up, just under the ceiling, so that little or nothing was visible from it ; there was no chair, only a small narrow bench without back or sides. I asked the wardress if a chair was never provided. She replied with some asperity that the ratepayers (pronounced ritepires) could not be expected to provide ' luxuries ' for prisoners, adding, however, as an afterthought, that the prisoners were provided with luxuries ; I made no comment on this, but I did not forget it. I saw the workroom, the chapel, the infirmary, the exercise yard, and then was taken for my interview with Mrs. Cobden Sanderson. I had brought her a few flowers ; she was not allowed to accept them, but I observed with satisfaction that the mere handling of them for a moment appeared to give her pleasure. The wardress of course was present all through. My friend, whom I had always seen most daintily and charmingly dressed, was in the coarse and clumsy prison garb marked with the broad arrow. She had a dark-coloured coarse cloth hanging from her waist. ' What is this ? ' I asked, taking hold of it. She laughed and said it was her handkerchief. No pockets were allowed, and this cloth, which was virtually a duster, was fastened to her side. She said it was lucky she had not a cold, as the allowance was only one a week. I believe it was one of the regulations that the prisoners were allowed neither pockets nor garters. She was a vegetarian, and her dinner in prison consisted of three potatoes. However, the doctor had recently ordered her two ounces of butter daily. ' That makes an enormous difference,' she said cheerfully. She uttered no syllable of complaint or dissatisfaction. I thought of : ' As shines the moon in cloudy skies, she in her poor attire was seen.' One word would open her prison door. That word she refused to speak. There was a light in her eyes, a self-forgetting enthusiasm in her voice that cheered and refreshed me. She had done nothing morally wrong, and she was sustained by the belief that what she was enduring would hasten the day of women's freedom. When I left her the wardress asked me if there was anything else I wished to see. ' Yes,' I replied, ' I should like to see the luxuries you spoke of just now.' The woman was for the moment taken aback, but could not deny her statement that the prisoners were provided with luxuries. She stammered that the luxury provided for the inhabitants of Holloway was cleanliness.''

This account was written twenty years after the event, and when it was published Mrs. Cobden Sanderson wrote at once to thank Mrs. Fawcett again for that long-past act of friendship.

" I remember how touched I was by your sympathy," she wrote. " Prison discipline was beginning to have the desired effect of killing my rebellious spirit, and then you came and gave me the encouragement I needed ! I do not know whether I ever thanked you enough, but I do now thank you with all my heart."

Mrs. Fawcett came away from that visit to Holloway greatly troubled in mind. The prisoners were suffering, and suffering unjustly ; and it was for the cause to which her own life was devoted. It did not matter if the actions which had brought them to prison were ill-judged ; wise or unwise, their courage and self-sacrifice were the same, and accordingly she decided to act as she had acted in the case of Mr. Stead, and to appeal straight to the King. On October 30, she accordingly addressed the following letter to Lord Knollys :

" May I draw your attention to Mr. Cobden Sanderson's letter in to-day's *Times* describing his wife's treatment in prison ; and may I be allowed to convey through you a dutiful and respectful petition to His Majesty the King that he would be graciously pleased to order that the whole of the prisoners sent to Holloway Gaol in connection with the recent disturbance in one of the Lobbies of the House of Commons should be made first-class misdemeanants. I say the whole of them, because I know Mrs. Cobden Sanderson well enough to be quite sure that she would accept no indulgence which was denied to her comrades. Mr. Stead, Mr. Yates, Colonel Baker, Sir Edward Verney and Dr. Jameson (to mention only a few cases that occur to my memory) were made first-class misdemeanants, and I feel very strongly that the sense of justice throughout the country is outraged by Richard Cobden's daughter, for a far less serious offence, being treated worse than the men I have mentioned. The women now imprisoned have committed no moral crime ; their offence is a technical one which has irritated the House of Commons by reminding it of its unredeemed pledges, and the punishment of two months' imprisonment as common convicts savours of petty vindictiveness."

Six days later the answer came.

" I submitted to the King," Lord Knollys wrote, " the letter which I had the pleasure of receiving from you, and I did not write to you at once in reply (for which please forgive me), as all the ladies to whom you referred have been made first-class misdemeanants."

Again, as in the previous case, there was no explicit confirmation of royal intervention ; but again Mrs. Fawcett was satisfied that it had taken place. And in any case, however it was brought about, the object was achieved.

Even this, however, did not seem to Mrs. Fawcett quite enough, and so, after much thought and anxiety, she decided, on her own responsibility, and without involving the National Union officially, to make a gesture of friendliness to the prisoners when they should be released. Accordingly, she sent out from her own house an invitation to a banquet to be given in their honour at the end of December.

The invitation explained the occasion for the banquet, and continued :

" I need hardly say that I am convinced that the work of quiet persuasion and argument form the solid foundation on which the success of the Women's Suffrage Movement is reared ; and I, in common with the great majority of suffrage workers, wish to continue the agitation on constitutional lines ; yet we feel that the action of the prisoners has touched the imagination of the country in a manner which quieter methods did not succeed in doing. Many of us desire, therefore, to offer the prisoners some public mark of the value we attach to their self-sacrificing devotion. . . ."

This circular, and the banquet which followed in due course, brought down upon Mrs. Fawcett a great deal of criticism. Many of her fellow workers thought that she, as President of the National Union, had no right to take such action, even in her own name, without their consent. Many more felt that, while she had the right she was, nevertheless, making a very serious mistake ; and for months she was much occupied with the controversy.

However, this did not trouble her nearly so much as the original perplexity. Once she knew what she thought it right to do, it was easy to do it and to defend it ; and to the end of her life she never regretted this action.

In the following year, however, a new development
of militant tactics took place which, to Mrs. Fawcett's
mind, made it impossible to do anything but dissociate herself entirely from their organisation. Until
that date the breaches of the peace for which the militants had suffered imprisonment had been merely
technical offences, and their claim to suffer violence but
to do none had been justified. But in the summer of
the year 1908 their campaign was intensified, and the
Women's Social and Political Union began of deliberate
purpose to damage Government property, attack
public men and commit other genuine breaches of the
law. And when this took place Mrs. Fawcett felt that
the time for public protest had come. At the Council
Meeting of her society that year she supported a resolution " strongly condemning the use of physical
violence in political propaganda," and ever afterwards
adhered to that position. In a letter written to Mr.
Lloyd George, two years later, she explained her view
with complete clarity.

" I have no difficulty in stating positively," she wrote,
" that I have not expressed or felt any sympathy with
militant tactics since the time when the Women's Social
and Political Union began to practise stone-throwing
and other forms of personal violence. I foresaw the
possibility of such action being taken in the summer
of 1908, and spoke against it at our Council Meeting in
Edinburgh. In November of that year the National
Union of Women's Suffrage Societies issued a protest,
of which a considerable part was written by myself.
Everybody who knows me knows exactly what my attitude has been. As long as the so-called militants only
did eccentric things calculated to rouse discussion, such
as trying to make speeches in the Lobby and so on, I
defended them, though I never joined them. But as
soon as they embarked on personal violence of any kind
I never failed to point out that the arguments which
justify these proceedings could also be adduced to
support serious crime."

The protest which the National Union made against militancy in 1908, and which they repeated in 1909, while it cleared the position in some ways, involved a great deal of difficulty within the organisation. As Mrs. Fawcett said in her history of Women's Suffrage :

" It is notorious that differences of method separate people from one another even more acutely than differences of aim. . . . It was a most anxious time for many months when there seemed a danger that the suffrage cause might degenerate into futile quarrelling among suffragists about the respective merits of their different methods, rather than develop into a larger, broader and more widespread movement. . . .

"The National Union of Women's Suffrage Societies endeavoured to steer on an even keel. They never weakened their conviction that constitutional agitation was not only right in itself, but would prove far more effective in the long run than any display of physical violence. . . . But the difficulties for a long time were very great. A few of our own members attacked us because we were not militant ; others resigned because they disapproved of the militantism which we had repudiated."

Storms on this subject were not infrequent on the Committees, and in the internal development of the societies. There was a tremendous agitation in 1909, for example, when the militant sympathisers in the London Society (of which Mrs. Fawcett was at that time Chairman) endeavoured to capture the organisation and break it away from the policy of the rest of the Union. Many an anxious hour had she to pass, and many a letter had she to write before she was able to steer safely through the turmoil.

Besides those who defended or attacked militancy with fervour, there were, throughout the whole period of the controversy, a good many well-meaning people who continually urged the advantages of unity, and spent their time deploring the differences of opinion among their colleagues. As a rule Mrs. Fawcett bore patiently with these somewhat impractical idealists, but at one of the National Union Council meetings she was moved to answer them seriously ; and she chose a simile which it was difficult afterwards to forget. " There are," she said, " great and obvious advantages in unity, but I think we should not forget that there may be disadvantages too. The most striking example of unity which I know is that of the Gadarene swine, of whom it is recorded that they ' ran violently down a steep place into the sea, and perished in the waters.' "

Mrs. Fawcett's trouble over the militant question was intensified at this time by the fact that her sister Elizabeth took a different line from her own. Between 1908 and 1911, while Mrs. Fawcett judged them to be acting mistakenly, Mrs. Garrett Anderson supported them, and this was inevitably difficult and painful for her sister. It was not indeed the first time that they had disagreed upon important subjects, and it could have no effect upon their personal relationship. But all the same it was a grief to them both ; and when in 1908 Mrs. Garrett Anderson actually joined one of the " raids " upon Parliament, her family grew exceedingly anxious. Lady Frances Balfour, who called unexpectedly upon Mrs. Fawcett on the morning before the raid, found her walking up and down her room in great agitation. She explained to her visitor what was about to happen, and added that Elizabeth was over seventy, and was not fit to be arrested, and that she dreaded the outcome. Without saying a word of her intention, Lady Frances left the house, and immediately approached the Home Secretary and secured a promise that Mrs. Garrett Anderson should not be arrested, and this she showed to Mrs. Fawcett. It was, of course, an immense personal relief ; and yet it threw a curious light upon the other arrests. If private influence, and age, and social standing could secure immunity, surely there was something wrong with British justice ! And Mrs. Fawcett hated the whole business even more than before.

A year later the lack of principle with which the suffragettes were treated was even more clearly exemplified in the case of Lady Constance Lytton. Three times she was arrested, and three times imprisoned. On the first two occasions it was known who she was, and she was medically examined on arrival at the prison, and at once sent to the infirmary. But the third time she was arrested under a disguised name, and then she was not examined, but was sent to the ordinary prison cells, and under this treatment her health was permanently destroyed.

Such things as these roused Mrs. Fawcett's deep indignation. She did not approve of the militants, but she approved still less of the outrageous way in which they were mishandled, and both then and later she was positive that the blame of the whole thing rested as much upon the Administration as upon the women concerned.

Mrs. Fawcett's difference of opinion with her sister continued for several years, but it was a great happiness to her when, at the time of the Conciliation Bill, Mrs. Garrett Anderson came over to her own view. The correspondence which passed between them at that moment shows how straightly these two sisters dealt with each other ; and, underneath the rather curt phrases, it reveals how intensely they cared both for each other and for the cause.

" My dearest Elizabeth," wrote Millicent on December 3, 1911; " I feel I ought to write you a letter to explain that the N.U.W.S.S. and I personally feel that the attitude of the W.S.P.U. about the prospect of W.S. next session is a very big blunder, and that we shall lose no opportunity of disowning it and making people understand that we condemn it. It is horrid to do it, but I feel we have no choice. . . . I hope we shan't drift apart over this, but I believe the chances of this misfortune (which would be a very great one to me) are less if we are quite frank with one another."

To this letter Elizabeth replied the next day.

" DEAREST MILLY,—I am quite with you about the W.S.P.U. I think they are quite wrong. I wrote to Miss Pankhurst before (no, I think it was the day after) the demonstration, but she took no notice. I have now told her I can go no more with them. It is dreadfully sad to have to be divided, but I cannot help it. I was meaning to write to you to-day. I had waited several days in case C. P. answered."

This reconciliation of view between the sisters did not entirely end the family difficulties over militancy, for Elizabeth's daughter, Dr. Louisa Garrett Anderson, continued to support them, and was herself imprisoned in 1912 ; but it was the family tradition to be independent, and each member had to judge for herself.

During the early years of the militant movement, and again in 1910 when a truce was arranged, and when all the organisations of suffrage workers united in a joint demonstration, a number of letters passed between Mrs. Fawcett and some of the militant leaders. The tone of these letters, while perfectly explicit, was always friendly.

" I feel differently from you about what is necessary to the success of our movement in this strange and critical time," she wrote to Mrs. Despard in 1908 ; " but I shall always have the same admiration and affection for you personally ; and I hope that when this coil is over we shall be able to meet on common ground."

And again to Mr. Pethick Lawrence in 1910 :

" I feel now and always that we are united as regards our object, and that what unites us is stronger than that which has separated us."

This was her profound feeling ; and in consequence, though criticism of the militants sometimes became very severe among some of her followers, it never went far in her presence. She was ready enough to say they were mistaken when she thought they were; but she refused to think they were anything more.

The controversy about methods raged from 1906 till 1914, and during those years Mrs. Fawcett's letters contain constant references to the subject. It was indeed impossible for anyone who was watching public affairs to ignore the militants, and the Press eagerly recorded everything they did. This publicity, while it gave a tremendous impetus to the whole movement, was not without its drawbacks. It was often malevolently inclined, and Mrs. Fawcett herself heard a reporter seated at the Press table at one of her meetings remark in a disgusted voice to his neighbour, " I shan't stay any longer. These women are only talking sense ; there's no news in it."

Journalism conducted in this spirit very naturally failed to give an accurate representation even of the militants, whose deeds were neither so hysterical nor so dangerous as the Press made out. The following letter, from Lady Frances Balfour, with Mrs. Fawcett's reply, give a typical example of what was actually going on.

" I am just back from a night with the militants," Lady Frances wrote in June 1909. " Lady Betty and I went to the Caxton Hall first. The speeches were of a very serious nature, almost like a service of dedication. There was no excitement. We were all asked not to move as the deputation left the Hall, to ' remain seated in silent thought for three minutes, and then to follow and cheer our comrades on in the Square.' The deputation consisted of nine, led by Mrs. Pankhurst. . . . They all looked very high-strung and nervous. They passed out, their band marshalled on the stair to play them out. We followed some time after. The police in solid lines turned us into Victoria Street. We slowly battled our way to the west side of Parliament Square and up to Whitehall ; here we saw several arrests, the women all showing extraordinary courage in the rough rushes of the crowd round them. The crowd neither for us nor against, merely interested in it as a spectacle. The police kept us all moving, mounted men continually at work. We were finally driven up to the north end of Whitehall. B. and I stood on the Treasury steps watching the crowd slowly driven up by a wedge of police. The police on the pavement asked us to come down, and as we did so two women exactly in front of us threw stones at the windows. Poor shots ; I don't think the glass was even cracked. A policeman flew on them, and had his arm round their necks before one could think. Crowd and police made a rush together, and B. and I were both knocked flat, falling in a rather ignominious heap ! I was afraid the crowd would fall over on us, but we were quickly picked up and walled in by police and kept moving. The two women were swept away with incredible speed. The police naturally hustled rather more, and we got away by the Horse Guards. The courage that dares this handling I do admire. . . . We saw one tall girl driven like a leaf up and down Whitehall. . . . There is a fine spirit, but whether it is not thrown away on these tactics remains a doubt in my mind. . . . I wonder much what happened to them all. The ministerial *mot* was arrest and avoid charging them afterwards."

To this Mrs. Fawcett answered the next day :

" The physical courage of it all is intensely moving. It stirs people as nothing else can. I don't feel it is the right thing, and yet the spectacle of so much self-sacrifice moves people who would otherwise sit still and do nothing till the suffrage dropped into their mouths like a ripe fruit. *The Times* article is as bad as ever ; but the report of what happened strikes a more subdued note than formerly. I am told that the reporters who actually see what takes place in the street are impressed ; but they are not allowed to report things as they actually happened. What you tell me of ' a tall girl driven like a leaf up and down Whitehall ' is a case in point. Nothing is reported except what can be turned into ridicule. Thank God you were not seriously hurt ; but it is hateful to think of you being knocked down in a rowdy crowd. There is no doubt that the militant women are fighting this through in the spirit of a religious revival movement. The more they are imprisoned and punished the more they go on."

But for all that Mrs. Fawcett had no temptation to change her opinion.

" Although," as she wrote to Miss Merrifield in this same year, " they really did a great deal for us at one time, they appear now to have stepped over the bounds between justifiable and unjustifiable. It is easier for those who thought them wrong all along ; but I did not, though I felt that the main work must always be done on constitutional lines. Now it seems to me that there is only a slight distinction between their recent action and positive crime."

And so, once and for all, the question in her own mind was settled. The only thing to do was " just to keep on and do what is right," as Harry had said. And to the best of her ability Mrs. Fawcett did it.

While this militant controversy was going on, and in large part because of it, great developments were taking place in the rest of the suffrage work, and Mrs. Fawcett's life was being seriously affected by them. She had always been a hard worker, and had devoted the greater part of her time and thoughts to the movement, but now there came into it all the elements of rush and hurry, which were new.

Other kinds of work and writing were driven out, and even things which were themselves part of the women's movement had to give way to the increasing importance of the suffrage campaigns. Mrs. Fawcett resigned from the Council of Newnham College, and drastically reduced the time she gave to the East Anglian sanatorium. She refused almost every opening for work which came to her unless it was direct suffrage work, and although she did give evidence before the Royal Commission on Divorce in 1910—urging of course that the laws should be equal as regards the grounds of divorce and the guardianship of children as between men and women—she felt obliged to refuse an invitation to serve on the Royal Commission on Venereal Disease three years later. More than ever as time went on she believed that the disfranchisement of women lay at the root of many social evils. Until that was put right, improvements would be slow and hard to gain ; and in working for votes for women she knew that she was working for all the other things as well.

And now at last, after forty years of preparation, the Women's Suffrage movement had begun to secure a wider backing. The National Union, which had had 16 societies in 1903, had 70 by 1909, and 305 by 1911, and each one of them was expanding fast. Secretaries were worked off their feet arranging meetings, enrolling new members and supplying information ; money came pouring in, and every effort was made to try and back up by adequate and solid argument the notoriety which was now attaching to the cause. In all this propaganda Mrs. Fawcett was, of course, deeply involved. She received constant calls to important meetings all over the country, she had to see and welcome innumerable distinguished converts, and to draft more and ever more of those weighty letters to the Press at which she was such an adept.

Among the other elements of the suffrage revival was the formation of a large number of specialised Women's Suffrage Societies. The Men's League, which was formed in 1909, was one in which Mrs. Fawcett was particularly interested, but she welcomed them all, and her genuine courtesy and goodwill prevented from the outset any feelings of rivalry or competition. She was as glad to see the formation of the Catholic Society as of the Jewish League, and welcomed the Artists' League and the Actresses' League and all the others with the greatest satisfaction. Her main efforts, of course, continued to be devoted to her own huge organisation, but she was always ready to do a good turn to any of the Constitutional societies which were working for the same end.

Money-raising, which is always a disagreeable part of any propaganda work, was easy to the National Union in those days. Mrs. Fawcett herself received a continual stream of gifts, ranging from quite small sums to very large ones, and this in itself involved her in much correspondence. In her reminiscences she gives a description of the unexpected way in which these presents sometimes reached her :

" I was sitting at home, rather tired and cross after an exhausting Committee," she wrote. " A new little maid, named Martha, came in and said, ' A lady to see you, M'm. She won't give her name, but she wants to see you on business.' ' Now, Martha,' I replied, ' that is what beggars always say. You must learn to know when people are beggars and not let them in.' Then I went downstairs and found the supposed beggar standing on the doormat. I saw at once that she was a lady, and asked her in, and was, I hope, welcoming to her before she spoke. Her first words were, ' I have brought you £1,000 to use in any branch of your suffrage work you may think most needs it.' She gave me her name, but said I must not make it known. The generous gift was, she assured me, not from herself, but from a friend whose name she was not allowed to reveal. Imagine my joy. It was the first time that such a magnificent gift had been made to our cause, and its unexpected arrival made it all the more welcome. I am glad to say that immediately the front door had been shut upon this ministering angel my first thought was at once to find Martha. ' Martha, Martha,' I cried, ' it was not a beggar, it was a lady who brought us a thousand pounds for our work ! ' "

Gifts as large as this did not come every day, but they were fairly frequent. Four times in her life Mrs. Fawcett was asked to dispose of £1,000 for the advantage of the cause, and sums of £500 and £100 very frequently reached her. In 1910 the National Union was raising and spending well over £20,000, and this sum increased substantially in every succeeding year until the outbreak of war in 1914. The proportion which was spent

upon salaried workers was small, since the supply of
eager and devoted voluntary workers was magnificent,
and in consequence the income was spread over a really
enormous amount of activity. As early as 1907, when
Mrs. Fawcett was leading one of the many deputations
to Mr. Lloyd George, he was kind enough to suggest to
her that it would be a good idea to hold some public
meetings. They were, as she promptly told him, already organising over 200 every week in the year.

Besides all this, which was the propaganda side, Mrs.
Fawcett was very much occupied with the internal
development of her organisation, and this in itself was
by no means an easy matter. The constitution of the
National Union had been drawn up in 1897, and it was
recast on a basis of complete internal democracy in
1906. The policy and affairs of the Union were decided
at Council Meetings of representatives of all the self-
governing societies within the Union, and Mrs. Fawcett
attached great importance to this procedure. She
really believed in democracy, and felt that it was worth
while to take all the trouble needed to secure reality in
its functioning ; but it became no simple task. For
the truth was that the suffrage societies were collecting
together thousands of women of strong character and
decided opinions, and it was not easy to combine
autonomy for the different societies with unanimity in
general policy.

Gone were the days of quiet drawing-room meetings,
and the comfortable committees where everyone was
more or less of the opinion that everything had better
be left to Mrs. Fawcett. Instead, there were hosts of
intelligent and eager women, drawn from all parts of
the country, armed with all sorts of varied experience,
and well able to express themselves and to argue their
case. Nothing but their intense and unanimous devotion to their cause, and their implicit trust in the
reliability of their leader could have made them shake
down together as they did in these years ; and nothing

16

in Mrs. Fawcett's whole career is more remarkable than the way in which she controlled, without coercing, this rampageous army. She did it, apparently, without an effort. She did not say very much at committees, or enter with any great enthusiasm into the internal controversies which went on. Sometimes she seemed even not to know that quarrels were immanent, and appeared to ignore all their details. And yet her followers were aware that the essential points were firmly fixed in her mind. They believed that her judgment was disinterested and sound, and they often saw the heat and fury go out of their concerns under her quiet treatment. She developed at this period a very useful habit of telling stories. When things got too heated round the committee table she was almost sure to intervene with an illustrative anecdote, which forced everyone to pause in their argument, and first smile unwillingly, and then laugh outright. And the effect was extremely salutary. When she could not lay hold of an appropriate anecdote, Mrs. Fawcett had no hesitation in introducing some perfectly irrelevant matter. Anything to stop too much attention going to a dispute, she seemed to feel ; and again and again she would drag the unwilling combatants away from the business of the moment, just to give them time to cool down before reaching a decision.

But all this, of course, meant much expenditure of time and effort on her part. The work became fast and furious, the number of her colleagues increased, and the business which required her personal attention grew to inordinate volume, and yet she continued to live in the same quiet individual way. She refused to install a telephone in her house, or to employ a private secretary. She refused to own a car, or even to travel much in taxi-cabs, and she still insisted upon holidays abroad and concerts at home. She knew that nothing would be gained by over-excitement, and that she could best make haste slowly ; and her mind, in consequence, was always free.

The very deliberation of her methods, however, must have added enormously to her personal toils. She still prepared every speech with the greatest care, and made her notes with her own hand. It was her habit, when she had an important speech to make, first to work over it at her desk, taking notes and arranging her ideas, and then to sit down somewhere else with a piece of needlework in her hands and go over it again carefully in her head. In that way, she said, she stitched the outlines firmly into her mind, so that there was no danger of losing them. The facts on which she built up these important speeches she collected for herself. She read the papers without the aid of Press-cutting agencies, and never allowed anyone to " devil " for her. She still answered every letter personally, and was punctual for every appointment. She rose early in the mornings, and sat at her desk writing terse post-cards for hours every day, always carefully punctilious to inform her colleagues of every important fact which she thought they should know, and always remembering her scores of private friends and their personal interests. When it was time to start for some engagement she would set off on foot, walking very fast, and glad of the exercise, and only when time pressed very hardly would she mount into an omnibus. In and out of the offices she would come almost daily, with a bundle of small things to be attended to, a fresh store of jokes to enliven the workers, a comment on the happenings of the moment to recall first principles, and the most detailed friendliness in any personal trouble. If an office messenger twisted her ankle Mrs. Fawcett would visit her in her home to enquire how it did ; and everyone who came into contact with her, even for a moment, felt that they had met not only a leader but a personal friend.

In 1907, while the propaganda work was assuming such formidable dimensions, the method of public processions and open-air demonstrations was first adopted. Mrs. Fawcett herself led the " Mud March " from Hyde

Park to the Albert Hall in February 1907, and although at that date many people seemed to think this a very daring and unconventional experiment, she took it quite simply. Her small figure ploughed along—a great deal too fast—at the head of 3,000 women, as unperturbed as if she had been walking to church ; and neither that, nor the great Albert Hall and Hyde Park meetings which followed, seemed to disconcert her at all.

Once, indeed, her composure was shaken. It was in 1908, after a great procession, 15,000 strong, had marched to the Albert Hall with the beautiful banners of the Artists' Suffrage League flying over their heads. Unknown to Mrs. Fawcett the marchers had provided themselves with bunches of summer flowers ; and when she came on to the platform to preside over the vast meeting, the young girls who were acting as stewards came forward and heaped them at her feet, until she was almost buried behind them.

" I felt like Freia behind the mass of the Niebelungen treasure," she said afterwards ; but everyone could see that she was moved, and found it difficult to open the meeting.

Mrs. Fawcett's speaking in these years was as careful and statesmanlike as it had always been. There was no monotony now, since the political position of the cause was always changing, but she still kept very close to the old arguments, and preached justice and co-operation as she had always done. The nervousness which had been so acute in the 'nineties still troubled her, though with the incessant speeches of these years it diminished, and the rather dry quality which had sometimes been apparent before was melted away in the enthusiasm with which she was now surrounded. As her sister Alice wrote to her in 1910, it was evident that she spoke with " impassioned fervour." " I felt, dear sister," Alice wrote, " that the cause is to you what religion was to dear mother. Of course we all know this, but you are speaking so much more now

MRS. FAWCETT WITH LADY FRANCES BALFOUR AND OTHERS LEADING PROCESSION TO
ALBERT HALL, 1908.

that I think you must be glad to know that you can touch other people with the flame that burns in your own heart."

The atmosphere of enthusiasm and success which attended most of the propaganda meetings at this time was occasionally interrupted by violent disturbances and riots, provoked, of course, by misconceptions about the militant movement. When Mrs. Fawcett was herself involved in such a scene she always appeared rather to enjoy it. She was as calm and as ready to smile when missiles were hurtling round her head as when sitting in her own drawing-room at home, and the only thing she would say about disturbances was that they could be turned to advantage for the cause. She was, indeed, delighted at one rowdy meeting in South London, when a man approached her and offered his protection, saying he was an ex-prize-fighter, and supported votes for women ; but it was not because she wanted protection. She believed, with justification, that disturbances could be managed best without the use of force ; but she loved to think of the suffrage prize-fighter.

In 1909 Mrs. Fawcett was involved in a considerable riot which broke out during a big demonstration at Nottingham. To Miss Sterling, who wrote anxiously to know if she had been hurt, she sent the following answer :

" Very many thanks for your kind letter ; but you have evidently heard a very exaggerated account of the Nottingham scrimmage. I had no difficulty whatever, and I do not think I was ever exposed to the least risk. My host, Mr. Kentish Wright, urged me to leave the platform some minutes before I did. He was on the ground behind the platform, and I could see better than he could. I did not want to scurry away before putting our resolution. After the resolution had been put and carried, I just walked down the steps and through the crowd, one of the few policemen on duty in the market-place preceding me and Mr. Wright. I heard that one of our speakers was pursued and would probably have

been maltreated if she had not been able to take re-
fuge on a tramcar ; but I did not know this till the next
morning. The police arrangements were very inadequate, and the Nottingham people are very angry about
it. . . . I never was in any danger at all. It needed
much more courage to send a message to Edward Carpenter to ask him NOT to speak or to appear on our
platform, and to converse with him the next morning
and to tell him why."

In the next year, 1910, the disturbances still continued, and the actions of the militants seemed to be
provoking them. Many members of the National
Union feared that their constitutional agitation might
be brought to a complete standstill unless something
was done, and urged that very strong measures should
be taken to dissociate the two organisations. Mrs.
Fawcett, however, was not at all afraid of this contingency, and believed that the best way to meet the
emergency was to go on quietly as if it did not exist.

" I am going to speak this afternoon," she wrote to
Lady Frances Balfour on March 5, " and shall say
frankly what I think of the W.S.P.U.'s recent proceedings. We (the N.U., I mean) have so repeatedly
passed formal resolutions setting forth our disapproval
of violence of all kinds that I am not inclined to do it
again. Our last resolution was passed at the special
Council Meeting last December. There is something
rather ridiculous in saying we opposed violence in
December and we still oppose it in March. But I suppose we must consider the subject at our next Executive
Committee on Thursday.

" I never believe in the possibility of a sex war. Nature
has seen after that ; as long as mothers have sons and
fathers daughters there can never be a sex war. What
draws men and women together is stronger than the
brutality and tyranny which drive them apart. I am
for going on with all our work just as before. If we are
mobbed or our meetings wrecked it won't harm our
cause.

" A stone was thrown against the windows of the

office last Friday when we were having a Board meeting. It did not come through."

With such a leader it was almost impossible to toss in imaginary storms, and the ship of the National Union rode on an even keel.

There was one element of the propaganda of that time which greatly helped to steady the ship, and which Mrs. Fawcett used quite deliberately for that purpose, and that was the organised Anti-Suffrage movement.

In 1908 a Woman's Anti-Suffrage Society was founded, and in 1910 it was united with a similar body of men, and under the leadership of Lord Cromer, Lord Curzon and Mrs. Humphry Ward, a good deal of active agitation against Women's Suffrage was set on foot. A weekly paper was published, and for many years Mrs. Fawcett was one of its constant readers, drawing much entertainment and many useful arguments from its absurdities. She never tired of pointing out the inconsistency of maintaining that " political ignorance was imposed on women by nature," whilst at the same time encouraging women to work actively in elections, as some of the leading " antis " did, and the more she could entice their speakers into the open the better pleased she was.

In February 1909 a formal meeting was arranged at the Passmore Edwards Settlement, when Mrs. Fawcett and Mrs. Humphry Ward met each other in public debate. The result was a decisive victory for the suffragists, and Mrs. Ward was much discomposed.

" She said to me with violence in the little room at the back of the platform, to which we were both shepherded when the meeting was over," Mrs. Fawcett wrote afterwards, " ' I shall NEVER do this sort of thing again, NEVER ; and I shall write to the papers to say so.' "

Mrs. Ward did this in due course, and the treat of a pitched battle with their opponents was very rarely available for suffrage speakers thereafter. A good deal of controversy was provoked by this occasion, not only on the suffrage issue, but on a point of organisation, the antis declaring (without a shadow of justification) that the meeting had been packed. But, of course, it was true that their supporters were less keen and much less vocal than the suffragists, and that the mere fact that they thought woman's place was the home, and only the home, must have tended to keep them away from public meetings.

In spite of this passage at arms, Mrs. Fawcett always retained a certain friendly feeling of respect for Mrs. Humphry Ward. She thought her opinions extremely silly, but she admired much of her public work, and completely trusted her honour and honesty. Not so however was it with all the antis. More than once she came upon evidence of very questionable methods employed in their propaganda—secret circulars to collect money, misrepresentations prepared for canvassers in poor districts, and referenda taken upon unfair questions. When these things came to her notice Mrs. Fawcett hastened to proclaim them, and, when necessary, she took them straight to Mrs. Humphry Ward herself.

One such occasion, which reveals a good deal of Mrs. Fawcett's courage and energy, occurred in 1909. One of the organisers of the Anti-Suffrage Society, a certain Mrs. S., made use of the expedient of dropping dark hints about the immorality of the things advocated at suffrage meetings, and the " pornous vices " there approved. This came to the ears of one of the local secretaries of a National Union Society. She at once indignantly denied the charge, and Mrs. S. offered to come and see her to give her the " facts " which were being hinted at ; but she did not do so. The secretary then passed on the correspondence to Mrs. Fawcett, who took the matter up with vigour, and endeavoured, without success, to induce Mrs. S. to meet her. Under her onslaught the accusation began to dwindle, first as not applying to Mrs. Fawcett's own society (a line of

retreat which Mrs. Fawcett indignantly declared made
not the slightest difference), and then to involving no
more than the possibility of a reference to prostitution
at public meetings. Mrs. Fawcett required Mrs. S. to
sign a statement that her words had not been intended
to bear any further implication, and that the interpretation given to them was unwarranted ; and when
this was refused she appealed to Mrs. Ward, and asked
her to lay the matter before the Executive Committee
of the Anti-Suffrage Society, and at the same time she
consulted her solicitor (who was her brother Sam), and
informed Mrs. Ward that she was so doing. These
prompt measures completely scotched the scandal ; and
Mrs. Pankhurst, to whom Mrs. Fawcett had written as
soon as she found that the accusation was being shifted
to the Women's Social and Political Union, was quite
content to leave it in her safe hands.

Twice again the same method of discrediting the
suffragists made its appearance, and on both occasions
Mrs. Fawcett sprang to the defence.   It was an imputa-
tion which made her angry, not so much in itself, since
it was patently absurd, but because it was a base
method of conducting political controversy. She never
forgave, or attempted to forgive, those who were responsible for these attempts, and sixteen years later she
took great and open pleasure in refusing an invitation
from one of them.   " Dame Millicent Fawcett regrets,"
she wrote in her note of reply, " that she does not feel
she can accept the hospitality of XXX. She is ready
to explain her reasons if desired. They relate to events
which took place in 1912, and possibly Dame Millicent's
recollection of these is more vivid than that of XXX."

The two incidents are worth recording, since they
afford excellent examples of Mrs. Fawcett's trenchant
style of controversial letter-writing. The first arose
from the statement made in the Press by a leading anti-
suffragist peer, that " suffragists of all shades " were
welcoming the appearance of an obscure little periodical

which, among other "advanced" subjects, advocated free love. Letters of enquiry about this statement at once began to reach Mrs. Fawcett, and the following is an example of her replies :

" The peeress who says she knows as a fact that I wrote to express my approval of the *Freewoman* when it first appeared, and said it was a most valuable paper, is saying what is absolutely untrue. I never saw the *Freewoman* until some time in March, when it had been appearing for some months. A copy was sent to me anonymously, and this is the only copy I have ever seen. I looked it through, thought it objectionable and mischievous, and tore it up into small pieces. I did not express publicly any opinion about it, because to do so would only have had the effect of advertising the paper, but in my own family I freely expressed my dislike. I know nothing of the printers of the paper. I once enquired who was at the back of it financially, and a well-known peer was mentioned, but I do not repeat his name, as the example of your peeress is a warning against repeating hearsay as fact.

" I wonder if the Anti-Suffragists think they are advancing their cause by the circulation of these inventions."

Nothing could be more explicit, or more convincingly true. Anyone who knew Mrs. Fawcett could see her tearing the paper up into " very small pieces," telling her sister Agnes how disagreeable she thought it, and then dismissing the subject from her mind. There were much more important things to attend to.

The second incident was less easily disposed of. It arose when a Member of Parliament put down a question to the Home Secretary asking if it was possible for the Home Office to prohibit the sale of a pamphlet by the National Union of Women's Suffrage Societies which he characterised as " disgusting," " indecent " and " obscene." The pamphlet in question was a serious treatise, written by a well-known medical woman, upon the subject of prostitution and venereal disease. It was stocked by the National Union, and by a number of other societies, and distributed only on demand for special use when wanted. The Home Office could not by any stretch of the meaning of words proceed against it, as was ultimately stated in the House ; but the question was not only asked, but repeated more than once, and the suggestion that the suffragists were using obscene pamphlets was thus kept before the public for eleven days. A good deal of notice was attracted to the matter in the Press, and Mrs. Fawcett's last letter, which appeared in the *Manchester Guardian*, summarises the results.

" Sir," she wrote, " there are one or two points in XXX's letter which call for a reply. After his question charging the National Union of Women's Suffrage Societies with circulating an ' obscene ' pamphlet had been twice repeated in the House of Commons, on November 21 and November 26, and had been twice postponed, I asked the advice of an eminent member of the present Government, pointing out to him the position we were in, of thus labouring under an intolerable insult for a period of time which might to all appearances be indefinitely prolonged. He said,' Write direct on the subject to the Home Secretary.' This I did, and, whether consequently or accidentally I know not, the question was at once finally answered in the House.

" XXX states, towards the end of his letter, that he had never up to the present time taken an active part for or against Women's Suffrage, but that my letter in defence of this pamphlet has caused him definitely to enroll himself among the anti-suffragists. So be it. But I happen to have a little book which gives an account of the votes of all Members of Parliament for and against suffrage, and the entry in his case stands thus :

" ' XXX : Has been continuously in the House of Commons since January 1910.

" ' Voted against Conciliation Bill 1910 (twice), 1911, 1912.'

" Therefore I cannot say I have it on my conscience

that, if he votes against us in future, my letter in defence
of the National Union of Women's Suffrage Societies
has been the unhappy cause of losing a vote in favour
of Women's Suffrage."

This was the last of the attempts to discredit the
suffragists by hints of their immorality. Either the
inherent absurdity of the attack became too evident,
or the raps over the knuckles which Mrs. Fawcett was
ready to administer were too hard. There were, doubtless, some people still left who really believed that the
idea of the enfranchisement of women was itself indecent
and scandalous, but they kept quiet ; and the cause
passed out from the harbour of theoretical controversies, and made its way into the political ocean, to
navigate amid the rocks and storms of the party system.

With courage and with firmness Mrs. Fawcett steered
her course and the course of her societies through these
preliminary tempests. She sailed before a freshening
wind of public approval, and with the tide to help her ;
and her ships travelled on, freighted with enthusiasm,
aspiration and hope.

CHAPTER XI

THE STRUGGLE WITH THE LIBERAL PARTY

Value of the movement—International work—The Dickinson Bill, 1907—Dr. John Massie—Deputations to the Government—The "adult" danger—Conciliation Committee—Announcement of Reform Bill—Renewed militancy—Defeat of Conciliation Bill—Change of election policy—The Reform Bill fiasco—Renewed effort—The Pilgrimage.

MRS. FAWCETT's life between 1906 and 1914 cannot be disentangled from the Women's Suffrage movement. She was closely involved in every step which was taken, her days were filled with its activities and her thoughts taken up with its problems ; but the bond was even closer than this. For she cared intensely for her cause, more intensely than for anything else. As her sister Alice said, it took the place in her life that religion had taken in her mother's, and she would have died for it gladly, if dying would have been of any avail.

She did not appear fanatical, and indeed she was not. Her judgment kept her to rational and normal paths, and her sense of humour never deserted her ; but an absolute and unwavering conviction that her cause was supremely right and supremely important became the very core of her being, and she was profoundly glad to devote her strength and her life to it.

Many strange suggestions for advancing the cause were made to her in the course of these years. Enthusiasts of all kinds found their way to her with proposals which were sometimes practical but more often foolish and wild. There was one in 1912, very seriously propounded, to the effect that a band of ten thousand women should be collected, pledged to adopt the hunger strike in their own homes, and to carry it on until they died if no satisfactory Government action were taken to ensure Women's Suffrage before then. Mrs. Fawcett was asked to head this band of martyrs, and her answer was as follows :

" The objection which I feel to your voluntary starvation plan is that all the inconvenience and suffering it would cause would fall on suffragists and their families, and that it would not inconvenience the Government in the slightest degree. I can in my mind's eye see Mr. Asquith chuckling at the thought of the suffrage ranks being depleted by the suicide of whatever number of women decided to adopt your plan."

Mrs. Fawcett wrote this, guided by her sense of the ludicrous ; but she would have welcomed any sacrifice which could usefully be made ; and there is a letter of hers to Lady Frederick Cavendish, written in 1913, which reveals some of the passionate intensity of her belief. Lady Frederick had written to Mrs. Fawcett saying that she thought it more important to put a stop to militancy than to proceed with Women's Suffrage, and she answered at length :

" Your letter confirms me in what I previously thought," she wrote, " namely, that you have never grasped the meaning and importance of the women's movement. I, and I think the great majority of the men and women who are working for our cause, look upon it as one of the very greatest things that has ever happened in the history of the world, immensely larger and more important than any merely national movement can be. The demand for the vote in England, U.S.A., Sweden, Denmark, Hungary, etc., is part of this bigger movement which is gradually changing the status of women all over the world, even in the East. It is the greatest step towards freedom which the human race has ever yet made, and it is greater because it is not confined to any one nation or to any rank or class in society ; it is the uplifting of our entire sex all over the world.

" The only thing at all like it that I can call to mind is the gradual triumph of Christianity in the third century, and of the ideals and aims of Christianity even where the forms of paganism were still adhered to.   Therefore, when you and others advise us, who have dedicated our lives to this great cause, to lay it aside on account of militancy, it is like advising a Christian to lay aside Christianity because of Kensit, or because of the reactionary policy of Pius X and the Vatican.

" Militancy is abhorred by me, and the majority of suffragists.   None of the great triumphs of the women's movement, such as the defeat of the Contagious Diseases Acts, have been won by physical force : they have been triumphs of moral and spiritual force.   But militancy has been brought into existence by the blind blundering of politicians who have not understood the women's movement.   I cannot wonder that people of excitable fiery temperament have been goaded almost to madness by the ' shuffling and delay ' (as Mr. Birrell called it) with which our question has been treated in Parliament.   If men had been treated by the House of Commons as women have been treated, there would have been bloody reprisals all over the country.   I do say most deliberately and with the utmost conviction that what is called militancy is ' political unrest ' caused by mishandling and misunderstanding by politicians of one of the greatest movements in the history of the world."

When Mrs. Fawcett wrote these words, there was a growing number of people, but there were still not very many, who agreed with her estimate of the importance of the women's movement.   Her correspondent was shocked by so extravagant a claim, and not only the politicians who were mishandling the matter, but most of the men who supported it, would have felt that Mrs. Fawcett was putting its value too high.   The antis were more nearly right, for once ; they declared that the suffrage movement was the beginning of a change which would revolutionise society ; and in that Mrs. Fawcett agreed with them.

The international aspect of the movement, which is stressed in this letter, was constantly present in Mrs. Fawcett's mind.   Ten, and even twenty years earlier,

before the idea of international work was at all pre-
valent, she had realised its importance, and had got
into touch with the leaders of women's causes in every
part of the world. Their letters came to her in scores,
from America, from the British Colonies and from
European and Eastern countries, written some of them
in quaint and halting English, but bearing witness to
the vicissitudes of the cause in every part of the globe,
and to the trust which the English leader inspired in
women whom she never met. As soon as any advance
came, or any depressing setback, they wrote to tell her,
confident that she cared as much as they did and that
there would be help as well as sympathy in her answers.
And even when her own work was at its busiest, and
when the excitement at home was running highest, she
never failed them. For she *did* care as much as they
did. She knew that progress in Tasmania or Montreal,
in Norway, Greece or India was as necessary to her
ideal as was victory in Great Britain itself. She knew
that when enfranchisement came in her own country
it would help the cause in Germany, in South Africa
and everywhere ; and that its echoes would reverberate
round the world until even the harems of Turkey would
hear them.

" It is not confined to any one nation or to any rank
or class in society ; it is the uplifting of our entire sex
all over the world."

The international aspect of the movement, which
Mrs. Fawcett felt so keenly, found expression early in
the twentieth century in an organised form. The first
meeting out of which the International Women's
Suffrage Alliance grew was held in Washington in 1902.
Only six National Societies existed to send delegates,
though the separate State organisations in Australia
combined to send a seventh ; but two years later eight
national delegates met formally in Berlin. Mrs. Fawcett
attended this meeting from Great Britain, and there
began the personal friendship which united her with

the leaders of the other countries, and in particular with Dr. Aletta Jacobs from Holland, and Susan B. Anthony from the United States. Mrs. Fawcett was made a Vice-President of the Alliance at this meeting, and served upon the Board of Officers from that time onwards, attending every meeting with regularity ; and after the office was opened in London she became personally responsible for the greater part of its work.

In 1906 the Alliance met in Copenhagen, with eleven countries represented, and two years later there were fifteen for the Amsterdam Congress. By the next year there were twenty, and that year they met in London. Mrs. Fawcett worked very hard to make this Congress a success. She arranged banquets and receptions, as well as business meetings, and secured a special service at St. Paul's for the delegates. She felt that it was extremely valuable for the English movement, as well as for the foreigners, that the Press should realise the importance of the occasion, and nothing which it lay in her power to do was neglected.

Two years later, in 1911, she attended the conference in Stockholm, and again in 1913 she went to Budapest for the International meetings. By that time the number of National Societies was twenty-nine, and the international work was well established. A monthly paper appearing in French and English was edited from the London headquarters, and the dream of world-wide co-operation among the leaders of the women's movement was a reality. But even so, and even when the organised work had grown so important, Mrs. Fawcett still maintained her personal touch with the workers in remote regions. She knew that though congresses and newspapers and resolutions were good and necessary, personal friendly interest was needed too. And she continued to give it unsparingly.

Mrs. Fawcett was not, of course, the only person in the British National Union to appreciate the importance of international work. There were some of her colleagues

17

who devoted themselves whole-heartedly to it, and who spent time and money and anxious thought upon its problems. Nevertheless, it is true to say that to the majority of those who were caught up in the enthusiasm of that time this side of the movement seemed rather tiresome. The crisis of the day was always so acute, and there was so much that was urgent to do every hour that it was a nuisance to be stopped short and obliged to listen to some trifling advance or failure at the other end of the earth, which couldn't be properly understood without a lot of explanation, and which only dealt with education, or the municipal vote, or something elementary of that kind anyway ! This was how most of the workers felt when Mrs. Fawcett insisted on calling their attention to foreign news ; and nothing but their respect for her, and their strong affection, could have made them listen at all.

Mrs. Fawcett, of course, knew all this, but she was not in the least affected by it. If they were not interested, they ought to be ; and she hammered away, quite undisturbed, upon the closed doors of their international understanding.

The rush and hurry of the suffrage work between 1906 and 1914 are now forgotten, and only those who lived through them can realise the intensity, the romance and the glorious excitement of those enthralling days. The women who plunged themselves into this enthusiasm, and who became as it were submerged in it, served it with a passionate devotion. For them, and above all for Mrs. Fawcett who was at its very centre, the cause became the most absorbing thing in life. Everything seemed to hinge and turn upon it, so that it was never far from their thoughts. They read into their suffrage work all their other ideals and beliefs. It stood to them for progress, real, immediate and profound, and they were prepared to dedicate everything they possessed to its service, and to sacrifice not only money and time and effort, but all their ambitions and all their lives. Up and down the country there were scores of these women who toiled and spared themselves nothing, devoting their leisure, their health and strength and all that they had to the service of the women's movement. They did not work for glory or for personal reward ; they did not shrink from the hardest and most uncongenial tasks, but they were happy in their devotion because of their intense and burning belief that what they were doing was imperatively right.

Mrs. Fawcett, the leader of these women, shared their faith and their devotion, and they all knew it. She made no parade of self-sacrifice, she made light of the long journeys, the hard work and the heavy strain ; but every worker, from the most responsible officer to the most obscure follower, knew that their leader was one of themselves. They counted upon her in every emergency as they counted upon the rising of the sun. They expected much from themselves and from each other, but even more from her. And she never failed.

The greater part of all this work was direct propaganda. Women's Suffrage was a symbol, a peg on which to hang the whole claim of women to their full share of the things of the world—the good things and the bad things alike, the responsibilities and the pleasures, the toils and the rewards. To convert people to see and understand this claim was, in the eyes of the true believers, as important, or more important than the actual winning of the vote. It was that—the recognition of their full claim—which was going to change the world for men and women both ; it was that which would be the real social revolution, and which would bring the progress towards civilisation for which they strove. And so their propaganda work went on, no matter what the situation of the Suffrage Bills in Parliament, gathering impetus as it went, and gaining ground all the time.

In order to understand Mrs. Fawcett's life this element of her movement must never be forgotten. It was always there, inspiring enthusiasm and rekindling hope.

When the political outlook of the cause was at its worst this essential aspect was still unchanged, and even if the Parliamentary progress had been fifty times as slow, no one would have been discouraged or turned aside. For all that, however, the actual political events had very great importance, and the history of the Suffrage Bills, and of the slowly changing attitude of the Government towards them, is essential to an understanding of Mrs. Fawcett's work. For she was intimately concerned with both sides of the effort, and no account of her life would be complete which did not show the wisdom and force of her leadership and the statesmanlike quality of her guidance during these important years.

The main struggle during the whole period was with the Liberal Party. In 1906, when they came into power with a huge majority after the Tariff Reform election, there were 400 Members who were pledged, many of them by their own election addresses, to support Women's Suffrage ; but the Government as such had made no pronouncement on the subject.

Four hundred supporters in the House might seem a safe number, but Mrs. Fawcett, remembering the events of 1884, did not put any overwhelming faith in their trustworthiness. And when Mr. Dickinson's Bill was tabled, early in 1907, actually bringing a concrete proposal before the House, the instability of the position began to be apparent. One example of many is worth recording, namely, the case of Dr. John Massie, Liberal M.P. for the Cricklade Division. This supposed friend of Women's Suffrage wrote to *The Times* complaining that Mr. Dickinson's Bill would " force the hand of the Government and the House of Commons," and when challenged by Mrs. Fawcett as to his meaning, he sent, also to *The Times*, the following extraordinary reply :

" I can assure Mrs. Fawcett," he wrote, " that when I spoke of Mr. Dickinson's Bill as ' forcing the hand of the House of Commons,' my words were not without meaning. I had chiefly in mind those Members—not a few in number—who have, lightly and casually, from one motive or another, talked (mainly to women friends or women questioners) about their sympathy with Women's Suffrage, and have, lightly and casually, from one motive or another, even voted for a resolution in its favour, feeling in both cases that the question was rather academic than practical, while both political parties were split up on the subject. But now light casual good-humoured complaisant talk is coming home to roost, and they are being called upon to redeem what they are told were their pledges, and that not by any mere academic resolution, but by practical legislation, where both Government and Liberal Party are still divided. If Mrs. Fawcett were a Member of Parliament and moved about in the lobbies, she would hear it said, not infrequently, that Mr. Dickinson's action has ' put Liberals into a difficulty.' But I cannot, of course, expect this difficulty to trouble Mrs. Fawcett.

" I admit at once that the question of Women's Suffrage has been in a sense ' before the country.' But I still unreservedly maintain that it has not been a real live issue in the constituencies. . . . The voters, like the Members of Parliament I referred to above, have largely regarded the question as academic, and not very serious. As constituents they did not trouble about it, and, if their candidate mentioned his sympathy with the idea, they put his view down as a harmless fad.

" Much the same reflections apply to the meetings of the National Liberal Federation. As a committee man and an officer of that body for years, I was well acquainted with the nature of those discussions and divisions which Mrs. Fawcett has observed from a greater distance. . . ."

It is easy to imagine Mrs. Fawcett's reaction to this outburst, and the contempt which she felt for its author. It is easy, too, to see why the Liberal women came out so rapidly from their party fold, and refused to be beguiled any longer. There was a story of which Mrs. Fawcett was fond, and which she used sometimes to tell at her meetings with application to the Liberals of 1884. It concerned a negro chapel, and a negro girl who was the leading spirit in the choir. After one of the services the pastor, so the story ran, had gone up to this girl full of thanks and delight. " Sally, yo' sing fine. Sally, yo' sing bootiful " ; and then, while the girl was smiling and pleased, he added in another voice, " But, Sally, yo' done put nuffin in de plate."

Dr. John Massie, however, was not to get off lightly with an apposite joke. Mrs. Fawcett realised that the situation as he described it was too serious for such treatment, and she sent a further letter to *The Times*, as follows :

" SIR,—A cutting from a West Country paper sent to me to-day by a correspondent throws rather a new light on the annoyance of Dr. John Massie with Mr. W. H. Dickinson for putting down the Women's Suffrage Bill for Second Reading on March 8.

"The cutting describes the first appearance of Dr. Massie at a great meeting at Swindon as prospective Liberal candidate for the Cricklade Division. It is dated December 19, 1905. Only two questions appear to have been asked him. One of these enquired his views upon the enfranchisement of women, and he is reported to have declared himself in favour of it.

" Is it possible that this is what he had in his mind when in your columns to-day he speaks of members who have ' lightly and casually, from one motive or another, talked (mainly to women friends or women questioners) about their sympathy with Women's Suffrage ' ? . . . A public reply to a public question put to a prospective candidate at his first meeting with a constituency is not generally regarded as light, casual conversation. There is, unfortunately, nothing new in promises given ' lightly and casually from one motive or another,' possibly to gain the support of women's electoral organisations, being lightly and casually broken as soon as the election is over. That is one of the reasons why women want votes. It is more serious to break pledges to voters than to non-voters."

After that, of course, Dr. Massie was found among the antis ; but he can have been no great asset to them.

Other similar incidents occurred from time to time, but nevertheless, when the same Bill, introduced, this time, by Mr. Stanger, came forward in 1908, it was carried through its Second Reading by a majority of 179. It could go no farther without Government support ; and of that there seemed to be no prospect, since the Cabinet was divided on the subject, and Mr. Asquith, who was then Prime Minister, was a bitter and unrelenting opponent. Mrs. Fawcett therefore realised that it was now the Government, and not the private Member, which mattered, and she bent her energies to putting pressure upon them.

The Women's Social and Political Union met this situation by a policy of open opposition to the Government. Their workers went down to the constituencies at election times with the cry, " Keep the Liberal out ! " believing that in this way they could force Mr. Asquith's hand. But Mrs. Fawcett and her colleagues did not take the same view. They, too, wanted to force his hand ; but they believed that it was better to do so by bringing evidences of growing strength than by threats which, until women were voters, could not be clearly substantiated ; accordingly, the National Union continued its election policy of giving what help it could to the best friend of Women's Suffrage among the candidates, regardless of party, and the only change which was made was in tightening up the definition of " best friend," and making the pledges upon which support was based as binding and explicit as possible.

With this election policy Mrs. Fawcett combined a great deal of Parliamentary activity. Those M.P.'s who were really sincere—and in spite of Dr. Massie's assertions there were many of them, even within the Liberal Party—worked readily and confidentially with the National Union, and deputations to Cabinet Ministers, and to Mr. Asquith himself, were frequent.

These deputations were accorded very diverse receptions, and Mrs. Fawcett was often very greatly amused by them. Her description, given in the little history *The Women's Victory and After*, is worth repeating.

" I well remember the long series of suffrage deputations which it fell to my lot to introduce to Mr. Asquith, and his gradual change of manner in receiving us. Some of the incidents of these interviews were extremely amusing, and we laughed over them as soon as we were by ourselves. The first was when he was Chancellor of the Exchequer in Sir Henry Campbell-Bannerman's Government. We had with us Miss Emily Davies, the founder of Girton College ; Lady Strachey, wife of the well-known Indian administrator ; Miss Frances Sterling ; Miss I. O. Ford ; and other well-known suffrage leaders from our various societies. While we were still in the waiting-room, I was sent for, by myself, for a preliminary interview with Mr. Asquith's private secretary. I found him a rather agitated-looking young man who said : ' I want you, Mrs. Fawcett, to give me your personal word of honour that no member of your deputation will employ physical violence.' ' Indeed,' I replied, ' you astonish me. I had no idea you were so frightened.' He instantly repudiated being frightened, and I rejoined : ' Someone must be frightened, or such a request would never have been made of me ; but as it is made, without hesitation I give you my most solemn word of honour that no member of my deputation will either employ or threaten violence.' The idea of it, considering who they were, entertained me, and I took no pains to conceal my amusement. I rejoined my deputation, and almost instantly the gentleman I had just left reappeared to conduct us to the reception room, I walking first, side by side with the secretary. As we entered the room, where Mr. Asquith was sitting with his back to the light on our right, I observed in the opposite corner on our extreme left a lady I did not know. So I said to the secretary in a clear voice, ' I give no guarantee for that lady ; I do not know her.' ' Oh, that,' he rejoined, and again showed some agitation—' that lady is Miss Asquith.' Members of the deputation told me afterwards that they had also seen Mrs. Asquith sitting behind her husband's chair, but I did not see her myself. I remember the extremely forbidding expression of Mr. Asquith's face, and how, after a little, when I was speaking to him, I ceased to look at him on this account, and looked at the space just above his head. Of course he gave us no encouragement. One of his expressions was that ' he had yet to learn that there was any widely-spread desire among women themselves for their enfranchisement.' A member of the deputation, Miss I. O. Ford, of Leeds, who all her life had been very much in sympathy and in constant communication with industrial women in the North of England, replied to this that if Mr. Asquith would come with her to meetings of working women in Yorkshire, she could show him that there were thousands of women who keenly desired the vote. He replied, in his most forbidding air : ' The prospect does not greatly attract me.'

" This interview was a specimen of Mr. Asquith in his most hostile mood. It was our lot to taste the insolence of office and the proud man's contumely. It was part of our job. We rather resented being made a show of for the benefit of his family ; but this, after all, was a small matter. His manner, probably adopted to impress his wife and daughter, was indicative of his deeply seated opposition to our aims, and it was extremely interesting to watch how by slow degrees it was modified until it became, even while he was still in opposition to us, cordial and pleasant. Once I remember, I could not resist saying to him that I had never seen a man so much improved. But this was very near the time when our victory was a certainty."

It was on one of these occasions, in 1908, before the " improving " process had gone very far, that Mr. Asquith, then Prime Minister, announced his intention to introduce a new Liberal Reform Bill, including what was practically adult suffrage for men, and he promised that if an amendment including women on democratic lines were added to the Bill, his Government, as a Government, would not oppose it ; though he added that his own personal opposition was and would be unaltered.

He was clearly in agreement with Mr. Pease, the Liberal Member for Saffron Walden, who had said at the election of 1901 that what he wanted was adult suffrage " with some slight modifications, such as women, and those men who are not in full possession of their faculties " ; and the announcement therefore did not sound like a very firm offer, and did not give much comfort to the suffragists.

Mrs. Fawcett always attached the utmost importance to the fact that the support for the suffrage movement was drawn from all parties.   If its underlying principles were to be accepted by the whole nation this was essential ; but from the point of view of immediate political tactics, it seemed at times to be a disadvantage. It was clear, for example, that such a democratic amendment as Mr. Asquith foreshadowed would not muster the maximum vote, while, if it were a legislative possibility, any narrower measure was likely to lose Radical support.

The fact that the first of these dangers was a reality was proved in 1909, when a Private Member's Bill, drafted to secure adult suffrage for men and women, was found to command a majority of only 36 in the same House which had given Mr. Stanger's Bill a majority of five times that number ; and this result caused the suffragists to look with more suspicion than ever upon the so-called opportunity which Mr. Asquith held out to them.

Besides the great difficulty of carrying such a measure, there was involved in it the additional misfortune of a division of the forces.   If once the suffragists could be made to quarrel among themselves about the precise terms on which women were to be enfranchised it would be easy for their enemies to hold them off ; and this danger Mrs. Fawcett fully appreciated. It seemed imminent at one moment, when a body called the People's Suffrage Federation came into existence ; but Mrs. Fawcett refused to be perturbed.

" I do not feel much alarmed by its formation," she wrote. " I do not believe there is much general demand for universal suffrage. I certainly have not met with it when I have been about the country speaking ; and I noted that at the general meeting of the Women's Co-operative Guild a resolution favouring adult suffrage in lieu of Mr. Stanger's Bill was only carried (although the influential members of the society spoke strongly for adult suffrage) by a majority of 6. In any case, our position is clear. We have nothing to do, and can have nothing to do with a general alteration of the franchise as it affects men. Our line is simply ' the suffrage for women on the same terms.' Any change in the direction of adult manhood suffrage would make our task infinitely more difficult of attainment."

Of course Mrs. Fawcett knew that if all the Labour and Liberal supporters went off in this direction the cause would be put back for years ; but she had greater faith in the sincerity of politicians than to believe this likely ; and she was proved to be right. The Labour men stood firmly by the original demand, and refused to be sidetracked, and all the strongest of the Liberals did so too. Only those who thought it more important to stave off Party dissensions than to stand by their beliefs adhered to the new movement, and it had no great political importance.

When the first election of 1910 was over, and the Liberals had returned again to power, the friendly Members set to work in earnest. An all-party committee, with Lord Lytton as Chairman and Mr. Brailsford as secretary, was formed in the House of Commons. It was named, from its object, the Conciliation Committee, and its members drafted a Bill which met with general approval from suffragists of all parties. The terms of the Bill would enfranchise women householders, not excluding married ones, and the effect of its passage would have been to give votes to about a million women of all classes of society. This Bill was introduced by Mr. Shackleton on June 10, 1910, the Government having been persuaded to allow it two clear days of Parliamentary time ; and, in a House where everyone was free to vote without the Party Whips, it obtained a majority of 110.

Everything now depended upon whether time for the further stages would be granted by the Prime Minister, and the National Union undertook a great series of public demonstrations to encourage him to do so.

" After pondering much on the situation," Mrs. Fawcett wrote to Lady Frances Balfour on the eve of one of the great Albert Hall meetings, " I feel quite sure our best line for to-morrow is to emphasise what we have gained thus far and make the best of it. We must be very careful not to say anything irritating to the Government or to the Liberals in the House. Don't give them any more excuse for throwing us over. Place an implicit and childlike faith in their vague promises. Above all, we must not chaff Asquith for being squeezable. It is the very way to prevent successful squeezing. What we have especially to press for is an early day ; this will back up our friends in the H. of C. . . . The Antis," she added, knowing the sharpness which Lady Frances sometimes allowed to her tongue, " offer a splendid field for chaff."

This line was faithfully followed, and in addition much impressive evidence of support was collected. A hundred and thirty Town and other Councils petitioned Parliament, including those of the great cities of Manchester, Birmingham, Edinburgh, Glasgow and Cardiff, and the Mayor of Dublin was authorised by the Corporation to go in person to London with his official robes and his attendant officers to present their petition at the bar of the House. But neither these things, nor the public demonstrations, seemed to affect Mr. Asquith ; and when, in November, the Government decided to go to the country again upon the issue of the Parliament Bill, he would say no more than that he would give facilities for " proceeding effectively " with a Women's Suffrage Bill, provided that it were open to free amendment.

This was not a very substantial promise, but it was more than had ever been given before, and Mrs. Fawcett made the most of it. To her impatient followers she would say at this time, " Remember if we are not winning as fast as we could wish, our opponents are not winning at all " ; but to the world at large she proclaimed an advance which she hoped would really prove to be one.

When the new Parliament assembled early in 1911, with the Liberals still in power, all the effort in the Suffrage camps was directed to passing the Conciliation Bill. After protracted negotiations the militants were persuaded to declare a truce, and in May the Second Reading of the Bill was passed once more, this time by the increased majority of 167.

The time for Mr. Asquith to fulfil his election promise had arrived, and the Suffragist Cabinet Ministers (who were anxiously questioned by Mrs. Fawcett as soon as the debate was over) reiterated that it was " a real opportunity " and not " a bogus offer," and even Mr. Asquith himself asserted in August that his offer of facilities for effectively proceeding with a Suffrage Bill applied to the Conciliation Bill which was already so far on its way.

All this was promising, and the autumn began with high hopes, when there came, quite unexpectedly, what Mrs. Fawcett called " a characteristic blow " from the Prime Minister. On November 7, 1911, he announced that his Government intended to introduce a Male Franchise Bill to give the vote to " citizens of full age and competent understanding," but all he would say about Women's Suffrage was that his views on that subject were well known.

" Even the mildest and most pacific of suffragists felt that she had received from the Prime Minister a personal insult," Mrs. Fawcett wrote. " If it had been his object to enrage every woman suffragist to the point

of frenzy he could not have acted with greater per-
spicacity."

And this being so, no one was much surprised when
the militants, in rage and indignation, called an end to
their truce, and embarked upon a campaign of increased violence.

Mrs. Fawcett's opinion was, however, " that it is
never safe to act under an impluse of blind rage," and
she set herself to look for what good might be extracted
from the new situation. There was a great deal that
was confusing about it, for the whole basis of the
franchise now seemed to have become uncertain.
Mr. Lloyd George, in an important speech at Bath,
announced that the Conciliation Bill (which he had
never liked) was " torpedoed," and a great many disillusioned women at once sprang to the conclusion that
the Reform Bill had been expressly invented for this
purpose. There was no widespread demand for adult
male suffrage, and they thought its appearance at that
particular juncture could be nothing else than a device
to escape from Women's Suffrage, and they were cor-
respondingly indignant.

Mrs. Fawcett, however, would not admit this view.
She was as disillusioned and as experienced as any of
them ; but she was slow to admit motives of bad faith ;
and before jumping to any conclusion she determined to
make quite certain what the intentions of the Government and of the Suffragist Ministers were. Accordingly, she at once took an influential deputation to the
Prime Minister and forced him to clarify the position.
In answer to her ingeniously explicit questions he said
that the Reform Bill, which would be passed through all
its stages in 1912, would be so drafted as to allow of
amendments including women, and that such amendments would not be opposed by the Government, and, if
passed, would become integral parts of the Bill. So far
as it went this seemed clear (though events were to prove
that it was the hollowest of all the shams ever offered

to the women), but Mrs. Fawcett did not rest satisfied.
She approached both Mr. Lloyd George and Sir Edward
Grey, and obtained from them assurances that if
amendments enfranchising women on democratic lines
were not inserted into the Bill, they would support
amendments giving votes to women on the narrower
Conciliation Bill lines instead.

With these public assurances, the prospects of including women in the Reform Bill seemed fairly good ; but
even so the whole outlook was less promising than it
had been before the Reform Bill came on the scenes at
all ; for the " torpedoed " Conciliation Bill had been
backed by men of all parties, and had seemed almost
certain of success. Mrs. Fawcett, therefore, finally
decided that the wisest course was to work for both
alternatives, to try and get the Conciliation Bill safely
passed, and, if that was impossible, to concentrate upon
the Reform Bill amendments ; and it was to these two
ends that the National Union directed all its efforts
during that winter.

The militants, however, were differently minded, and
their attacks upon the Government for breach of faith
proved very irritating and unfortunate. Many of the
Liberals were only too glad to make them an excuse for
shelving the whole thing, and there was more talk than
ever of the unwisdom of giving in to force, and of the
impossibility of granting Women's Suffrage while violent
methods of propaganda were proceeding in the country.

All this made Parliamentary work very difficult, and
the friendly M.P.'s were anxious and troubled. Mr.
Lloyd George, whose own meetings, even when they
were suffrage meetings, were being constantly interrupted
by the W.S.P.U., was deeply concerned, and he wrote
to Mrs. Fawcett at the end of November as follows :

" I have been very unhappy about the prospects during the last few days. The action of the militants is
alienating sympathy from the women's cause in every
quarter : I felt the depressing influence even at the

meeting at Bath. Tuesday's violence and last night's indecent exhibition, when the Prime Minister, supporting a charitable institution, was howled down in a place of worship, have between them created a very grave situation. If next year's chances of carrying either a women's amendment or a Bill are not to be totally ruined, some emphatic action must be taken at once. You can hardly realise what the feeling is even amongst Members of Parliament who have hitherto been steadiest in their support of Women's Suffrage. I feel confident that if these tactics are persisted in, our hopes of being able to secure the insertion of a Women's Suffrage amendment in next year's Bill will be of the slightest. I have consulted Sir Edward Grey and other friends of the movement, and they take an equally serious view of the situation. What do you suggest ? Anti-Suffragists are, of course, exultant. They feel confident that the effect of our agitation will be neutralised by the antics of the militants."

Mrs. Fawcett in answer agreed, of course, that the effects of the militant campaign were deplorable, but she urged Mr. Lloyd George to remember that these disturbances were the outward sign of a real and well-grounded unrest.

" The disorders," she said, " are symptoms of a social and political disease. You may punish the offenders, but mere punishment does not affect the causes of the disease. Force is no remedy. You must seek the causes and endeavour to remove them." . . . " If I may venture to advise," she went on, " I would suggest your taking all possible means to make widely known what you are prepared to do next session to secure the enfranchisement of women. . . . As your desire to secure this becomes clear, the supporters and perpetrators of violence will be more and more isolated, they will have little or no public behind them. . . . People will begin to laugh at riot and tumult when it is abundantly clear that the reform desired can be obtained by the ordinary constitutional channels."

This answer was not very comforting ; and it was not meant to be ; for in her own way Mrs. Fawcett was as angry with the Liberal Government as the militants were themselves. Nothing but good solid proof of a determination to treat the question fairly would satisfy her, and such proof did not seem to be forthcoming.

The next two years, indeed, put her optimism and patience to a severe test, and what was more, they gave her a contempt for the workings of party politics which nothing she had yet encountered had prepared her to feel. The Women's Suffrage question cut straight across party lines, and rested upon nothing but its own merits ; and the only thing which stood out clearly from the Parliamentary subtleties of 1912 and 1913 was that party advantage was the mainspring of political action.

The first opportunity which the suffragists expected was the Conciliation Bill, which was reintroduced in March 1912. This identical Bill had been carried in the existing Parliament not a year before by a majority of 167, so that it might have been thought to be fairly safe, at any rate for the Second Reading, but it soon appeared that this was not so. The shadowy and as yet undrafted Reform Bill was skilfully used against it, and it was suggested to Members that it would be futile to pass such a limited measure immediately before the complete overhauling of the electoral system which the Government proposed. This was tiresome enough, though it could have been met with argument, but a much more insidious rumour was also put about to the effect that the passing of the Conciliation Bill would lead to the resignation of the Prime Minister. Liberals were told that he would be put into " an intolerable situation " (namely, the situation of having to keep his pledges to the women to give facilities to the Bill to become law), and they were assured that it would be much better for everyone concerned to let the matter wait over until it could be radically dealt with in the Reform Bill. Exaggerated estimates of the additional Conservative voters who would be enfranchised under

18

the Conciliation Bill were made, and of course the militant outrages were used for all they were worth.

Much of this talk was insincere, and none of it was officially authorised ; but it was continuous, and its effect was seriously to alarm the rank and file Liberals, and still more the Irish Members. These men, whose only interest in Parliamentary affairs was the advancement of Home Rule, were not prepared to let anything endanger their cause. Any disturbance in the Liberal Party would be fatal to their immediate chances, and so small a matter as their personal convictions or their pledges about Women's Suffrage could not be allowed to stand in the way, and so their support was successfully detached from the Bill.

The atmosphere of the House was thick with rumours as the date for the Second Reading approached, and although women were most strictly excluded from the precincts, Mrs. Fawcett was fully informed of them all. In vain she and the other officers of the National Union interviewed important Liberals and talked to private Members ; in vain they wrote letters and explained facts. When the vote came 42 of the Members who had supported the Conciliation Bill before " ratted " and voted against it ; 91 of them abstained from voting at all, and the Second Reading was consequently lost by 14 votes.

This defeat was a most crushing blow to all the suffragists.

" I remember what I felt when I heard the bad news," Mrs. Fawcett wrote in her reminiscences ; " I was one of a crowd of some hundreds of women walking up and pacing down Palace Yard and Parliament Square on that March evening. I felt that what I had been working for for forty years had been destroyed at a blow ; but I also felt what beavers feel when their dam has been destroyed, namely, that they must begin all over again, and build it up once more from the beginning. While I was in that frame of mind I met Mr. Stead. It was the last time I ever saw him, for the *Titanic* disaster followed

in two or three weeks.   He spoke some cheering words
to me, but I was at a point where cheering words were
meaningless, and I remained in a state of great depression, from which I had much difficulty in rousing
myself."

Mrs. Fawcett undoubtedly felt depression ; but she
did not show it.   The beaver qualities were what her
colleagues saw, and with one accord they all set to work
to build up their dam again, to make it stronger than
before.   To this end the National Union now changed its
election policy.   It was proved beyond discussion that
the " best friends " had failed them, and that until
pressure could be put upon the Government nothing
would be accomplished ; and the only unsettled question
was how a body of people, almost all of whom were voteless, could put pressure upon the political parties.

A great deal of thought and discussion went to the
solution of this question, and finally it was decided that
the best thing to be done was to support not merely the
staunch individuals, but the party which, as a whole,
advocated Women's Suffrage.

In 1912 the only such party was the Labour Party ;
and the fact that Labour candidates were drawing votes
mainly from the Liberals did not lessen the attractive-
ness of supporting them in suffragist eyes.   The value
of support which outside bodies could give to a candidate
was much greater at that time than it became after the
passing of the Act of 1918, and in the conditions which
then prevailed the turnover of even a few hundred votes
might be enough to alter an election result.   The
National Union was thus in a position to help its real
friends and to injure its real enemies by the same
stroke, and its able and ingenious workers exploited the
position to the full.

The National Union was, as has already been described, a highly democratic body.   The decision to
change the election policy could only be arrived at with
the full consent of all the societies, which by now

numbered 411 ; and in consequence Mrs. Fawcett gave much attention, in the months after the defeat of the Conciliation Bill, to the internal politics of her Union.

She had not originated the new policy, but she warmly supported it, and defended it against all comers. It was exceedingly difficult for many of the suffragists to bring themselves to the point of accepting it ; for it did indeed test the loyalty of those whose sympathies were not with the Labour movement. Some people found a difficulty in grasping its essential non-party character, and much plain-spoken argument and explanation were needed before it was fully understood. Once grasped, however, the new policy was fully accepted by women of all shades of political opinion, and it was put into effect from the summer of 1912 with great vigour. A number of by-elections occurred most conveniently, and the immediate results of the intervention of the National Union appeared to be the loss to the Government, through a split vote, of two seats, Hanley and Crewe. This result was followed, as time went on, by many other similar campaigns, and the organisers soon had reason to know that their intervention was being seriously troublesome to the party machine. And, of course, the more they saw this the better pleased they were.

Besides the election work, which was naturally intermittent, the Union increased once again the volume and intensity of its propaganda. Mrs. Fawcett spoke night after night to huge gatherings, and the evidences of public support grew overwhelming. But Mr. Asquith still remained unimpressed, and as the time came round for the discussion of the Reform Bill the Parliamentary anxieties were renewed. The interviews, the consultations and the careful preparations began again ; and now there were new problems, introduced by the new form of the opportunity, which complicated the situation.

Lobbying Members in the House of Commons was a weary business, and not only because the results were so unsatisfactory. The actual conditions under which it could be done were tiresome in the extreme, since no women were admitted into the precincts without elaborate guarantees of good behaviour dated and countersigned by an M.P. Without such passports—which were very sparingly issued—the process of seeing a Member involved hours of waiting, and Mrs. Fawcett spent much time sitting upon the stone benches of the outer hall. She did not spend the hours in fretting against the regulations, and she wasted no anger upon them, but filled her mind as pleasantly as she could, reciting over to herself the poems with which her memory was stored. But for all that it was a tiresome business, and one which added greatly to the practical difficulties of her work.

Mrs. Fawcett and her associates, however, were not daunted by practical difficulties. They saw everyone who was likely to be helpful, and with the aid of the Conciliation Committee the three possible amendments including women in the Reform Bill were most carefully drafted and arranged so as not to interfere with each other. Everything was meticulously prepared for the Parliamentary struggle, which was expected at the end of January 1913.

On the whole the signs were favourable. It was true that when the Second Reading had been taken in the previous July, Mr. Asquith had done his best to destroy the chances of the Women's Suffrage amendments by dismissing as " altogether improbable the hypothesis that the House of Commons is likely to stultify itself by reversing in the same session the considered judgment at which it had arrived " on the Conciliation Bill. But this phrase of his had been unfortunate, since the " considered judgment " of the House of Commons had twice been given in opposite senses on that very Bill in that very Parliament ; and Mrs. Fawcett was quick to drive the discrepancy home. She was in no mood to deal gently with Mr. Asquith or his Government, and her speeches during the months preceding the Reform Bill were lucidly clear and trenchant. Tangled though the position was, and intricate as its history had been, Mrs. Fawcett's leadership at that time allowed no misunderstanding to arise in the public mind. The exact political position was clear not only to the House but to the Press and to the great body of suffragists as well ; and all over the country they were making it plain to the general public.

It was, therefore, in an atmosphere of tension and excitement that the appointed days drew near. Mrs. Fawcett could not feel confident, but she did feel hopeful. The beaver's work had been very well done, and the dam had been built up ; but the flood of Parliamentary chances might overwhelm it again.

And this in fact was what happened. On January 23, in answer to a question on quite another point, the Speaker made it clear that none of the Women's Suffrage amendments could be carried at all. His ruling was that the Reform Bill would be so altered by their inclusion that it would become a different measure, and would have to be reintroduced and go through all its stages again as a fresh Bill.

Gone at one blow were the Prime Minister's promises that his Bill would be open to amendment ; gone were the chances for which the Conciliation Bill had been destroyed ; gone, in fact, were the last hopes of getting anything from the existing Parliament. It was an unexpected and acute crisis.

The hours which immediately followed this pronouncement were troubled and uncertain. Mrs. Fawcett and her colleagues consulted each other and their friends in the House, and were at once beset by journalists clamouring to know what line they were going to take. As Mr. Philip Snowden wrote to Mrs. Fawcett, the situation was " chaos."

" I know," he said, " that all sorts of cross-currents are flowing, and the great danger is that we may be

swept into one which is going straight to the rapids.
Certain members of the Government are sounding
various people and submitting all sorts of proposals.
No doubt you will be consulted. I am sure you will
exercise your invariable wisdom and discretion. . . .
The present crisis is the women's great opportunity.
The new situation has aroused interest and sympathy,
and if we press hardly enough, I think we can force
a decided advantage. . . . To have forced Women's
Suffrage into the position it has to-day as the over-
thrower of Cabinet unity and constitutional procedure is
almost as great a success as winning it. No question
since 1886 has dominated politics as women's suffrage
does to-day."

That was true ; the whole thing, and the public's
reception of it, clearly showed that Women's Suffrage
was come much nearer. But that was not a consolation
for losing the chance of its coming at once, and the
suffragists were bitterly disappointed.

Mr. Asquith's Government—which was guilty either
of a base deception or of an incompetent blunder—were
obliged hurriedly to withdraw the whole Bill. Mrs.
Fawcett at once declared that this action should be
accompanied by the offer of some equally good alterna-
tive opportunity of passing Women's Suffrage in the
existing Parliament, but Mr. Asquith would make no
such move. Though of course pressed very urgently,
he refused to do more than offer facilities for another
Private Member's Bill in the next session, and these
offers the National Union and all the other suffrage
societies indignantly rejected. They were done with
Private Members' Bills for ever.

It was now evident that so long as the Liberals
remained in power there would be no Parliamentary
progress. Mrs. Fawcett and her societies therefore
turned back once more to their task of organising support in the country, and to their intensive preparations
for the next election. The rest of 1913 was spent in this
way, the only development being that the propaganda

grew easier and easier, and the meetings more and more enthusiastic.

The account of this effort is not, strictly speaking, part of Mrs. Fawcett's life. She did, of course, play a most prominent part in it all, and fill her thoughts and her days with its activity ; but the movement had grown so vast, and had attracted so many hundreds and even thousands of eager workers that it was impossible for her to be so much as aware of all that was on foot. The machinery of her National Union, which had been devised so as to stand indefinite expansion, was now tested, and the results well justified the care which had gone to its construction. Its Executive Committee, which had to meet continually, and for very long hours, was truly representative of the whole body, and among its members Mrs. Fawcett found colleagues capable of sharing and easing the burden of leadership. She remained, however, very definitely the central figure of the whole organisation, and aroused an intense personal loyalty. Her judgment was profoundly trusted, and the admirable balance of her outlook steadied her followers again and again. Her advice was constantly in request on every variety of problem great and small, and she remained as accessible, as friendly and as simple as she had always been. She disliked ovations and public tributes intensely, but had to endure them continually ; and her public as well as her private manners were unfailing. No occasion at which she was present ever seemed to go wrong. If others forgot or overlooked some expression of gratitude, or made some *faux pas*, Mrs. Fawcett could always be relied upon to put it right, so that everyone was at ease when she was present. Her little formal speeches, her replies to toasts or requests for reminiscences were models of their kind ; for she seemed to have the gift of saying just the right thing in just the right way. She could indeed be stern on occasion, but within her own societies her influence was strongly felt for toleration, good humour and peace ; and hundreds and hundreds of the workers whom she hardly knew obeyed, revered and loved her.

The suffrage cause had, as Mr. Snowden said, sprung into such prominence that it almost dominated politics. Everyone knew of it and discussed it, and the controversy raged in private homes as well as on public platforms. People felt passionately, and spoke passionately for and against Women's Suffrage, and the members of the suffrage societies took the utmost advantage of this general and intense interest, and intensified their efforts day by day.

The long series of Parliamentary disappointments had naturally affected the militant societies as much as they had the National Union, though in a different way. Ever since the truce had been ended in the autumn of 1911, their " outrages " had been growing more and more desperate, and by 1913 they had become a serious administrative problem. The adoption of the hunger strike had for a time reduced to a farce the sentences passed on the prisoners, and the passage of the so-called " Cat and Mouse Act " in this year neither put an end to their activities nor raised the prestige of the Home Office. Many law-abiding suffragists, of whom Mrs. Fawcett was one, considered that the passing of such a law, applied as it was only to one class of offenders, was a blot on British justice ; and numerous protests were made in the House about the treatment which the suffragettes were receiving.

For all that, Mrs. Fawcett did not attempt to conceal her opinion that the extreme violence of the militants, and the wild and irrelevant nature of the damage they were inflicting was harmful to the cause. She repeatedly said that the only remedy for the trouble was the granting of Women's Suffrage, and that the blame for the disturbances lay as much with the Government as with the militants ; but she regretted their spirit and their whole action profoundly.

" There seems very little probability that the militants will cease from outrage," she wrote in a private letter at this time. " I think they would rather lose Women's Suffrage than give up their own way of demonstrating. . . . There is no doubt that X and a hundred others slept until the sensationalism of the militants awakened them. Of course I recognise that this is a feat on the part of the W.S.P.U. But I also feel that blessed are they who do not need to be awakened by stone throwing and bombs. . . . I wonder the way the Antis gloat over their disturbances doesn't open the eyes of the militants to the fact that they are on the wrong track."

Again, a little later, she wrote to Dr. Jane Walker :

" I never can feel that setting fire to houses and churches and letter boxes and destroying valuable pictures really helps to convince people that women ought to be enfranchised. That half-savage men did worse things half a century ago does not make it any better in my eyes. I consider all first-class social and professional work done by women, such as yours in your profession and outside your profession in helping numbers of men and women to be better human beings, is the finest kind of propaganda for Women's Suffrage. You know I am not saying this to flatter you. But I do so intensely believe in the sort of work that helps to evolve a finer kind of civilisation, and so intensely disbelieve in the work that helps to push us back into barbarism and the reign of brute force."

It was clear in 1913 that the policy of the militants was indeed leading to an increase in the use of force in politics, for not only was the Government attempting to apply violent coercion to the suffragettes, but the hooligan elements in the country felt at liberty to attack them. Disturbances at meetings, which had practically died out, began again, and the police did their best to discourage open-air speaking. The result was, very naturally, that the National Union made a point of holding as many open-air meetings as they possibly could. They were not going to be frightened off by anybody, or prevented from going on with their propaganda, and they soon proved that the expected violence was not directed against their cause, but only against the methods of the militants, and that it melted away as soon as the difference between the two things was made clear.

Mrs. Fawcett did a good deal of the special open-air speaking which this emergency required. She did not like it ; not because she was in the least afraid, but because the open air called for a style of speech which was uncongenial to her, and for a louder voice than she could command. But all the same, she turned out, Sunday after Sunday, into Hyde Park, and clambered on to the back of a cart, or mounted an inverted packing-case to defend representative institutions and the right of free speech.

In the summer of this year the constitutional societies decided upon a new and gigantic form of peaceful open-air demonstration, and organised a great pilgrimage in which bands of women from all over the country marched to London, holding meetings in every village and town through which they passed. Mrs. Fawcett, of course, was required to rush from route to route to be present at the largest of the demonstrations ; but she insisted on walking, whenever she could be released, along the East Anglian route with the neighbours and friends of her childhood.

The great march brought innumerable incidents, some comic, some rowdy and disagreeable, and others exceedingly touching. But the impression of it all was strikingly encouraging.

" I have a photograph of the pilgrims sent me from Stratford-on-Avon," Mrs. Fawcett noted, " by a man who heard me speak at the Pavilion, Brighton, forty years ago, who has been a suffragist ever since. So one goes on casting bread upon the waters."

But now at last it was coming back to her a hundred-fold. She and all the marchers had ample proof of the friendliness of the whole countryside, and they knew that it was at last true to assert that the bulk of the people were with them.

The great demonstration ended in a gigantic meeting in Hyde Park, and this was followed the next day by a special service in St. Paul's Cathedral. This service gave great comfort and encouragement to Mrs. Fawcett.

" Were not the Psalms wonderfully appropriate ? " she wrote to Dr. Jane Walker that evening. " ' When the Lord turned again the captivity of Sion ' I have always in my own inside called the Suffrage Psalm. And then, ' Except the Lord build the house ' does so touch the spot about ' methods.' I knew Canon Simpson was not going to mention suffrage outright in his sermon, but it was there all the time. The only criticism I made on what he said was that he seemed to think we were in deep depression. We are not. We have got on at a really wonderful pace when we re-member what a tremendously difficult job we have tackled without an ounce of direct political power to back us up. Our job is far more difficult for this reason alone than that of any other reformers."

The job certainly was difficult, even now when such widespread public support was secured. On the day following the service in St. Paul's Mrs. Fawcett wrote once again to Mr. Asquith " on behalf of the immense meetings which assembled in Hyde Park " to ask him to receive another deputation.

" The law-abiding suffragists have been pilgrimaging through England and Wales for the last six weeks," she wrote, " and they have some facts which they would be glad of an opportunity to bring before you. . . . They can hardly believe," she added, " that you and your party can regard coercion, unaccompanied by any remedial measures, as an adequate response to the demand of women to share in the advantages of repre-sentative government."

To this Mr. Asquith replied that he would see the deputation.

" I feel bound to warn you," he added in his accustomed manner, " that I do not see my way to add anything material to what I have lately said in the House of Commons as to the intentions and policy of the Government."

In spite of this the deputation of course went forward, and Mrs. Fawcett, who led it, pressed the Prime Minister very hard upon the unfulfilled pledges.

" The Government is now meeting the demand of women for free institutions with coercion and nothing but coercion," she added. " It is not thus that the victories of Liberalism have been won."

There was, Mrs. Fawcett thought, " a notable improvement in his attitude and language," but she came away as unsatisfied and empty-handed as ever, and with no change in her conviction that the movement had come to a deadlock which nothing but a change of Government could end.

All through the winter of 1913 and the early months of 1914 this situation prevailed. Progress was evident in the parties and in the Press, and public sympathy was steadily increasing, and even the Antis seemed to be aware of it. In May 1914 Mrs. Fawcett wrote in some amusement about the signs of their uneasiness.

" Mrs. Humphry Ward's proposal," she said, " is that we as Women's Suffrage Associations should abandon our main object and purpose in return for her giving her personal adhesion to votes for women for local parliaments. It is as if she proposed that the Church of England should abandon Christianity in exchange for her withdrawing *Robert Elsmere* from circulation."

That sort of thing was entertaining ; but still there was no change in the Parliamentary outlook. However, everyone felt that the existing position could not last long, and Mrs. Fawcett began to look ahead. She was positive that the franchise would be carried very soon, and her thoughts turned more and more to the things which were to follow it, the social reforms and the liberations to which Women's Suffrage was the key. She studied what had happened in other countries after enfranchisement, and in her speeches she dealt not so much with the rights of the case, or with its tactical position, as with the evils against which enfranchised women must fight, and the solid work and help which they must bring to their country's affairs. The rights of citizenship were approaching, and she felt that its duties must be understood.

CHAPTER XII

THE EUROPEAN WAR

Outbreak of war—Decision of N.U. to " sustain the vital forces of the nation "—War work—Objections to international congress—Differences of opinion in the N.U.—The Kingsway Hall meeting—The Birmingham Council—Co-operation with the Labour Party.

BETWEEN July 8 and July 25, 1914, the Board of officers of the International Women's Suffrage Alliance met in London, and so little did any of them realise what lay immediately before them that their main business was the discussion of the arrangements for a full meeting of the Alliance in Berlin in the following year. As usual, Mrs. Fawcett made careful plans for the entertainment of the foreign guests ; she arranged receptions for them, at the House of Commons and elsewhere, and when they parted to return to America, France, Germany, Denmark or Finland, no one of them suspected what terrible misfortunes would have befallen them before they could meet again.

Events moved with disastrous swiftness in the immediately following days, and before some of the delegates could have reached their homes the European War was beginning ; and before a week was out the possibility that Great Britain would be involved was apparent.

Mrs. Fawcett was in London during these anxious days, and, like everyone else, she was at first incredulous, and then profoundly moved. The catastrophe was so tremendous and so utterly unexpected.

When fighting actually began, and when the Germans advanced into Belgium, Mrs. Fawcett was one of those who realised that English intervention was inevitable, and with a desperately heavy heart she turned to the consideration of what she and her societies ought to do.

On Sunday and Monday, August 2 and 3, the Executive Committee of the National Union sat all day in anxious consultation. They had to decide what guidance to give to their 500 societies, and what to do with their paid workers, their organisation and their funds. It was clear to them all that definite suffrage work must be suspended, but it was also clear that their active and vigorous body could be used, and would long to be used, in the national emergency. These problems therefore they discussed, for they had to be settled at once ; and yet it was difficult, and almost impossible, to attend to them, since every moment was fraught with the swift and deadly news.

While there yet seemed hope for peace, and before Sir Edward Grey's negotiations had finally broken down, three of the great organisations of Labour women had approached the International Women's Suffrage Alliance and the N.U.W.S.S. to try to secure a demonstration in favour of the preservation of peace. When it was conceived this meeting was to be a call to statesmen—

" to leave untried no method of conciliation and arbitration." " In this terrible hour," the manifesto ran, " when the fate of Europe depends on decisions which women have no power to shape, we, realising our responsibilities as the mothers of the race, cannot stand passive by."

But by the time the meeting could be held, namely, the evening of Tuesday, August 4, all such pronouncements were too late.

Mrs. Fawcett, who presided, knew this well. " We, being voteless, are not responsible for the complicated series of political events which have led up to the war," she said. " We could neither prevent it nor permit it." War was " insensate devilry," and must be a blow to the whole fabric of civilisation. " The highest and most precious of national and international aspirations and hopes will have to be set aside, but we as citizens have now our duty to perform."

That was, to her, the obvious and inevitable reaction, and though she agreed from her soul with the passionate protests against war which the other speakers made, and although she united with them in the longing to abolish hatreds and misunderstandings, she had no thought but to stand by her own country in its hour of need.

The meeting ended, and Mrs. Fawcett came out of the hall into the summer night to hear the newsboys calling the late editions with war news, and with the reports of the fateful speeches in Parliament. She walked along the Strand, and down Whitehall into Parliament Square, and there joined the anxious throng waiting outside the House. Up and down she walked, as before in the days of the Conciliation Bill, with a heavy heart. She had no doubt of what was coming, and she believed it to be inevitable and even right. And yet war was so terrible a necessity, so overwhelming a horror that only when it was a fact could she fully believe it. She waited, consequently, for the irrevocable news ; and when it came she went silently home, walking slowly, for once, her thoughts busy with dread of the future.

" The day on which we knew that we were actually at war with the greatest military nation on earth was the most miserable day of my life," she wrote. " I do not think I ever doubted that in the end we should win. The idea that Great Britain should ever really be crushed by the iron heel of German militarism never found a place in my mind ; but so ill did I read the future that I thought the hope of women's freedom was indefinitely postponed, and that this was the supreme sacrifice asked of us at this stupendous moment. Black indeed the outlook seemed."

Mrs. Fawcett believed that her life-work was destroyed and that the hope of the civilising influence of women's

19

enfranchisement was to perish, along with so much else, in the ordeal of war ; but still there remained the call of duty, which seemed to her transparently clear. The message which she sent out, on that miserable day, to her followers sounded the unmistakable note :

" Women, your country needs you," she wrote. " As long as there was any hope for peace most members of the National Union probably sought for peace, and endeavoured to support those who were trying to maintain it. But we have another duty now. . . . LET US SHOW OURSELVES WORTHY OF CITIZENSHIP, WHETHER OUR CLAIM TO IT BE RECOGNISED OR NOT."

That this message expressed what the women of the country were feeling was evident the next day, August 6, when the Executive Committee again met to consider the replies to the letters they had sent out earlier in the week. The secretaries wrote agreeing wholeheartedly to the necessity of suspending the normal political work of the Union, and to the proposal to devote their energies, as a corporate body, to the relief of distress arising from the state of war, and to all other such activities as might "sustain the vital forces of the nation" in the time of crisis. This therefore became the policy of the National Union, and within a few hours plans and preparations were on foot which rapidly developed into a great sum of organised effort all over the country.

The forms of work varied greatly from place to place. Where there were military camps, the greatest need at first was for the welfare of the soldiers in training, for rest rooms, canteens and the like. Where there were voluntary hospitals the need was for V.A.D.'s, and for the organisation of supplies. Elsewhere maternity centres, workrooms for unemployed women, hospitality for Belgians, local relief committees, or Red Cross centres were arranged. All these things, and the myriad other forms of effort called out by the emergency were immensely simplified when they could be undertaken by an organised body, whose members were accustomed to working together, and although of course thousands of the members of the societies also carried on whatever other work came their way, these things were done on a large scale by the organisation.

As time went on the needs changed somewhat. The unemployment problem very soon ceased to exist, and instead there came the great shortage of workers due to the enlistment of so many men. Then it fell to the lot of the societies to supply women recruits for all kinds of work hitherto done only by men ; and in this branch of the work the London Society, with which Mrs. Fawcett was always in very close touch, became specially expert. Their Women's Service Bureau, which was opened early in August, was the means of drafting thousands upon thousands of women into new work, of the most varied kinds, and Mrs. Fawcett watched this development with the deepest interest.

She realised that in the changed conditions of women's employment there lay great hopes for the future, and she knew, even from the first, that the way they bore themselves would have a profound effect not only upon the war itself but upon their own future position in the State. There was indeed no danger that women would not respond with enthusiasm to the call for their work ; but Mrs. Fawcett feared that their very enthusiasm might be turned against them, and that in all ignorance they might be forced into doing harm.

" I feel it is most important," she wrote to Miss Mary Lowndes, who was one of those most active in training women for some of the new work, " that women should not be put in the position of undercutting men, or being the means simply of supplying employers with cheap labour. These things would lead to bitter sex-antagonism, the very thing we want to travel away from. The comparison with the men who enlisted in such splendid numbers is not at all on all fours with the women whom the Government are now calling for. In the case of the men it was a new need they were called upon to supply ; there was no question of displacing or underselling other labour, and this makes all the difference.''

There was no disagreement among the National Union Societies on this point, and none among the Trade Unions. The two movements worked along the same lines in trying to secure for women war workers the same rates of pay as the men they were displacing ; and although this was very imperfectly achieved, the progress towards it was a very important feature of the economic situation in Great Britain during the war.

Of all the members of the suffrage societies, of course, the ones who were the most immediately ready to help their country at the beginning of the war were the doctors and the nurses. These latter were at once used, but the medical women were at first utterly rejected.

When Dr. Elsie Inglis approached a high official at the War Office to ask what she and the other women doctors could do to help, she was told in plain words that her best course was " to go home and keep quiet.'' She went away, not indeed to keep quiet, but to consult with Mrs. Fawcett and her other colleagues as to what could be done to change this preposterous attitude, and, as early as September 1914, the project of forming special medical units, to be called " the Scottish Women's Hospitals,'' was on foot. These units, which were financed and staffed entirely by women, and were composed mainly from members of the various suffrage societies, were offered to and accepted by the Allies, and were sent, some to France, some to Russia and some to Serbia and elsewhere ; and before the war was over they had made a magnificent contribution to its medical history.

The brave deeds and the great success of the Scottish

Women's Hospitals do not form part of Mrs. Fawcett's life, nor does the important work which Dr. Elsie Inglis herself did for the Serbian people. Although she could take no personal part in all this, however, Mrs. Fawcett was very closely interested in it, and followed every detail with admiration and enthusiasm. So, too, with the medical unit which was raised and commanded by her sister Elizabeth's daughter. When Dr. Louisa Garrett Anderson, after working splendidly in hospitals equipped by herself, first in Paris and then at Wimereux, was invited by the British War Office to take over the military hospital at Endell Street, with the rank of Major in the Army, her aunt felt that she was not only doing good and important work but also carrying on the family tradition of pioneering. Had Elizabeth not opened the door to medical studies her daughter could not have been so useful ; and other women in the generations to come would advance farther still because of that daughter's work.

Mrs. Fawcett's personal share in all the war efforts was inevitably limited by the number of hours in the day. She heartily supported and encouraged every one of them by letters and speeches, by articles in the Press, and by suggestions and contributions of her own ; but she could only come into personal contact with a small fraction of it all, mainly what was being done at the Headquarters of the Union and in the London Society. She did, however, still influence her followers, in spite of the widely varied forms of their work, in the direction of steadiness and reasonable feelings. In September, when the " white feather " movement was beginning, and when there was much outcry about the cowardice of men who did not immediately enlist, she wrote a protest in the *Manchester Guardian*.

" I do not think it is the function of men and women to lecture each other on the special duties of the opposite sex," she said. " These duties are sufficiently obvious."

And again, in the same month, when there was an outburst of wild reports on the subject of atrocities, she published a serious protest :

" It is surely no part of patriotism to stir up by speech or writing ungovernable rage and fury against the whole German people. . . . After nearly 2,000 years of Christianity we have but imperfectly learned one of its lessons if we think we can drive out cruelty by cruelty."

There was much exaggerated talking, in those early months of the war, upon almost every topic, but Mrs. Fawcett would tolerate none of it. Sometimes there were women, fresh from losses and bereavements, who would assert that women had the hardest lot in the war, and that action, even if it meant disablement or death, would be easier to bear. But Mrs. Fawcett felt that this was a false sentiment, and she took occasion to rebuke it at one of the many meetings to raise money for war work at which she spoke.

" We often say and feel," she asserted, " that nature and society combine to put a heavy handicap on women. However true this may be in many cases, it is not true of women's work in war. This is one of the few cases in which nature and society combine to give women the best of it and not the worst. Far be it from me to minimise the awful sufferings of women in war time. But they have one immense overwhelming blessing in this, that while the necessary, inevitable work of men as combatants is to spread death, destruction, red ruin and sorrow untold, the work of women is the exact opposite. It is, when we have the strength to understand it, to preserve, to build up the desolate house, to bind up the broken lives, to serve the State by saving life rather than by destroying it. When it is looked at from this broad point of view will not everyone agree that the work of women in war is more enviable than the work of men ? "

The energies of the suffragists were, as Mrs. Fawcett said, directed to preserving the life of the State, and their days and nights, like those of all the other women in the country, were absorbed in the task. They were not, however, able to forget the principles in which they believed, and when, in the winter of 1914, the military authorities began to talk of reintroducing the C.D. Acts in certain areas, their protests were vigorous and emphatic. The older workers knew how dangerous and insidious such regulations were ; they were convinced that the compulsory examination of prostitutes was not only unsound in principle, but also useless and worse than useless in practice, and they endeavoured, with a considerable measure of success, to resist the reimposition in this country of the discredited system of the State regulation of vice.

In guiding and encouraging all this mass of work, Mrs. Fawcett remained moderate and reasonable, as was natural to her, but like all her fellow-countrymen, she could not but be troubled and anxious about the course of public events. She was desperately anxious to see the success, and the early success, of the Allies. It seemed to her that they were fighting for civilisation and for their own existence, and that there was no course open but to continue until victory should be won. When reverses came, as they did so fast in the early months, she was oppressed, not because she feared the outcome, but because of the losses and casualties they involved, and because she knew they must delay the end. Sunday, August 23, was, as she said, an—

" overwhelmingly miserable day." " Terrible rumours reached London," she wrote, " of the retreat from Mons and the supposed destruction of our Expeditionary Force. I thought and thought of all those departed from this life whom I had most loved, and thanked God they were no longer here to endure the misery through which we were passing."

To the general anxiety there was of course added the personal trouble which no one in those years escaped. The Garretts did not worry much over Zeppelin dangers, even though so many of them lived on the East Coast ; indeed, Alice wrote to her sister in 1915 that she thought they were " probably safer than inland places, for they would have to take such nice aim not to drop their precious bombs either into the sea or on the marshes." But their sons and grandsons went to the war, and Millicent felt acute anxiety for the safety of these " splendid young men " of her own and Harry's family. Twenty-nine of them were killed, including several whom " Aunt Milly " had known and loved well, one of whom was her brother Sam's son Harry, and another her sister Alice's son Maurice Cowell. The loss of these young lives was but a part of the great tragedy ; but it was a part which it was heavy to bear, though Millicent tried to remember that " he that findeth his life shall lose it, and he that loseth his life for My sake shall find it."

There were many letters of sympathy to write, during these terrible years, to friends who were in mourning. Mrs. Fawcett, who had always found helpful words to say, wrote now more certainly than ever.

" Look up and take courage," was the note she struck. " The pure note of idealism is a real help in these times of sorrow. Anyhow, it is what the human spirit almost automatically seeks, and what poets only are able to express. ' For Lycidas your sorrow is not dead, sunk though he be beneath the watery floor.' "

Mrs. Fawcett's mind during the last months of 1914 was completely filled with thoughts of the war itself, and the efforts which it was possible for women to make to support and strengthen their own country. She knew, of course, that there were people whose outlook was different, who were so fundamentally opposed to all war that they could not do the smallest thing to support it, and some of those of the Quaker community, such as Isabella Ford of Leeds, were among her own friends. She knew, too, though without much attending to it, that there were sections of opinion which were already demanding a negotiated peace, but she believed these to be no more than a mistaken or impractical handful, not worth much serious attention. By the end of the year, however, she began to realise that there were several among her own colleagues on the Executive Committee, and among the leaders of the National Union Societies, whose attitude towards the war and the duties of the National Union was profoundly different from her own, and she became aware that there was serious danger of disagreement and disruption.

The actual point at issue, when the divergence of opinion in the Union first became apparent, concerned the international aspects of the movement. Mrs. Fawcett was strongly of opinion that it was impossible to hold a Conference of the Alliance while the world was at war, and in this she was at one with the French, German and Belgian auxiliaries, who all intimated to the American President, Mrs. Chapmen Catt, that they would refuse to attend a conference even if it were called.

Mrs. Fawcett's view was put before the President of the Alliance very clearly in December 1914.

" I am very strongly opposed to your calling any international convention, mainly for the reason that women are as subject as men are to *national* prepossessions and susceptibilities, and it would hardly be possible to bring together the women of the belligerent countries without violent bursts of anger and mutual recrimination. We should then run the risk of the scandal of a PEACE Conference disturbed and perhaps broken up by violent quarrels and fierce denunciations. It is true this often takes place at Socialist and other international meetings ; but it is of less importance there : no one expects the general run of men to be anything but fighters. But a *Peace Congress of women* dissolved by violent quarrels would be the laughing stock of the world.

" It would be impossible to discuss the principles on which Peace should be made without discussing the causes of war, the value or otherwise of arbitration and international treaties, and these could not be discussed without bringing in the question why the past treaties have not been observed. Prussia's pledge, for instance, to observe the neutrality of Belgium—and there you have all the elements of a furious discussion and quarrel.

" I give another instance. I heard recently, on good authority, that Aletta Jacobs had heard recently from Elsa Luders, who had complacently remarked how much for the welfare of the world the victory of Germany would prove, because it would enable Germany to impose her culture upon all the other nations of the world. Aletta Jacobs was furious : here we have an example of the sort of thing that might happen during every day and hour of the proposed international conference.

" I feel so strongly against the proposed convention that I would decline to attend it, and if necessary would resign my office in the I.W.S.A. if it were judged incumbent on me in that capacity to take part in the Convention.

" This is not at all a nice Christmas letter, but you know, dear Mrs. Catt, how cordially and affectionately I think of you and rely on your leadership."

This letter was written when some of the societies in neutral countries, and the Americans in particular, were urging that such a gathering might be advantageous. Mrs. Fawcett could understand that those who were at a distance from the conflict, and unaffected by its passions, might take this view ; but she was amazed and dismayed to find that there was within her own British society a strong group of people who not only agreed with it, but even went farther, and maintained that it was their positive duty to discuss the war, and to give international expression to the detestation of it which they believed animated the women of the whole world.

When the matter came to a vote on the British Executive Committee Mrs. Fawcett was in a minority in opposing the calling of a conference. This was not very important as regarded the actual point at issue, since the decision rested finally with the International Board, whose members nearly all took the same realist view as herself. But it was important as showing the trend of opinion among the officers and leaders of her own society ; and Mrs. Fawcett began to feel anxious. She roused herself, unwillingly, from her preoccupation with the national emergency, and freed herself, as best she could, from the multitude of war activities in which she was involved, in order to give her attention to what was going on within her society on the subject of war and peace.

The six months which followed were in many ways the most difficult and painful of Mrs. Fawcett's whole life, complicated as they were by the strain under which everyone was living, and by the sundering of many ties of personal friendship and affection. In later years she was most unwilling to refer to these troubles, and she gave them no place either in her published account of the movement or in her own reminiscences. Yet this internal crisis in the affairs of the National Union was without question a great test of her leadership, and a matter whose outcome was of deep importance to the suffrage cause.

Mrs. Fawcett found, as soon as she began to attend to the matter, that the things which she had taken for granted were by no means universally accepted among her followers. She had thought that the phrase which had covered all their war work, namely, the effort " to sustain the vital forces of the nation," had clearly expressed their intention to back up their own country in its struggle, and to give all the practical help they could in the emergency. She now found, however, that some of the National Union speakers and workers were interpreting it differently, and were objecting to any activity which could be considered as promoting the continuance of the war. These people maintained, she found, that the vital interest of the nation was peace, and that the best service they could do their country was to promote the discussion of the ethics of war and the possible terms of peaceful settlement.

There were, of course, many different shades of opinion among those who took this general view. Some were out and out " pacifists," who frankly opposed all forms of fighting and war work ; others, while admitting the necessity of continuing to fight, tried to promote an early negotiated settlement ; and others again, less practical still, wished to devote their strength, and that of the National Union, to general propaganda against war as a means of settling disputes. They maintained with passionate sincerity that every principle upon which the suffrage case relied was involved in this problem. The women's whole claim presupposed the triumph of right over might, they said, and pacifism, in its widest sense, was implicit in, and quite inseparable from, a belief in the women's movement.

The whole of this attitude was profoundly uncongenial to Mrs. Fawcett, and although she tried to understand it she was never fully able to do so. She could not clearly distinguish between the many shades of opinion, and thought the whole thing far-fetched and visionary ; and it was with difficulty that she preserved her belief in the good faith of her colleagues. She knew them to be honourable and intelligent women, and she had trusted them implicitly for years ; and it was a very serious blow to her to find them now following a course of action which was violently opposed to her sense of what was right.

It did not for one instant occur to Mrs. Fawcett that her view of the duties of the National Union was wrong. She felt that she was right with every fibre of her being ; she knew it practically, theoretically and instinctively too, and the controversy did not so much as approach the seat of her judgment. In a sense, therefore, she was unperturbed, untroubled by hesitations or doubts, unafraid of being put in a false position, and inwardly secure. But for all that she was very unhappy and anxious, and the position at the headquarters of the Union was exceedingly strained. Mrs. Fawcett was not,

nation," and she referred in detail to their hospital units and their work with the Allies. She said, too, that they, like all the world, longed for peace, and for the abolition of all future war, and she explained their deliberate acceptance of the principles Mr. Asquith had laid down. And then she came to the pronouncement which she had determined to make. Speaking for herself, she said, it was clear to her that the greatest national duty of all those which faced the country at the present moment was the duty of driving the German armies from French and Belgian land. " *Until that is done,*" she said, " *I believe it is akin to treason to talk of peace* " ; and with that, amid the thunderous applause of the audience, she sat down.

Mrs. Fawcett's colleagues upon the platform looked at each other in dismay. Many of them were already preaching peace with all their strength ; many others were hoping to use the Union itself for that end, and all of them were fresh from a Council meeting where no such sentiment had been endorsed. What is this, they thought, that our President has done ? Has she taken leave of her senses, under the war strain ? And what will happen next ?

They had little time for such thoughts, for Mme Vèrone, the pacifist of pacifists, was on her feet, and while she paid the correct and beautifully worded compliments with which French orators necessarily begin their speeches, they looked apprehensively at each other and at the Press table.

In a few moments the substance of Mme Vèrone's discourse became clear ; and then once more the pacifist members of the committee looked at each other in dismay. For she was saying just what Mrs. Fawcett had said, only with a passion and violence such as the older woman could never display. " Plus nous sommes pacifistes, plus nous devons aujourd'hui demander l'écrasement, non pas de l'Allemagne, mais du militarisme allemand." It was a complete and a most disconcerting surprise.

What Mrs. Fawcett thought as she heard the rousing words no one knew. She sat there quite quietly, and carried the meeting through to its end with her accustomed competence and courtesy ; and afterwards, in the green room behind the stage, she said not a word about it all. While her colleagues were clearly moved by strong emotions, some angry, some apprehensive, and all excited and at a loss, Mrs. Fawcett remained apparently unaware that anything unusual was going on. She was perhaps a trifle flustered, a little troubled about whether she could get a cab, and obviously anxious to get away quickly ; but of the crisis she said nothing. She had made it clear where she stood, and the consequences would follow all in good time.

They were not long in coming, and it can easily be imagined how strained and difficult the next moves were. All the parties to the dispute were wholly sincere, all were acting from deeply conscientious motives, and all were very intimately acquainted with each other. There was not much possibility of misunderstanding, and although in the intricate manœuvres which occupied the next few weeks there was a good deal of very indignant accusation, and a good deal of passionate feeling, the heart of the matter was, and remained, a difference of opinion as to what it was right to do.

The details of the controversy which followed the Kingsway Hall meeting are not very important or interesting now. All the officers of the Union, except the President and Treasurer, resigned early in March, and a week or two later ten of their colleagues on the Executive Committee followed their example. The pacifist group went out, and Mrs. Fawcett was left to carry on without the help of those who had been her chief advisers in the past.

It was interesting, and important, that it should have been the pacifists, rather than Mrs. Fawcett, who resigned. In actual numbers, they had at the time a clear majority on the Committee, and it would have seemed natural for the larger group to retain control, and to force the smaller one out until the main body of the membership should decide between them. But this was not what happened, and the reason lay in Mrs. Fawcett alone. She stood like a rock in their path, opposing herself with all the great weight of her personal popularity and prestige to their use of the machinery and name of the Union, and they could in no way get the better of her. As they had seen from the Kingsway Hall meeting, she could and would make personal pronouncements which would inevitably be taken by the public to represent the opinions of the organised suffragists, and nothing which anyone else could publish would carry anything like the same weight. Moreover, since she was now fully alive to the situation, she was watching every move with attention, and upon the committee it was very difficult to vote her down. The majority against her was not entirely unanimous : there were shades and differences among the pacifists which were useful to the other side, and the stormy weeks which led up to the resignations were very trying for all concerned.

The chief reason, however, why Mrs. Fawcett was successful, and the chief reason why she was so impossible to shake, was that the feeling in the Union as a whole was strongly behind her, and everyone in their hearts knew that this was so. The balance of argument might go this way or that, and the " pacifists " might, and did, believe with religious intensity that all women ought to feel with them ; but the facts were evident and irresistible. England was at war, and the people of England, the women as much as the men, were standing by their own country. Hateful, sickening, tragic though it all was, that was the mood of the country, and no other aim or ideal, however generous or fine, could stand in the way of the determination to win the war.

Mrs. Fawcett, of course, was English to the very

20

depths of her being. All her East Anglian stubborn-
ness, all her national pride, and all her deep love for her
own land rose up in the time of danger ; and her sense
of justice and of right came to the aid of her nature.
As she saw the war, it was fought in defence of noble
principles—for the sanctity of treaties, the rights of
small nations, and the overthrowing of military tyranny.
She could not compromise or give way : " Until the
German army is driven from France and Belgium, it
is akin to treason to talk of peace."

In the face of this attitude there was nothing her
opponents could do. They were, indeed, extremely
angry ; they said quite freely that she was acting
unconstitutionally, and imposing her own personal view
upon the Union. They said that she was losing her
grasp of principles, and that she no longer understood
policy and argument ; but that was of no avail. Mrs.
Fawcett stood four square in their path, and they had
to resign.

The resignation of the officers and of the majority
of the committee was naturally followed by a great
commotion within the societies of the Union. It was
not, however, and never had been, an ordinary political
society. The members were not only enthusiastic and
loyal, but they were vividly interested and excited by
its internal affairs, and there were hundreds and hundreds of them to whom suffrage had been the major
interest of life. It was impossible for these women,
therefore, even in the midst of their war preoccupations,
to ignore so dramatic a development, and letters of
expostulation, of enquiry and of congratulation poured
in upon Mrs. Fawcett and upon the headquarters office.
A special Council Meeting was at once summoned to be
held in Birmingham in June, and great preparations
began among the societies. Letters and circulars
defining the position were drafted and sent about, resolutions and explanatory statements passed to and
fro, and efforts were made on all sides to arrange the

business for the meeting so that the issues should be perfectly clear, and no possibility of an ambiguous decision arise. The members who had resigned and those who were standing for election in their places all published statements of their views, and no effort was spared to ensure that the subject should this time be settled once and for all.

When the Council assembled it was found that there was an unusually large number of delegates, and they were all serious and anxious and moved. They were all aware that the outcome was important, not only because of the actual issue at stake, but because of the inevitable reactions which their decisions must have upon the suffrage cause. Although the war was going on, and suffrage work was in abeyance, every one of the delegates was as ardent and passionate a believer in that cause as they had been before, and everyone knew that upon the issue of that Council the future of the Union depended. The " pacifists " believed, with desperate sincerity, that if the National Union turned away from the spirit of peace it would be denying its own cause. They thought that their ideals were the very truth and substance of the women's movement, and that it would be disgraced and stultified if women were to take the narrow shortsighted view. Mrs. Fawcett and her followers could not admit this argument. To them it seemed no more than plain necessity to stand by their country while the war went on, and they would feel both shocked and shamed if the Union they had built up were to take any other line. Moreover, they knew quite well what would follow if the pacifists won the day. The general public would, however unjustly, brand their society as pro-German, and it would be henceforth covered with odium, and politically outcast. They feared, moreover, that it would be not only their Union, but their whole cause which would suffer. If the organised suffragists deliberately refused to stand by their own country in its hour of need they thought that the cause would be irretrievably damaged, and that men would say, with some reason, that women were politically impracticable, and unfit for the vote.

The actual issue which faced the National Union when this critical Council met was not, strictly speaking, the rights or wrongs of the war itself, though it was closely entangled with them. What the Council was called upon to decide was whether or not the machinery, funds and organisation of the Union should be used for education and propaganda against war in general, or whether they should still be confined only to the relief works and the war emergency undertakings which were already on foot. But this was too academic a point for most of the disputants. On the one side, any talk of peace, while war was still going on, was considered to be damaging and anti-national ; on the other, any kind of relief work was considered to be helping directly in the prosecution of the war. And so the conflict was in substance, though not in technical exactness, a conflict between those who wished to assist the prosecution of the war and those who were unwilling to do so.

There was, however, one very important cross-current which swept in on Mrs. Fawcett's side. The Union had been essentially, and until that moment exclusively, a union of suffragists. Its members differed, and were accustomed to differ, upon every other topic, political, religious or social. Their very strength in the past had come from their diversity in all but the one cause, and consequently now there were many who held that the war was entirely irrelevant to the objects for which the Union existed, and that, whatever might be the right course for individuals to pursue, the Union as such was clearly debarred from undertaking propaganda upon any controversial subjects. This view, which was held by many who were in personal sympathy with the " pacifist " group, found strong adherents among the rank and file and carried great weight at the Council.

Mrs. Fawcett herself did not advance this argument, and did not appear to appreciate its force. She was deeply anxious, and deeply moved, but she gave little sign of her feelings. She had taken her stand, as they all knew ; and it was now for the Societies to make their decision. She did not speak very much while the deliberations went on, knowing perhaps that there was little use in argument or discussion at that stage of the proceedings. She just sat quietly upon the platform, watching the faces of her old friends and colleagues, and waiting for the vote to be taken. Perhaps, in her heart, she knew that all was well.

The vote, when at last it came, was overwhelmingly on Mrs. Fawcett's side. The silent, inarticulate voters and the smaller country societies were unanimously with her, and the pacifists, eloquent, devoted and beloved as they were, had but an individual following in some of the big towns. They retired almost entirely from the affairs of the Union, and thenceforward the controversy within its ranks was at an end, and the societies went back to their war work, a little weakened here and there by the loss of their officers, but on the whole as strong and vigorous as before.

As the months went on the need for their corporate activity grew increasingly urgent and important. The demand for munition workers created a series of new problems which closely affected women, and the subsequent enrolment of women in the W.A.A.C.'s, W.R.E.N.'s, and W.R.A.F.'s, developed this still further. The thrift campaigns, the food shortage, and the Land Army all offered wide scope to the energies and abilities of the suffrage workers, and as the demand for national effort widened so did their enterprise and self-devotion.

All this, of course, Mrs. Fawcett watched and assisted with profound satisfaction, but she was no longer as happy and serene as before. She had been personally hurt and disillusioned by the troubles within the Union, and by the complete estrangement of so many of those

with whom she had worked. " The painful events of
the spring of 1915," she wrote, some years later, " are
really the only part of my fifty years' work for Women's
Suffrage which I wish to forget. . . . The whole business caused me acute regret and anxiety. It was a
bitter blow." " I think it was George III who began
a day in his diary with the words, ' Remember to forget '
something," she added in a private letter nearly two
years after the troubles began. " Perhaps the best
thing I can do is to try to remember to forget." But
it was no easy matter to do it.

At the time she said nothing at all about her feelings,
but those who watched her closely could tell that some
of the elasticity had gone from her spirit, and that she
was sometimes tired and sad. At sixty-eight a few
strands of white showed at last in her thick brown hair,
and, although she still worked as hard as ever, it was
not always without effort.

The year 1915 was difficult and trying enough, without personal troubles, for the prolongation of the war
was very hard to bear. At that time the victory of the
Allies seemed indefinitely remote ; the hope of a short
conflict was over, and preparations were being made for
a long-drawn-out struggle.

" We had Esther's saying in our hearts," Mrs. Fawcett
wrote : " If we perish, we perish " ; but whatever the
cost or the consequences might be she would not contemplate surrender. " My dearest wish, now and
always, is to help by any means within my power the
cause of my country," she wrote in one of the rare letters
in which she spoke of herself. " This is the deepest
and most passionate feeling of my heart."

It was this feeling which prevented Mrs. Fawcett from
opposing the introduction of conscription, profoundly
though she disliked and disapproved of the principle.
" I wish," she wrote to a friend, " that we could have
got through without even this mild measure of conscription ; but the main business is not to please me

and others who feel with me, but to win the war." It was useless and wrong to let even one's convictions stand in the way of that necessity, she felt ; and when the conscientious objector agitation arose she had no sympathy with it. When one of her friends asked her to sign a memorial for the release of these prisoners, she explained her view fully :

" I am sorry I do not feel I can sign it," she wrote. " If a man resists the payment of taxes the State can destrain upon his property and recover the amount ; but if a man refuses personal service there is nothing that the State can destrain upon except his person. No State could ' carry on,' especially during the crisis of a world war like this, if men were allowed to be the judges in their own case and defy on their own responsibility the law of the land. Every Government must under circumstances such as the present consider the effect not only on the little handful of ' conscientious objectors ' at present defying the law, but on the great body of men throughout the country to whom for various reasons the giving of personal military service is irksome and repugnant to the last degree. We are all, including the conscientious objectors, enjoying the safety and security which millions of our countrymen have bought for us at the risk of their lives ; and I don't feel any of us should grumble at some hardships and inconveniences which they have not been able as yet to save us from ; though we confidently believe that future generations will be saved from them by these very sacrifices which the conscientious objectors decline to share."

Mrs. Fawcett held these views very strongly ; and, in the year which followed the controversy within the National Union, they became relevant once again to the decisions of the suffrage societies.

Ever since the adoption of the new election policy in 1912 their relations with the Labour movement had been very close, and under the agreements which had been made the Union was pledged to give support at the next general election to Labour candidates (subject to their personal views being satisfactory, and to their opponents not being " tried friends "). In addition to this general understanding, there were certain constituencies where active work was already in progress, and although an election was a remote contingency, it became necessary in 1916 to decide whether or not this work was to be continued.

The war and the pacifist controversy had affected the Labour movement much as it had the suffragists. There were at that time two distinct groups of Labour people, the majority who supported the war, and the minority who denounced it. Mrs. Fawcett, of course, approved the action of those Labour men who took their stand upon the "patriotic" side, and when Mr. Arthur Henderson entered the first Coalition Cabinet in 1915 she immediately wrote to him to express this view. His answer showed how similar was the tactical problem which faced the two organisations ; and though, of course, it was no consideration of tactics which animated either of them, the similarity is interesting.

" Your letter," Mr. Henderson wrote, " is an inspiration in view of the fact that some of our close friends in the Labour movement take such a strangely different view to that held by yourself. Personally, I am quite satisfied to rely on your judgment, which is in strict harmony with my own. At any rate I am convinced that, had we followed the minority during the past ten months, the Labour Party would now be in a most unfortunate position indeed."

Although the majority of the Labour Party endorsed Mr. Henderson's action, there still remained within it a great many leading men and women who took the other view ; and the National Union found itself in a position of some difficulty, since their policy might easily result in working for a candidate who was supporting the view which the National Union had itself rejected. This difficulty was not an academic and remote contingency, but was raised in a very dramatic

form when the candidate for one of the special constituencies where work was already in progress came
out as a conscientious objector and was imprisoned in
Wandsworth Gaol. The local society from which he
came pointed out that if they continued to work for him
it would be impossible to make anyone understand that
they were not themselves a pacifist society ; and yet
they admitted that definite promises had been given
and that these had been to some extent a deciding
factor in his candidature.

Mrs. Fawcett was genuinely troubled by this difficulty.
She did not at all like the idea of using the funds and
the name of the Union to promote the candidature of
a man who was in prison as a conscientious objector ;
and yet she was even more unwilling to break an undertaking formally given by her society. She arranged
therefore to see and discuss the matter with the Labour
leaders, and, after full and frank conversations with
them, the Executive Committee, and, later, the Council,
decided that the policy should stand unaltered, the only
proviso being that if the three-party system were not
in force when the election came the matter would be
open to reconsideration. This decision was communi-
cated to the Labour leaders and to the imprisoned
candidate, and their answers showed how genuine and
real was the tie which bound the two movements.

" I think that the decision reached," wrote Mr. W. C.
Anderson, " is in the circumstances the only one you
could have reached. Personally I had felt that as the
war had so entirely changed the situation you were
not bound, as I think, by any pre-war understanding.
I should not have felt the least aggrieved whatever
action you had decided to take or whatever new policy
you had adopted. What you have to think of first is
the advancement of your own movement and all that
you are standing for. You may be quite sure that
whatever you decide to do in the future there will be
no change in our attitude on a question which is to us
a matter of principle and not expediency. I am very glad,

however, that there is every prospect of cordial relations in the future between the National Union and the Labour Movement."

The candidate wrote from the guard room of his place of detention.

" May I say how deeply I appreciate the action of the Council, and also of yourself. I can understand how deeply you feel on the great war question—as keenly as I feel in the opposite direction. That only emphasises the breadth and generosity of the spirit behind your action. To me, it is full of profound import for the success of the women's movement ; and I trust the time is not far distant when I shall be able once again to do my little towards its complete achievement."

Mrs. Fawcett answered this letter ; and the stern things she said were as honest and straightforward as the decision she had taken.

" I thank you for your letter," she wrote, " and especially for your perception that several of us have not been able to arrive at the decision we recommended to our Council last week without great pain and difficulty. What finally weighed with us was that our organisation had given pledges in regard to specified constituencies (of which yours was one) which could not be disregarded except by consent on both sides. It is, as you plainly see, very painful to most of us to be in a position of helping a candidate whose presence in Parliament would (according to our conscientious convictions) be detrimental to the best interests of our nation in such a crisis as this. But in my judgment we really made our choice four years ago ; for I cannot see that what has happened since has materially altered the situation."

Through the whole of these difficult decisions Mrs. Fawcett was guided solely by her sense of what was right and honest. She hardly gave a thought to questions of tactics and expediency ; but the next two years showed clearly that the course she had followed was, in fact, both tactically wise and politically expedient. The attitude of the National Union in turning its strength to the service of the country put its leaders into a very strong position when the suffrage question again came forward, and enabled the suffrage movement to reap the benefit of the popular approval of women which their war work ensured. And the straight dealing with the Labour Party bore fruit also at the same time, when confidence among the various sections of suffragists was essential to making a united decision upon concrete proposals. Mrs. Fawcett, if she had thought of these things at all, would have considered them only a proof that honesty was the best policy. But, in fact, she brought other qualities as well as honesty to her leadership—a grasp of practical realities, and an innate understanding of the people of her own race. She was, as she wrote to a friend who stood by her through these difficult years, " a worshipper at the inner shrine, the holy of holies, all that England stands for to her children and to the world. It is because it is the holy of holies," she added, " that it is difficult to speak of it."

But there was no need for words. The whole course of her life, and the whole trend of her thoughts proved where her devotion lay. And it was by virtue of that dedication that she became so great a leader of her people.

CHAPTER XIII

THE SUFFRAGE VICTORY, 1918

Registration proposals—Change of public opinion—The Speaker's Conference—Lord Northcliffe—Interviews with members of the Government—The victory in the Commons—The victory in the Lords.

AT the time when the National Union Council meeting decided to follow Mrs. Fawcett's leadership, and for about six months afterwards, the question of Women's Suffrage appeared to be wholly suspended, submerged in the more pressing business of the war. Towards the end of 1915, however, the problem of adjusting the franchise to suit the fighting men began to come forward in Parliament, and the allied issue of Women's Suffrage inevitably arose at the same time. After all that had gone before, no one, however hardened in opposition to the women's claims, could discuss the basis of the franchise without remembering the demands of women, and consequently the various proposals for new Registration Bills called for attention and action by the suffrage societies.

This need awakened all Mrs. Fawcett's energy. It was just for such a crisis as this that she had guarded the life of her Union ; and she realised at once that its opportunity was at hand. There were some among her new colleagues who were timid and hesitating ; who said it would be unwise to make any stir about their own special question until the war was ended, and who clung to the idea that it was a patriotic duty to let everything remain in abeyance. But Mrs. Fawcett was quite clear that this was folly. If the new proposals with regard to the registration of men voters involved no change in the basis of the franchise, that attitude would be perfectly reasonable and right. But how could they collect the soldiers' and sailors' votes without changing the basis of the franchise ? To shorten the residential qualification (which was the first proposal) would be to introduce what amounted to male adult suffrage. And if this were done without the inclusion of any women, their chances in the future would be infinitely worse than they had been before. That would not be letting the question stand in abeyance, it would be letting the enemy steal a march on them ; and she stood out as strongly against these overpatriotic colleagues as she had stood out against the pacifists.

Intricate negotiations, of course, went on. Mrs. Fawcett interviewed the suffragist members of the Coalition Government, and took counsel with men of all parties, and a careful watch was kept upon the developments of the various expedients which were suggested, and in particular on the proposal to base a temporary franchise upon war service, both at the front and behind the lines. Although this plan never seemed likely to be adopted, it obviously offered a good basis for raising the women's claim, and it was noticeable that public discussion of Women's Suffrage began again in the Press some time before the National Union thought it wise to make any pronouncement.

When once the public discussion had begun it was amazingly friendly. On all sides people who had been opponents in the past now proclaimed their conversion, and the Press rang with loud praises of the patriotism, the national services and the heroic sacrifices of women. Mrs. Fawcett felt all this to be overstrained and exaggerated. To her it seemed that women were only behaving as she had expected them to behave, and that there was no special reason to be grateful to them any more than to anyone else. But she was not unwilling to profit by this wave of popularity, and she thoroughly enjoyed turning it to good account for the cause. So many times in her life she had known women to be unjustly slandered and abused ; it was only fair that for once they should experience the opposite extreme.

Mrs. Fawcett once described to a friend, laughing at herself as she did so, how her years of familiarity with the movement had taught her to pick out the word " woman " from a page of *The Times* the instant she opened the paper. It had been a faculty not very often called into requisition, at any rate upon the leader pages. But after 1915 it had plenty of exercise, and her daily study of the newspapers became a very different matter when there were all these hopeful and encouraging eulogies to read and enjoy. It really seemed, at last, as if the tide of popular sentiment had turned, and as if sympathy and goodwill were being added to the conviction of justice which had been growing so strong in the country just before the war. Mrs. Fawcett listened, therefore, with a very quiet smile when pompous people told her that women had now proved their fitness for the vote. Her task, as she sometimes said, was to provide convenient ladders down which opponents might climb, and to help them to save their faces while they changed their minds. She invariably restrained her younger colleagues when they showed signs of being irritated by well-meant lecturing on this subject. It would not hurt them, she said, to listen to what they knew already ; and the value of each sinner that repenteth is high.

The discussion of registration possibilities and of women's virtues continued through the first months of 1916, and by the beginning of May it seemed that the time had come for the suffrage societies to take public action. A letter was therefore sent to the Prime Minister and to the Press, and, as Mrs. Fawcett said, "We discussed every sentence of it before it was finally agreed upon." This letter set out the position plainly : the danger to Women's Suffrage from a change in the franchise for men, the increased support now evident, and the proved value of the help women were giving to the country.

" When the Government deals with the franchise,"
it suggested, " an opportunity will present itself of
dealing with it on wider lines than by the simple removal
of what may be called the accidental disqualification
of a large body of the best men in the country. We
trust," it continued, " that you may include in your
Bill clauses which would remove the disabilities under
which women now labour."

No immediate statement of the intentions of the
Government followed this letter ; indeed, it was many
months before any practicable method of dealing with
the franchise tangle was evolved. But Mrs. Fawcett
had reason to know that the claim it made was strongly
supported by Lord Robert Cecil and Mr. Henderson,
who were both in the Cabinet, and that Mr. Asquith
was at last convinced that it could not be resisted.
The whole election business might be left alone—if the
exigencies of democracy would permit it ; but if it
were once raised Women's Suffrage would have to be
dealt with.

This was the position in the spring of 1916, and during
the following months several attempts to find an agreed
basis for settlement were under consideration. Looking
back, when the outcome is known, these various proposals
seem to have little importance, since they were all
abortive, and for the most part wholly inadequate. But
in Mrs. Fawcett's life they loomed at the time very
large. Each one as it appeared had to be discussed
and examined. The consequences it would have, if
adopted, had to be estimated, and suitable steps had
to be taken to see that these were adequately guarded
against. Mrs. Fawcett and her colleagues had, therefore, to be constantly on the watch. They had to
maintain very close, and at times almost daily, contact
with their friends in the House and in the Government,
and yet to avoid being importunate. All their supporters, and they themselves no less than the people
they were seeking to consult, were overwhelmed with

war work. Many of them were sent abroad at short notice, and all were anxious about their friends and relatives, and liable to be suddenly plunged into private mourning and sorrow. The suffrage question, important as it was, had nothing to do with the war, and could not be allowed to interfere with its prosecution, and it was therefore more than usually difficult to arrange interviews, and quite impossible to do anything in the way of political demonstrations. Moreover, material conditions made things more complex. Moving from place to place was not easy, and Mrs. Fawcett, who at all times disliked wasting money on cab fares, entirely refused to do so during the war. Once, when she was hastily summoned to London from Yorkshire where she was staying with one of her sisters, she insisted on walking the six miles to the station rather than allow a man to be taken off the harvest ; and when she returned late at night, after the two long journeys and the intervening committees, she walked the same six miles back again and thought nothing of it.

It was in this spirit that Mrs. Fawcett met all the various difficulties of the work ; and certainly the fact that things were going so smoothly with her cause helped her to find everything easier. The chorus of popular approval of women continued to swell, and was reinforced from the most unexpected quarters.

Mrs. Fawcett had the joy of being at one of the meetings to promote women's work upon the land about this time and to hear Mr. Walter Long, hitherto a firm supporter of the antis, saying in the most innocent way in the world, that an unfortunate idea had got abroad among the village women to the effect that women's place was the home. " The idea," he added, " must be met and combated " ; and as Mrs. Fawcett noted, " There was a broad grin on the faces of all the suffragists round me as these words were uttered."

In an article written at this moment, and headed " Nearing Victory," Mrs. Fawcett said :

" Mid-August witnessed an immense advance in the suffrage movement. How great the advance was could be fully appreciated by those whose political instincts had been sharpened by contact with the facts of political life. . . . It is, I am aware, necessary for me personally to beware of my own tendency towards optimism ; but several months ago I was so certain that victory was near that I said, ' The battle is over, and we have won it.' "

Even though this was the truth, Mrs. Fawcett well knew that she could not afford to let anything slip by unnoticed ; and that same mid-August, which was so hopeful, was spent by her in London in steady and arduous work. On August 13 Mr. Garvin came out in the *Observer* with a complete recantation of his former anti-suffrage views, and before Mrs. Fawcett had had time to do more than thank him, Mr. Asquith followed suit. In introducing one of the abortive Registration Bills on August 14, he said :

" I have received a great many representations from those who are authorised to speak for (the women), and I am bound to say that they have presented to me— not only a reasonable but, I think, from their own point of view, an unanswerable case."

This important admission was followed on the next day by a conference in the House between the friends of the movement, which Mrs. Fawcett felt to be " very satisfactory." The point at issue, as it had been so often in the years just before the war, was what form of franchise it would be wise to go for ; and then, as previously, Mrs. Fawcett had explained that her Union " was favourable to any change which enfranchised any women, be they few or many, but if they were many, so much the better."

The leaders of this conference on the Parliamentary side were Mr. Dickinson and Sir John Simon ; and in accordance with the decisions arrived at, amendments were moved the next day in the House, and were accepted by the Government. The details of the tactics then debated speedily became unimportant, since the Registration Bill did not long survive ; but the result of all the thought and effort was apparent when, in the autumn, the whole matter, including the question of women's suffrage, was referred to the Speaker's Conference. It was true that the members of that body were supposed to be drawn equally from the suffragists and the antis ; it was true that the Speaker himself had been an opponent ; but no one could tell by then who was converted and who was not, and the chances were heavily on the side of there being a favourable majority among the members. Moreover, the first and most serious danger was already averted, namely, the danger that Women's Suffrage would not be considered at all. The attitude of the National Union on that point had been accepted as reasonable on all sides, and there was no possibility of a repetition of the Reform Bill fiascos of 1884 and 1912. Mrs. Fawcett knew that this was an enormous step forward.

The Speaker's Conference was in session from October 1916 until January 1917, and no hint of its proceedings was allowed to transpire. There were several staunch supporters of the suffragists among its members, but even Mrs. Fawcett's old friend, Mr. (now Lord) Dickinson, was not free to tell her what was going on. There was therefore little to do but to wait ; and the interval was filled with the agreeable task of collecting and recording the new backing for the movement, and preparing to make a full display of support if it should be required.

During the time when the Conference was sitting, Mr. Asquith's Cabinet fell, and Mr. Lloyd George became Premier, and Mrs. Fawcett most heartily welcomed this change. She had never liked or admired Mr. Asquith, and she did not think him wise enough or flexible enough to guide the country during such a crisis. Of Mr. Lloyd George she had a much better opinion. She had watched the two men for many years in relation to a cause which tested them both ; and although neither of them had an entirely blameless record, Mr. Lloyd George had at least been strongly on the right side, and had shown courage and energy in its support. She felt therefore that the national cause was better under his guidance ; and as for Women's Suffrage, there could be no question that the change would be an immense advantage.

Before the Speaker's Conference had reported, a very significant and important correspondence passed between Mrs. Fawcett and the previous arch-anti Lord Northcliffe. It began on December 22, with a letter from the great newspaper magnate to Lady Betty Balfour which opened with the words, " There is absolutely no movement for Women's Suffrage anywhere," and went on to suggest that the time had come for a big public demonstration. This letter was sent at once to Mrs. Fawcett, who confessed that it made her " very angry," and she wrote back " in a white heat " to Lady Betty, pointing out that there were no political demonstrations because the suffrage societies were devoting their strength to war work.

" I had no patience with people who could see nothing unless their heads were broken with it, and Lord Northcliffe's attitude was absolutely unreasonable."

This letter, which delighted Lady Betty, was duly sent on to Lord Northcliffe, who in his turn was delighted with it ; and he at once proceeded to see the Prime Minister, and as he said, " read it *at* him."

The consequence of this was direct communication between Lord Northcliffe and Mrs. Fawcett. On December 27—only five days after the first letter had been written—he was able to tell her that he had " talked for some time with the Prime Minister, who is very keen on the subject, and very practical too." He added the suggestion that a large and representative deputation should be arranged. " That will give the newspapers the opportunity of dealing with the matter.

I shall speak to the Editor of *The Times* on the question to-day. I believe he is entirely favourable." To this there was the following postscript : " Have done so. He is."

Mrs. Fawcett knew that the value of this support could hardly be overestimated, and as she looked back at the record of *The Times* she could hardly believe her memory. Again and again, through all those long years, it had been the implacable enemy. From 1870 onwards it had missed no opportunity of damaging the women's cause : it had come out with heavy leaders, long diatribes, inadequate news and bitter correspondence, until she had longed to be able to stop her subscription. And now Lord Northcliffe was taking trouble to advance the cause, was arranging opportunities for his paper to advocate it, and was reading her letter AT the Prime Minister !

With this knowledge behind her Mrs. Fawcett awaited the report of the Speaker's Conference with equanimity. There were a number of alarming rumours early in January, but she was not at all disturbed. She knew that the Prime Minister was " very keen on the subject and very practical, too," and though she well knew that all sorts of hidden dangers might yet emerge, she could not bring herself to fear them.

The Conference recommendations were published at the end of January 1917, and included, by a majority, a compromise proposal to give votes to women householders and the wives of men householders who were over the ages of thirty or thirty-five.

The following weeks were filled with consultations and negotiations. Mrs. Fawcett was no longer anxious. She knew that the inclusion of Women's Suffrage in the Report was an immense tactical advance, but she knew also that a great deal of effort must still be expended, and her first care was to try and secure the unanimous acceptance of the terms of the proposals by all sections of suffragists. The actual basis on which it proposed to enfranchise women was not logically defensible, and the high age limit which it suggested was patently absurd. But the reason for both kinds of limitation was the desire to secure that the women first enfranchised should not be a majority of the electorate ; and Mrs. Fawcett firmly adhered to her view that it was infinitely better to support an incomplete thing which could be won rather than to stand out for a perfect thing which could not. Moreover, she did not really dislike the proposed basis of enfranchisement on its merits as much as some other suffragists did.

" I felt that it marked an important advance," she wrote, " in that it recognised in a practical political form a universally accepted and most valuable social fact—namely, the partnership of the wife and mother in the home."

In any case, whether one liked or disliked it, the basis recommended by the Conference was clearly the one which would be brought before Parliament ; and it was extremely important that it should have all the backing it could. The section most opposed to it was the Labour women. They said, with great justice, that the industrial women, who most needed such protection as enfranchisement could bring, would be largely untouched by the proposals, and they very much wanted to secure amendments which would include these workers. The Parliamentary members of the Labour Party, however, knew that nothing but the Conference recommendations would have a chance of passing, and they urged the necessity for compromise ; and it was at this stage that the wisdom of the honesty of the National Union was apparent. For the Labour people had learned to trust Mrs. Fawcett ; and when she assured them that the suffragists would regard this as no more than a first instalment, and that they would continue to work for a democratic extension of the vote as soon as it was reasonably possible to do so, she was believed. All sections therefore came into line, and it was possible to assure the Prime Minister that if a

Bill were brought forward based upon the Conference recommendations it would receive unanimous support, provided the lower of the two ages was selected.

This assurance was given to Mr. Lloyd George at the big deputation which had been organised in accordance with Lord Northcliffe's suggestion, and which was received in March 1917. The day before it was seen a resolution calling for a Bill on these lines had actually been passed in the House, so that the meeting between the Prime Minister and the suffragists was largely devoted to mutual congratulations. Mrs. Fawcett, indeed, did not fail to make assurance doubly sure, by getting the Prime Minister to state definitely that the suffrage clause would be treated no differently from the rest of the proposals. But she did so, more because of the caution born of experience than because she thought it necessary. " The fight is over ; and we have won it."

From that point, as she said, " our Parliamentary success went forward rapidly, smoothly and without check. . . . It was roses, roses all the way, without the dismal sequel which Browning's hero had experienced."

In order to make perfectly certain that the members of the House of Commons did not share Lord Northcliffe's delusion that interest in Women's Suffrage was dead, a certain amount of the old activity of Mrs. Fawcett's societies was renewed. A War Workers' demonstration was held in the Queen's Hall, where women, representing every kind of occupation from railway engine cleaners, lamp lighters and omnibus conductors, to chemists, dentists and bacteriologists, demanded the vote ; this public meeting was followed by small private deputations from the constituencies to the individual Members, and Mrs. Fawcett herself made it her business to see every one of the members of the Government in order to impress upon each of them the strength and unity of the backing for her cause.

Owing to the war conditions it was not very easy to

see all these busy men, but Mrs. Fawcett made no
difficulty about going wherever and whenever it might
be convenient.   Some she saw very early in the morning,
and some late at night.   Others met her in the House,
or in Government offices, or in their own homes ; and
to each interview she arrived with exact punctuality.
Her manner in approaching these men was admirably
calculated to achieve her ends.   She began in every
case by asking for advice as to what was the best thing
to do to ensure the passing of the Women's Suffrage
clause, and she did this partly because she really wanted
to know what they thought advisable, but partly also
because she knew that important men love to give
advice.   This preliminary over, the interview developed
according to the peculiarities of the men she was seeing.
With the firm friends of the movement, such as Lord
Robert Cecil and Mr. Henderson, it became at once a
discussion of tactics.   From them advice was what she
wanted and all she wanted ; and they discussed ways
and means in detail.   With men who had been antis
in the past, and were now either wholly or partly converted, however, the interview proceeded differently.
In these cases her object was to make sure of them ;
and so she tried to draw them out upon the main question, and listened with admirable patience while they
told her why women ought to have the vote, or while
they explained how exceptional the situation was, and
how well justified their own change of opinion.   She
allowed them to explain the importance of the age limit,
and how dangerous a preponderance of women voters
would be, and it was not until they had thoroughly
relieved their minds that she said anything at all.
Then, very concisely and shortly, she told them what
the suffragists themselves thought ; that they would
take this if it were offered, and trust to the future to
show how far from dangerous women were.   She reminded them of the really overwhelming support which
her cause now commanded, and added a few words to

show that she was really expecting success and counted upon them to help her to win it.

In one case, where a Cabinet Minister (who was a life-long suffragist himself) expressed fears that the thing could not and perhaps ought not to be done in war time, she adopted a different method. She cut short his hesitations, and sat a little forward on her chair. " Mr. So-and-So," she said, " do you remember the state of the suffrage movement between 1910 and 1914 ? Do you remember that militancy arose then, even though the prospects of success were slight and opinion in the country divided ? What do you think will happen now, if this chance is taken from us ? Do you look forward with equanimity to the renewal of militant scenes during the war ? Do you think that anything short of an in-stalment of Women's Suffrage can prevent such an outbreak ? " She spoke without heat or violence, and made no threat ; but the Cabinet Minister turned quite pale. He looked uneasily round at the windows of his official residence, as if he half expected stones to come hurtling in, and he heaved a sigh. " Yes, yes," he said hurriedly, " I suppose it will have to go through " ; and then with all speed he showed Mrs. Fawcett to the door. And as the door shut Mrs. Fawcett turned smiling to her companion. " I think that settled him," she remarked. " Who is the next on the list ? "

In March Mrs. Fawcett took a series of meetings in the north of England, and at the end of April she had seven more in Yorkshire, which involved some awkward cross-country journeys. The weather had been severe all winter, and her tour fell in a very cold and blustering week. Mrs. Fawcett was nearly seventy, but it did not enter her head that she was not strong enough for anything, and she was completely dismayed when she found herself obliged to take to her bed on her return home with a severe attack of bronchitis.

" I have never had a week in bed in all my life before since Philippa was born," she wrote to a friend, " so I feel utterly unaccustomed to the situation. I am enjoying much more time than I usually have for reading," she added, " and I am getting well as fast as ever I can."

As soon as Dr. Jane Walker allowed it, Agnes took her sister away for a short change, and she reported that Milly behaved on the whole quite well, but that when she took her first walk she was " much astonished to find that she had to moderate her pace."

Letters from the office brought continual good news.

" We are all feeling extremely cheerful in spite of the struggle ahead," one of them runs. " You can't think how pleasant it was to hear the antis complaining that the Prime Minister would not see them, nor the papers put in their letters, nor the Government give them a straight vote in the House. I wish you had heard poor A. W.'s pathetic speech and the jeering and mocking with which the House received it. ' This amply repays all the wearisome days we have spent on the billowy ocean,' " the letter goes on, quoting from Mrs. Fawcett's old favourite, *The Hunting of the Snark.*

Even good news, and the conspiracy among her colleagues not to call her back, could not keep Mrs. Fawcett long out of town in the spring of 1917, for during May the initial stages of the Representation of the People Bill were passed in Parliament, and the critical debate on the Women's Suffrage clause was put down for June 19.

Mrs. Fawcett had often listened to debates upon Women's Suffrage Bills ; but never before had she gone down to the House with a feeling of real certainty. She sat in the Speaker's Gallery, visited from time to time by friends from the benches below, or by her anxious colleagues from the Ladies' Gallery next door ; the afternoon and evening were very hot, and up in the galleries the air was stifling ; but Mrs. Fawcett did not seem to notice. She listened to every speech attentively, she smiled serenely to every visitor, and she said very little.

No doubt it all seemed a little dream-like to her, as if it were too good to be real. No doubt she saw again some of the scenes long past—John Stuart Mill moving the first Bill, and John Bright sitting in his corner seat with his mocking smile. No doubt she looked at the place Harry had occupied, and remembered the faces of his friends ; and heard again the voices of the champions who were gone : Jacob Bright, James Stansfeld, James Stuart, Keir Hardie, Walter Mac-Laren and the rest. But she gave no sign of her thoughts as she listened yet once more to the familiar arguments put forth from the benches below her. It sounded much the same as ever, and yet it was strangely different. The principles were unaltered, the arguments were unchanged, and yet the whole atmosphere was unfamiliar. There was no ribaldry now, no scorn, only a chorus of approval from all sides, with a small minority of deeply serious opponents.

The result was, of course, a foregone conclusion, and the only uncertainty lay in the size of the majority by which the clause would be adopted. This indeed was important, since safety in the House of Lords mainly depended upon it ; and even Mrs. Fawcett, careful as her preparations had been, could not be quite positive what the figures would be. However, when at last the division came, it was better than her best hopes. By a majority of 7 to 1 the House of Commons put Women's Suffrage into the Representation of the People Bill ; and the leader of the movement went home content.

" The approaching triumph of our cause is so wonderful," Mrs. Fawcett wrote to Edith Palliser at this time, " one cannot help feeling that a sort of miracle is happening under our eyes. This may be the result of having struggled without success for so many years. But now that actual success seems so near, I feel strongly that it is the path of wisdom to refrain from any public manifestations of triumph until the Reform Bill is an Act of Parliament."

There was still a delay before this complete security could be attained, for an interval of six months elapsed between the passing of the clause in the Commons and its discussion in the Lords. And there was uncertainty, even yet, as to what the Peers would do. Mrs. Fawcett knew well that the strength of the antis lay in the Upper House ; she knew that Mrs. Humphry Ward would strain every nerve to secure at least the postponement of a decision, and although she was not exactly anxious, she realised that no effort must be relaxed. Of course, nothing in the way of constitutional agitation was possible, and the only approach to their Lordships seemed to be through the public Press. Accordingly she wrote even more letters and articles than usual, and caused her colleagues to do the same ; and she corresponded with those individual Peers and Bishops whom she knew to be at all friendly to the cause.

In spite of their leader's caution, Mrs. Fawcett's followers could not be altogether restrained from behaving as if the vote was won, and they marked the occasion of her seventieth birthday in June by a special Jubilee number of their paper, and by descending upon No. 2 Gower Street in large numbers, armed with flowers. Mrs. Fawcett was given a foretaste of the loving congratulations which were in store for her, and although she did indeed appreciate them, they obviously made her very much embarrassed.

" I am always troubled," she wrote after one of these occasions, " by the knowledge that I get so much more praise than I deserve : hundreds of splendid women are working, and I get the credit for their work, as well as for the ' bit ' I am able to do myself. But I do thank and bless you for your generous feelings."

That summer, unlike the previous one, Mrs. Fawcett went out of London for a reasonable holiday ; but it was a holiday overshadowed by the war. The long strain was telling severely upon the whole country, and there seemed no hope that it would soon be ended.

Even the approaching triumph of her beloved cause could not lighten this burden for Mrs. Fawcett. Though she firmly believed that Women's Suffrage would help towards preserving the future peace of the world, the existing war would be untouched by it, so that the two things were, in a sense, irrelevant to each other. The one was coming to success ; the other was still enveloped in tragedy and disaster. And so, in spite of all, the year was an anxious and a dreadful one.

Mrs. Fawcett, true to her own nature, tried to cling to her hopefulness and to look chiefly upon what was encouraging.

" Such wonderful things are happening in the world," she wrote to Dr. Jane Walker in this year. " Russia, the United States, Women's Suffrage—all pointing the one way, that autocracy is doomed, and a large advance in human freedom is being made. When I remember how I felt at the beginning of the war, and how I feel now, I wonder if I am the same person. I saw nothing but black failure then, and now I see all kinds of beautiful things."

Optimism was put to a severe test as the fourth winter of the war settled over Europe, and Mrs. Fawcett was glad to have plenty to do. The month of November was filled with the final stages of the Reform Bill in the Commons, during which a great deal of effort was expended on improving the basis of the local government franchise for women. In this effort the National Union and the Labour Party again worked hand in hand, and Mrs. Fawcett with Mr. Adamson led a joint deputation to the Home Secretary on November 14 which, after some anxious vicissitudes, resulted in the adoption of the desired amendment a week later. After this no further difficulty appeared, and the Bill went up to the Lords with Women's Suffrage as an integral part of it.

The debates in the Upper House began before Christmas, but it was not until January 8, 1918, that the real

tussle came.   There had been at the last moment a great
outburst of anti-suffrage protest in the Press.   Letters
and memorials signed by a number of leading " die-
hards " had made their appearance during December,
and some ingenious person had started the idea that
Women's Suffrage should be taken out of the Bill and
submitted to a special referendum.   Mrs. Fawcett only
laughed at this proposal.   Even as a tactical device
it came more than a year too late, and she found it very
easy to point out its absurdities.   Was it to be a
referendum to men or to women, she asked ?   If to men,
why use it at all, since men had already elected the
House of Commons, which had so emphatically passed
the clause ?   If to women, was it not tantamount to
giving them the vote ?   She thought it unnecessary
to say much more about this red herring, and did not
take it very seriously.   As she sat in the ante-room of
the House of Lords, however, waiting to be admitted
to the debate, Mrs. Humphry Ward came and sat
beside her, and raised the question, actually having the
temerity to ask her to support the plan.   " In the event,
which I do not anticipate, of the view I take being
unsuccessful," Mrs. Ward said, " would you support
me in an agitation for a referendum ? "

Mrs. Fawcett answered promptly and politely ; but
what she said was conclusive.   She would not support
such an agitation in any circumstances.   She had no
liking for the principle of the referendum, and personally
believed it to be most respected where it was least
known.   " I made at one time," she said, " a collection
of the sayings of the members of a former Government
on the subject.   One of them called it ' an expensive
way of denying justice,' and another described it as
' just the thing for female suffrage.'   If you had seriously
meant to raise this question," she added, " why did
you not do so when the Speaker's Conference was
appointed last year ? "

Mrs. Ward's answer was cut short by the opening

of the doors into the Chamber, and the two leaders went in together and sat side by side in one of the small pens under the gallery to watch the last stage of their battle as it was fought out by the Hereditary Peers.

The debate lasted for three full days, and all that time Mrs. Fawcett sat and listened. She heard once again the old, old arguments, and their old, old answers. She heard aged and learned men declare that women were politically untrustworthy, and that their proper place was the home. She heard her friends and her enemies speaking with passionate conviction, and she noticed, with growing delight, that all the younger men seemed to be on her side.

On the third day, just after Lord Selborne had made his splendid speech, Mrs. Fawcett turned to Lord Aberconway (the son of her old friend Mrs. MacLaren) who was standing near her at the bar, and asked him what majority he thought they would have, and his answer was " Thirty." And then Lord Curzon rose to sum up the debate—Lord Curzon who was the President of the Anti-Suffrage League, and Leader of the House of Lords. Mrs. Fawcett and Mrs. Humphry Ward both waited anxiously for what he would say, and both watched him earnestly. But, as he proceeded, their expressions entirely changed. All vestiges of nervousness faded from Mrs. Fawcett's eyes and Mrs. Ward grew white with anger. For Lord Curzon was taking the last step needed to ensure the passage of the clause. He did indeed say that Women's Suffrage would be a disaster, and that it would spell the ruin of the country, but he admitted that it was now inevitable. Their Lordships, he said, would not emerge with credit from a struggle with the other House, after so overwhelming a vote there ; and the only thing he could do, or could advise those who agreed with him to do, was to abstain from voting altogether.

When Mrs. Fawcett heard these words she knew that all doubt was over. " It was, I think, the greatest moment of my life," she wrote afterwards ; and at the time she knew that it was so.

Ten minutes later the figures were given out, and the majority for Women's Suffrage was 63 ; and then there followed a scene of great enthusiasm in the halls outside. The suffragists who had been waiting in the precincts crowded round Mrs. Fawcett, the friendly Peers came forward and shook her by the hand, and the police beamed with satisfaction. Members came out from the House of Commons to join the throng, and Mrs. Fawcett made her way to the doors amid a tumult of joyful congratulations. It was over at last ; the fifty years' fight was ended.

" When I returned triumphant on the evening of January 10 from the signal victory of the Women's Suffrage cause in the House of Lords," Mrs. Fawcett wrote in the *English Review*, " feeling that women's (at least one woman's) place was home, within an hour interviewers began to arrive from various papers. One of them, knowing of my fifty years' association with the movement, asked me to describe briefly its ' ups and downs.' I said I could not do that, because it had been all ' ups ' and no ' downs.' He looked so perplexed and incredulous that it is possible others may also regard my reply as misleading. . . . The history of the women's movement for the last fifty years is the gradual removal of intolerable grievances. Sometimes the pace was fairly rapid ; sometimes it was very slow ; but it was always constant, and always in one direction. I have sometimes compared it, in its slowness, to the movement of a glacier ; but, like a glacier, it was ceaseless and irresistible. You could not see it move, but if you compared it with a stationary object and looked again after an interval of months or years, you had proof positive that it had moved. It always moved in the direction of the removal of the statutory and social disabilities of women. It established their individual liberty and freedom ; they were in fact gradually passing from subjection to independence. That is why I said the history of the movement had been ' all ups and no downs.' "

CHAPTER XIV

STANDING AND STARING

The Victory Celebration—End of the War—General Election—Support for Mr. Lloyd George—Resignation from Presidency of N.U.—Visit to Paris—Work for the League of Nations—Opposition to Family Endowment—Opening of the Legal Profession—Magistrate's work—Visits to Palestine—Writing books—The Dame.

WHEN the victory had been won, and the long toil was over, congratulations, rewards and honours poured in upon Mrs. Fawcett. Her old friends wrote to rejoice with her, reporters crowded to interview her, and all kinds of celebrations and festivities were proposed. Mrs. Fawcett, however, somehow managed to turn all these things away from herself, and did not seem to realise that it was she, as much as her cause, that people were praising. She confessed that she felt " like unto them that dream," and when she was pressed to give accounts of the long years of work she could remember nothing but what was good.

" Things won are done," she would quote, " Joy's soul lies in the doing." " Looking back on the strenuous days of our fight for Women's Suffrage," she wrote to Mary Lowndes, " it really was a glorious time. ' To strive, to seek, to find, and not to yield.' I don't think life offers anything better than this."

The war, of course, was still in progress when the Bill was passed, but the suffrage societies felt that they must have one public thanksgiving, and a great meeting was held in the Queen's Hall early in March 1918, at which Mrs. Fawcett presided.

" Years before victory was in sight," she wrote in her reminiscences, " I had been accustomed to talk with my dear friend, the late Mrs. Arthur Lyttelton, about

322

the best way of celebrating our triumph when it came.
We had agreed that music alone could really convey
what we should feel. . . . She and I had agreed that
we must certainly have the Leonora Overture No. III
with its glorious burst of triumph, when freedom dis-
places captivity and the overwhelming power of love
overcomes the world of darkness. We had also hoped
to have the last movement of Beethoven's Fifth
Symphony, but that part of our dream never came true.
. . . Our friends among the great musicians came
splendidly to our help. Chief of them was Sir Hubert
Parry. He was ready to be our conductor. We had for
some years been using Blake's noble poem 'Jerusalem'
as our suffrage hymn. But there was no adequate
music for it that matched in any sense with Blake's
magical words, so we took this trouble to him and asked
him boldly to do the impossible. . . . The result was
his splendid setting of Blake's poem, which is now
known and sung wherever fine music and glorious words
are wedded. Its first performance was at our Queen's
Hall meeting."

Mrs. Fawcett was very happy that night. The
beautiful banners under which she had so often marched
hung round the hall, the triumphant music rang out,
and hundreds of her friends and fellow-workers were
there, rejoicing to be with her. Even Mrs. Fawcett
could not turn aside the great ovation which they gave
her.

The victory speech which she made on this occasion
was exactly what her followers expected from her.
" We do not triumph over our opponents," she said ;
" it is much better than that. We did not threaten
them ; it is better than that. But the great search-
light of war showed things in their true light, and they
gave us our enfranchisement with open hands." And
now, having won so much, they must go on steadfastly,
and use their new strength, believing, as the Council's
resolution had put it, " that the enfranchisement of
women will contribute to the true and permanent
welfare of the country."

22

Although this public celebration was held, and although Mrs. Fawcett's heart was filled with deep thankfulness, yet everything was still subdued by the national emergency. The war had been going on so long that its conditions had become entirely familiar, and such things as dark streets, food queues, and Zeppelin warnings were accepted as normal. But no familiarity could lighten the burden of the war itself. Mrs. Fawcett was as clear as she had been from the first that the struggle must be continued until the Allies were victorious, and now that the suffrage question was disposed of she turned back with fresh energy to the war work which her societies were doing. The direct recruitment of women into the services of the Army and the Navy and the Air Force was proceeding very fast at this time, and Mrs. Fawcett was frequently consulted as to the plans and arrangements which were under discussion. She did not, however, lose sight of the international movement. All through the war she had carried on, almost single-handed, such scraps of the work of the International Alliance as were possible. She took a great deal of trouble to ensure the continuance of the monthly newspaper, and she corresponded regularly with the leading women in the neutral countries. That spring she was in great anxiety over the position of her friends in Finland, where revolution was in full blast, and she heard most distressing accounts of what was happening there from Sweden and from Norway and Denmark, and, finally, from Finland itself. It was not, of course, possible to communicate with the enemy countries ; but if it had been Mrs. Fawcett would gladly have done so. There is an illuminating correspondence between her and the *Daily Mail*, dated April 18, 1918, which shows exactly where she stood on this point.

" MADAM," the *Daily Mail* wrote, " A reader of the *Daily Mail* has asked us to call your attention to the fact that the International Women's Suffrage Alliance notepaper contains your name and also those of two German women—Anna Lindemann and Marie Stritt. I have no doubt that, your attention having been called to this, you will give instructions that your name is to be removed, or those of the two representatives of the German people."

To this Mrs. Fawcett replied :

" The Board of Officers of the International Women's Suffrage Alliance was elected at its last Conference which met in 1913. I was then elected by the whole Conference to the First Vice-Presidency, and I have no intention whatever of resigning my trust. I may add that even if it were in my power to do so (which it is not) I should not dream of requesting the German women who were also elected in 1913 to resign. I should look upon such a request as an impertinence. It appears to me, not only from the international point of view, but especially from the point of view of the Allies, that it is to our advantage to stimulate the demand of German women for free representative institutions. We have no means of doing this at present ; but if such means presented themselves, I should unhesitatingly avail myself of them. The course which your anonymous correspondent suggests would have—so far as it went—a contrary effect."

The *Daily Mail's* suggestion was nonsense, and hardly to be treated seriously ; but the question of how to work for international aims was very often in Mrs. Fawcett's thoughts. Early in 1915, when the first League of Nations Society had been founded, she had been asked to join it, and had refused.

" I am in general agreement with the objects of the League of Nations Society," she wrote, " and yet I do not wish to become a member of it. My feeling is that there is a danger in the energies in our country being dissipated by this and a large number of similar schemes, when they ought to be concentrated on the gigantic task which we, as a nation, have undertaken, and which is at present unfulfilled, namely, to gain such a complete victory over Germany as will enable us, with our

Allies, to secure the civilised world against a recurrence in the future of the horror from which we are suffering now. Victory in this war is, and should be, our first national object, and this will be the foundation-stone of all such efforts as the League of Nations Society has in view."

This same thought was still with Mrs. Fawcett in the summer of 1918, but the after-war problems had evidently come closer. The entry of America into the war had made the victory of the Allies certain—though as yet no one knew how far away it might be ; and President Wilson's speeches were provoking not only intense popular enthusiasm, but also serious constructive effort in England. Mrs. Fawcett was guided, in approaching world problems, by her own instinctive nationalism, that " deepest and most passionate feeling " of her heart.

" A wholesome internationalism," she wrote at this time, " can only be developed from a grouping and mutual understanding and appreciation of a vital and healthy nationalism." " I don't hold," she wrote to another friend, " with the view that the better Europe and the better world is to be built up on the destruction of nationalism. Nationalism is one of the main facts of life, and the law-giver and the statesman, if they are going to build for permanence, must build in accordance with it and not in defiance of it. The R.C. Church has defied and endeavoured to root out (in many of its orders) the natural family affections, and it has always been against nationalism in the churches. ' Gallicism,' ' Anglicanism ' is anathema to it, but such attempts fail, and ought to fail. Of course we may mean different things by nationalism. Some people seem to think it consists in hating all countries but your own ; but this is only a diseased sort of nationalism. Love of one's own country and readiness to sacrifice one's self for her is quite consistent with friendliness and appreciation of other countries. No country is more intensely ' national ' than U.S.A., but none has done more to spread a really fine sense of internationalism. I don't believe we shall ever get internationalism worth having without the basis of a sound and healthy nationalism."

" I have no patience with people who pretend it is their Christian duty not to love their own country," she wrote on another occasion. " Loving your own country does not mean that you should hate and despise other countries. Each country has its own characteristics, excellences and defects. But a man is a cold-blooded beast if he does not love his own. There is plenty of love of country in the Bible, and I feel that the whole thing is ' placed ' by the text, ' If a man doth not love his brother whom he hath seen, how shall he love God whom he hath not seen ? ' "

If a League of Nations could be built up on these foundations, as she believed it could, she saw in it a hope for the peace of the world ; and the longer the war dragged on the more she longed for its establishment. But still, until the end had come, she was clear that the national effort must be supported, no matter what the cost.

The tremendous events which hurried so fast in the early days of November filled Mrs. Fawcett's heart with thanksgiving. The overthrow of the Hohenzollerns, the surrender of the German Navy, and the promulgation of the famous Fourteen Points and the declaration of the Armistice seemed indeed the beginning of the new era ; and she trusted, and believed, that it would be a clearer and freer world in which women would take up their new citizenship.

The General Election which followed in England was of the deepest interest to Mrs. Fawcett. For the first time in all her life she was taking part in it as a voter, free from the consideration of suffrage " policy." For the first time, too, women were being considered and consulted politically, and she took the keenest pleasure in every manifestation of the changed atmosphere. She watched with deep interest the candidatures of the women who had at the last moment been made eligible to come forward as Parliamentary candidates, and she herself went to speak for some of them. She was not, however, either surprised or distressed that none of them were elected, and when she received a letter of deep sympathy from Norway it made her feel, as she said, " rather an impostor."

" I do not feel I really have had this ' bitter sharp drop of disappointment poured into my cup of gladness,' " she wrote to the friend who had translated the letter for her. " I do not attach any great importance to the fact that no women were elected in December. There were only about four weeks between the passage of the Enabling Act and the General Election, and naturally there was next to no time to make a fair choice of constituencies (most of the seats women were asked to contest were forlorn hopes) and no time for working up an organisation. I must explain this when I write to the dear old thing, so that she should not pour out her affectionate sympathy under a false impression."

Mrs. Fawcett's reading of the political situation led her to give wholehearted support to the Coalition. Her view of Mr. Lloyd George was enthusiastic, and she strongly upheld him in wishing to continue the party truce as long as possible.

" I feel there is no doubt," she wrote at this time, " that Lloyd George has saved the country, and that his name will go down to history as that of a great war minister, worthy to be set by the side of Chatham and Pitt."

Many of Mrs. Fawcett's friends disagreed with her view, and urged her to refrain from active support, but she was not to be moved.

" Each one must vote in accordance with her own conscience, and for what she believes to be the best interests of the country," she said ; but for her part, if she had twenty votes she would give them all to the Coalition. " I do feel it was the Coalition Government that gave the vote to women," she added. " Mr. Lloyd

George's active support gave us deep water enough to float over the rocks of the House of Lords. When I am speaking of this subject I always say it is such an immense satisfaction to my non-party frame of mind that we owe the suffrage to no party, but to all parties combined. In such an immensely important national crisis as the present I should not allow my vote to be influenced by women's questions only. But I feel that the P.M.'s vigour, courage, insight and driving power have saved the country."

When, therefore, Mr. Lloyd George asked her to preside over his great meeting for women voters, she was proud and happy to do so, and counted it one of the great days of her life.

The Queen's Hall, where the meeting was held, was a place of many memories. How many concerts she had heard within its walls! And how many times she had herself stood upon its platform! It was from there that she had made many of her most important pronouncements, and from there she had seen many militant disturbers carried out. It was there that the War Workers' Demonstration had been held, and it was there, only a few months before, that the Victory was celebrated. And now she was again presiding over a meeting of women, but how different it was! On the eve of the first election after the Great War the man who had been Prime Minister was asking for women's votes. He was saying how important was the women's point of view, how necessary was their collaboration in the affairs of State ; and she herself, Millicent Fawcett, was taking the chair for him. Once again she must have felt " like unto them that dream."

When the election was over, and the Coalition once more firmly established, Mrs. Fawcett felt free to consider the affairs of the National Union. There had been, of course, a great deal of discussion as to its future work ; and the point which its President had emphasised, and the one which she really cared for, was to ensure that it should continue in active existence until the franchise should be extended upon truly equal terms. It was evident that this could not be worked for at that moment ; one or two elections must go by upon the existing plan ; but they must not forget that their cause was still uncompleted, and that there was straight suffrage work still to do. This view did not need much urging, for it was shared by the whole Union. But Mrs. Fawcett knew that it was important to make it clear and she did so. And then, at the end of 1918, she announced that she wished to resign from the Presidency.

" My reason," she wrote to the societies, " is to be found in my age. I feel that the time has come when younger women should lead the National Union. It has been my good fortune to remain at my post until the victorious end of the war, and until the great victory also for the cause of women's freedom. You know how intimately associated I have always felt these two great events to be.

" I am, and shall remain, a loyal and devoted member of the N.U.W.S.S. I highly value the political work of the Union, more effective than ever now that we have won the vote. I also particularly value its non-party character. . . . I mention these things that all societies may know that I am not retiring because I am dissatisfied, or because I think the work of the N.U.W.S.S. is accomplished and its organisation can be fitly brought to an end, but really on account of my more than three-score and ten years."

There were, of course, prolonged and violent protests, but Mrs. Fawcett stood quite firm, and at the Council meeting in January 1919 she laid down her task.

" I have come, as you rightly suppose," she wrote to Miss Lowndes at this time, " to hate committees with their endless talk, and I feel I can work for the women's cause in other ways that are less exhausting. But don't let me say anything which implies for a moment that I have not been happy in my work. It has brought me a large number of very dear friends with whom it is always a pleasure to be associated ; but I own it will be a joy to be free of committees."

The laying down of her office and the escape from tedious committee meetings did not mean that Mrs. Fawcett ceased to work for the National Union. Indeed, only a month after her resignation she went on their behalf to join a group of women from the Allied countries who were assembling in Paris to urge the claims of women's questions upon the attention of the Peace Congress. This gathering was not an offshoot of the International Alliance, which could not meet until peace had really been made. It was a special body, summoned together by the French and American feminists, and included women from Belgium, Italy and the British Dominions. From the moment of her arrival in Paris this informal group was led and directed by Mrs. Fawcett. She sought and obtained interviews with all the leading delegates : with President Wilson, M. Clemenceau, M. Venizelos and the rest, and though of course she recognised that Women's Suffrage itself was considered a domestic question, she urged them all to remember that the freedom they were hoping to establish in the world would not be soundly based if only half the human race were included. They all met her with attention and respect ; and although none of the international aspects of the women's movement were actually considered in the Congress, one very positive gain was secured. For, through the efforts of Lord Robert Cecil, the eligibility of women as delegates to, or officers in, all the positions under the League of Nations was written into the Covenant from the beginning.

Mrs. Fawcett did not like or enjoy this visit to Paris. She was troubled by the curious atmosphere which she observed in the delegations, and by the difficult and obscure negotiations which were evidently going on. She disliked, too, the rather hectic gaiety which was to be seen, and she went about the streets of Paris disregarding the traffic entirely, and walking faster and faster as the days went by, with a troubled and perplexed look upon her face ; and she was glad when her mission was over and she could return to her own home. Travelling was not easy at that time ; but Mrs. Fawcett paid little attention to the annoyances. While she was patiently waiting in one of the long passport queues, one of the British officers on duty in Boulogne station recognised her, and hurried up to see if he could help her. She wanted nothing, but when he told her that he had been a member of the Men's League, and that he rejoiced with her over the passing of the Bill, that was help indeed ; and the incident cheered the rest of her journey.

Mrs. Fawcett had been troubled by what she saw in Paris, and she anxiously watched the negotiations as they dragged on through the spring of 1919. When at last the announcement of peace came, at the beginning of June, she felt profoundly relieved.

" It is very blessed to have peace," she wrote to Dr. Walker. " I feel as if a big cloud had been rolled away. We heard it this morning at breakfast-time at Alde House, and we all jumped up and kissed each other."

But Mrs. Fawcett knew that peace must not mean idleness. She had brought back from Paris the clear conviction that there was an absolute world necessity for the League of Nations, and now that its Covenant was signed, and its existence formally secured, she was ready to work hard for its development. She was therefore glad to be asked to help in the formation of the British League of Nations Union, and made a number of public speeches, and even in the winter of 1920 went on a speaking tour on its behalf. Nineteen-fifteen had not seemed to her the time to do international work, but 1920 was ; and she did not spare herself.

The years immediately following the war had many things in them for Mrs. Fawcett besides international interests. Great developments were already following at home upon the granting of the vote, and what were known as " women's questions " were constantly under discussion in Parliament, so that all sorts of people came to her for advice upon all sorts of points, and reporters and politicians alike sought to find out from her " what the women think." Mrs. Fawcett generally refused to answer this question, maintaining that women thought all sorts of different things, just as men did, and that the idea of the existence of such a thing as a women's party was an absurdity. She did, however, maintain that there were some subjects to which most women would be likely to attach more importance than most men, and on which they might have a somewhat different outlook, and she believed that one of the chief results of women's enfranchisement would be the coming to the front of the political aspects of health, housing, maternity, education and social welfare.

Mrs. Fawcett's contention that all women did not think alike was speedily proved to be well founded, and the fear of a women's party did not outlast the first election. So far from uniting in a solid block, the immediate result of enfranchisement was to disintegrate some of the women's societies, which had a long and somewhat arduous reconstruction to go through before they found a working basis upon which to continue. Mrs. Fawcett naturally took a close interest in the affairs of the National Union, which in time altered its name to " the National Union of Societies for Equal Citizenship " ; but she was not in full agreement with all that it did. In a way this pleased her ; it was a sign of life and vitality, and of course she knew that the world must change. A good many people urged Mrs. Fawcett, as soon as the 1918 election was over, to make arrangements to stand for Parliament herself, but she did not for a moment consider doing so. She wanted to see women in Parliament, of course, and was more than delighted when Lady Astor was elected in

1919 ; but she knew it was no task for herself. In the by-election at Louth in 1921, at which the second woman M.P., Mrs. Wintringham, was returned, a curious and revealing incident took place. Some of the old suffrage workers, who had turned out to help the woman candidate, were driving through a remote Lincolnshire lane in a car decorated with the red, white and green colours of the National Union. A labourer, ploughing in a field far away on the sky line, caught sight of them, and waved to them to stop. He left his team and came down to the lane, and before they could say a word, he explained that he knew them to be " they suffrage ladies," and that he wanted to assure them that he was going to vote for Mrs. Wintringham. " I wish it could ha' been Mrs. Fawcett herself," he added ; " but I suppose she is too wise to go there. Likely she thinks it's for the young ones." And with that he returned to his ploughing.

Although Mrs. Fawcett did think Parliament was " for the young ones, " she watched every development of national politics with interest, and when the first Labour Government came into office in 1924, she felt very hopeful indeed. She congratulated her old friends who were now taking up Cabinet office, and wrote with particular warmth to Mr. Philip Snowden, whom she always both liked and admired ; and after they had been at work for a few months she confided her impressions to Dr. Jane Walker :

" I am VERY favourably impressed by Ramsay MacDonald's management and leadership of the recent debates in Parliament," she wrote. " Asquith, Austen Chamberlain and Co. seem to me to be content with mere debating-society points aiming at scoring off an opponent ; but Ramsay MacDonald produces a totally different impression, that of a good man in a difficult and perplexing situation (guiding the House without a majority) and anxious only to ' make reason and the will of God prevail.' You know that in our old suffrage

days we used to speak of Asquith as ' that old villain '
and sometimes as ' that old fox ' ; he is just the same
now. But clever as they are made.''

Mrs. Fawcett's readiness to accept change did not go
so far as to enable her to let pass without opposition
the things which she felt to be politically wrong. She
remained, as she had always been, a strong individualist,
distrustful of all State interference, and firmly convinced of the fundamental importance of private thrift
and personal responsibility. These principles, which
had been part of her philosophic radicalism in the
'sixties and 'seventies, seemed to her to have stood the
test of time, and to be essential to all self-respecting
government ; and she viewed with anxiety the increasing tendency to ignore them.   When therefore Miss
Eleanor Rathbone, her successor in the Presidency of
the National Union, began to advocate mothers' pensions
and family allowances, Mrs. Fawcett believed that she
was entirely wrong.   These schemes did not seem to her
to be the charter of women's economic freedom, but
rather to be the ruin of family life ; and she opposed
them with all her might and main. She went to the
council meetings of the National Union, at which
they were discussed, and spoke against them very
strongly ; but in spite of her great prestige, in spite of
the love and veneration which all the societies felt for
her, the view she advocated was not upheld ; and then,
in friendliness and without anger, but with absolute
finality, she gave up her personal membership of the
Union altogether.

Even after this separation, however, there remained
many points upon which Mrs. Fawcett and her old colleagues were in complete agreement, namely, all those
relating to the legal inequalities still obtaining between
men and women. Whenever these were attacked she
was ready and eager to lend her assistance, and they
consulted her as much as before. There was, moreover, one of her old societies which she did not wish to

leave, and that was the old London Society, which was now called Women's Service.[1]

This was the society of whose first committee she had been a member when she had entered the movement in '67 ; she had been in it continuously since that date, and for years and years she had been its Chairman and was now its President. This society was working entirely for the economic equality of women, and was carrying on both practical employment work and propaganda upon equal pay and opportunity, and Mrs. Fawcett felt entirely at home in its work. Indeed, she really loved it, with the love which was compounded of present unity and old loyalty, and she was glad indeed when in 1923 one of the splendid £1,000 presents was given to her on its behalf.

One of the tasks which this society and the National Union were jointly attacking was the opening of the legal profession to women. It was a subject which had always interested Mrs. Fawcett.

Thirty years earlier, when Cornelia Sorabji had first come to England with the hope of studying law and returning to help the Purdah women of her own country, Mrs. Fawcett had encouraged and helped her ; and she had taken part also in the unavailing efforts made at later dates to secure admission for women to the British courts. Now, when suffrage was an accomplished fact, success seemed possible, and Mrs. Fawcett became one of the leading spirits of a special committee which met frequently in the House of Commons. Her brother Sam, who had himself been President of the Law Society, agreed to be the Chairman of the Committee. He and his sister looked much alike, and spoke the same practical language, and it was obvious that they enjoyed working together even through the forms and formalities of committee procedure ; and when the business was over, the two of them would walk away

[1] The London and National Society for Women's Service, 29 Marsham St., Westminster.

through Parliament Square, and it was evident that they were happy in being together.

The work went well and easily, and when the Government introduced and passed the Sex Disqualification Removal Bill in 1919, it was possible to include in it the removal of all the legal barriers, so that women became eligible as solicitors, barristers, jurors and magistrates all at one stroke ; and in the following year Mrs. Fawcett herself was appointed one of the first women Justices of the Peace.

She found this work exceedingly interesting, and was a most regular attendant at her court, and formed a very high opinion of the " humanity and wisdom " with which the work was conducted.

" It seems to me," she wrote, when she was seventy-seven, " that the pessimists are altogether wrong, that the world is better and not worse than it was fifty years ago, more intelligent and more humane, and that the results of the comparatively gentle method of dealing with crime have not increased it, but the contrary. If I may refer here," she added, " to another little piece of my small magisterial experience, I may mention having sat occasionally over a period of some three years as a member of the Holborn Bench to hear education summonses. My colleague in this capacity not infrequently was the late Sir John Kirk. . . . This dear Christian gentleman was moved with compassion, not only for the defaulting parents, but also for me, inexperienced as I was in the more seamy side of the life of the London poor. . . . Sir John Kirk used to say to me in a low voice, so that no one but myself should hear him, ' You must not let these things make you too unhappy. These that come before us are the failures ; but the great mass is very satisfactory indeed.' "

Mrs. Fawcett did not let things make her " too unhappy " ; but neither did she take the troubles which came before her lightly. During the time that she sat on the Bench she took great pains to follow up the future careers of the young defaulters, and spent a great deal of time and thought, and took much personal trouble to secure good openings and a fresh start for some of the boys whose cases came before her.

Mrs. Fawcett attended to all these things, and continued to be active and energetic, because it was in accordance with her nature and her habits of life. But after her resignation from the Presidency of the National Union she did allow herself rather more time for enjoyment and relaxation than she had ever done before, and she indulged her love of hearing music with a good conscience.

" Our pleasure-loving natures," she wrote to a friend in 1922, " have led us to take tickets for the Ring " ; but the only guilt she felt about it was in staying out so late at night, which was a thing neither she nor Agnes cared to do. Mrs. Fawcett lived very quietly and contentedly, still getting up early and spending her mornings at her desk, still answering every letter by return of post, and still remembering all the interests of her friends. She generally went out in the afternoons, and came back to see her friends at teatime, or stayed to visit them. An hour or two with a book before a simple dinner followed, and then, unless she were tempted out by the opera, an early bed. When there was some engagement to be fulfilled she would set off, rather over-punctually, and walk through the streets, still going faster than was safe, and laughing at remonstrance.

There was one afternoon when she was sitting reading by the fire, and heard her sister come home from some expedition. After a moment or two Agnes came and sat down opposite her, but she did not seem disposed to say very much about what she had been doing, and a little silence fell between the two of them. Then Agnes suddenly said, " Milly, I think I ought to tell you that I was knocked over by a taxi-cab just now." " Oh, were you ? " her sister answered, looking carefully at her to see that she was not hurt ; " well, since you were, I'd better tell you that I was knocked down by a taxi-cab

too last week. I didn't mean to say anything about it."
That was all they said. Both were guilty, neither had
the right to scold the other, so they left it at that ; if it
had not been that they could neither of them resist telling
the story to Philippa, no one would ever have known.

Great as were the joys of freedom and leisure, Mrs.
Fawcett could not be happy in idleness. She had an
unending zest for facts and information, and discovered
in herself a real taste for meetings and lectures at which
she did not have to speak. She enjoyed such things as
the proceedings of the Statistical Society, and attended
occasional lectures on law or history or political economy
or international affairs with great satisfaction. She read
a good many solid books, too, as well as her old favourites
among the poets, and she went fairly often to church.
Her fundamental beliefs had not greatly altered, but as
she grew older she seemed to find more comfort in
the forms of religion, and she particularly enjoyed the
services and the sermons at the Temple Church.

" I have not found the process of growing old very
irksome at present," she wrote to Edith Palliser on her
seventy-fifth birthday. " I think it is because I
find it so pleasant to ' stand and stare.'

> ' What is life if, full of care,
> We have not time to stand and stare ? '

" When I was in the full rush of suffrage work my time
for standing and staring was very much curtailed."

The occupation of " staring " at the world in which
she was living was made easy and delightful after 1920
by a present which was given to Mrs. Fawcett by a
group of her friends. It had been a great perplexity
to all of them that she would accept no personal testi-
monial to her work, and although she herself had been
delighted with the scholarships for girls, and the endowment of hospital beds and the other so to speak public
rewards which had been collected in her honour, no
one else was quite satisfied. On New Year's Day 1920,

23

however, she received a gift which she could not refuse, when a cheque for £500 was delivered to her with the strict injunction that it " should not be given away to any cause or institution, but should be used entirely for your own pleasure and amusement. If you have any dream unfulfilled," the letter continued, " which this sum can accomplish, we should like to feel that we had helped to make it come true."

Mrs. Fawcett had a dream which was not yet fulfilled—a dream of travelling far abroad in the world, and she accepted this gift, and called it her " Travelling Scholarship " for that purpose.

" My dear Friends," she wrote in accepting it. " How can I thank you for the more than kind letter and the wonderful present. It quite took my breath away, and I do thank you again and again. I shall have to give myself a strict training in habits of luxury. The letter and the wonderful present did indeed give Agnes and me a keen pang of pleasure, and I do bless and thank you and all the donors for the love which prompted it, and especially for all the strong backing you and they have ever given me in all my work. What I have accomplished was really due to this. Without it I could have done nothing."

It was all very well for Mrs. Fawcett to say and to think this, but the gift had been given to her, and it was she who was to enjoy it.

" I asked and obtained leave to share it with my sister Agnes," she wrote in the introduction to the account of her travels which she published later, and in February 1921 the two of them set off for their first visit to Palestine.

They both loved travelling, and were indefatigable sightseers, and the fascination of the country so seized upon them that they returned again and again. Four times in all Mrs. Fawcett visited Jerusalem, becoming most deeply interested in the ancient and difficult problems of the government of the Holy Land. She made, at once, a score of friends there, and found herself in the closest touch with all those who were working for harmony and peace among the different communities. She stayed repeatedly with the American Colony in Jerusalem, whose work she greatly admired, and she visited schools and hospitals, and entered closely and eagerly into the details of the work of the British administration. Her opinions and conclusions upon the policy which should be adopted, and the way in which the promise to make Palestine a national home for the Jews could be carried out, were formulated and published in her book, *Easter in Palestine*,[1] which, though it gives no final judgment on the difficult problems, shows quite clearly the mixture of pilgrimage, sightseeing and political enquiry which made up her travels.

It was perhaps rather an adventurous thing for two ladies, both between the ages of seventy and eighty, to travel so far together without any younger companion ; but both Mrs. Fawcett and Miss Garrett were hardy travellers, who made light of every inconvenience. They were neither of them very good sailors, but they counted that as nothing, and Mrs. Fawcett filled her ship letters with praises of the vessels and their arrangements, always making the best of the weather, and of her own powers of resistance. In Palestine itself they insisted upon going for long expeditions to see the country, sometimes staying for the night at uncomfortable inns in out-of-the-way places ; and once, in 1927, they were completely snowed up at Amaan, on their way to visit Jesrah.

" We are having quite an adventure," Mrs. Fawcett wrote to her daughter. " We left Jerusalem in fairly good weather . . . but presently torrents of rain began to fall, and we reached this little caravanserai very much like drowned rats. It was all very primitive, with three or four beds in a room ; however, we have not had any strangers imposed on us so far. In the night the rain turned to snow, and we were really snowed

[1] *Easter in Palestine*, 1921–2, by Dame Millicent Fawcett. T. Fisher Unwin, 1926.

up. It would be most unsafe to attempt to travel by car . . . so we are spending the day here. Fortunately, we each have some kind of needlework, also writing materials and a *Manchester Guardian* (weekly edition). This latter is handed round by turns."

Their attempts to return to Jerusalem the next day were, as Mrs. Fawcett put it, " frustrated " ; that is to say, their car became completely stuck in a snowdrift, and they had to stand a long time in the snow while it was extracted, and then return to their primitive shelter.

" No tragedy has happened to us," Mrs. Fawcett wrote. " We have plenty of good food and oil stoves to keep us warm." And the rest of the party reported that no one was more cheerful or unconcerned at the mishap than the two old ladies for whose sake everyone else deplored it.

In a similar spirit, the reports of serious earthquakes in Jerusalem the following year did not deter them from returning.

" To be in an earthquake will be quite a new experience for us," Mrs. Fawcett wrote, " and one which we could willingly do without." But all the same they continued their journey, and insisted on repeating the attempt to visit Jesrah, this time without misfortune.

Apart from these voyages, which were usually undertaken in February and March, and one journey to Paris to attend a meeting of the International Alliance, Mrs. Fawcett did not leave England in the last ten years of her life. She spent her summers either with her sister Joey in Yorkshire, or with Alice at Aldeburgh, or sometimes at Salisbury, and she frequently spent a few days with Dr. Walker at the Nayland Sanatorium ; but she really liked best to be at home. There, in her familiar London, she had all her books and papers, and endless people to welcome and endless things to do. She had time, at last, for writing, which she had always disliked so much less than making speeches. In 1911, even in the midst of all the rush of the suffrage campaigns, she had put together an admirable little history of the movement,[1] and in 1919 she completed it and brought it up-to-date with the volume *The Women's Victory—and After*.[2] When she had finished this task many of her friends began to urge her to write her own reminiscences, but for a long time she refused to do this. " The book would have to be I, I, I," she said. " I don't like that kind of book." But her friends were importunate, and finally she gave way to an urgent appeal from the *Woman's Leader*, the paper which was the " organ " of her old society. The editor persuaded her that if she would write a few articles on what she remembered it would be a very great advantage to the paper ; and once she had brought herself to begin she found that she really enjoyed the task.

What I Remember ran serially in the *Woman's Leader* during 1923, and was published in book form in 1924,[3] and naturally brought to Mrs. Fawcett a great many welcome and delightful letters from her old friends and acquaintances all over the country, which gave her much pleasure. She managed somehow to prevent the book from being full of " I, I, I " ; and indeed, the only criticism which was heard of it was that she had remembered too little about herself.

This book was followed in 1926 by the one on Palestine, already referred to, and then in 1927 she set to work, with the collaboration of Miss E. M. Turner, to write a Life of Josephine Butler[4] for the celebration of her centenary in the following year. The writing of this book, while it involved a great deal of work, was a really great pleasure to Mrs. Fawcett. She was able

[1] *Women's Suffrage. A Short History of a Great Movement*, by M. G. Fawcett. T. C. & E. C. Jack (The People's Books), 1912.
[2] *The Women's Victory—and After*, by Millicent Garrett Fawcett. Sidgwick & Jackson, 1920.
[3] *What I Remember*, by Millicent Garrett Fawcett. T. Fisher Unwin, 1924.
[4] *Josephine Butler*, by M. G. Fawcett and E. M. Turner. The Association for Moral and Social Hygiene, 1927.

to look back upon the events of Mrs. Butler's life, and upon the progress of world opinion on moral questions since her death, and to bring out, as she set herself to do, " the meaning of her work and principles for the twentieth century." Although Mrs. Fawcett was eighty years old in the year when she wrote this book, it shows all her accustomed vigour and vitality. There is in it her characteristic grasp of principles, her keen understanding of political developments, and her serene optimism and faith in the future.

Mrs. Fawcett herself was rather doubtful about its success. She had put a great deal of work into it, but confessed that she " felt rather low about my J. E. B. book. It is not easy to transfer to print one's own vivid personal impression of a great personality." When, therefore, it was well received, and when the centenary celebrations led to its being widely quoted in the daily Press, she was extremely pleased and proud, though she still believed, and said, that she was getting a great deal more " glory " than she deserved.

She could not escape " glory," however, say what she might. Whenever there was a ceremonial occasion in any part of the women's movement—a dinner in honour of medical women, or women Members of Parliament— or any garden-party or meeting in celebration of any advance (and there were many in the years immediately following the granting of the vote) the first thought of everyone concerned was to secure the presence of Mrs. Fawcett, and to get her to make a speech. She did not like such functions, and she still hated making speeches, and even more being publicly praised ; but she knew it was her duty to do this sort of thing, and rarely refused. And each time that she spoke seemed to be better than the time before. Her mixture of dignity and personal humility was very impressive ; her sense of what was due to the occasion was un- failingly right, and the anecdotes which she produced were always new, appropriate and entertaining.

DAME MILLICENT AND MISS GARRETT TAKING FLOWERS TO THE STATUE OF JOHN STUART MILL, MAY 1927.

344]

In 1924 there appeared in some of the daily papers a paragraph announcing that Mrs. Fawcett's name was to be included in the Birthday honours list. To her old friend Miss Lucas, who wrote to her about this, she replied :

" I have no knowledge of what the newspapers say, so I am afraid you have congratulated me on what has NOT happened. I have not heard a syllable about it officially, but I heard last January that Lady Astor and some others were urging a request of this nature upon the Government. It obviously failed then, and I thought no more about it. I shall be ' more than natural calm ' (as Sir Walter Scott's little girl friend wrote) if this fails too. However, I get the best of it, any way, in your loving words, and the knowledge that you think kindly of me."

Six months later, however, the recognition came, and Mrs. Fawcett was made a Dame Grand Cross of the Order of the British Empire, henceforth to be known as " Dame Millicent." She was more proud and pleased with this honour than she had expected, but the first result was a perfect shower of letters of congratulation, which poured in upon her from all over the world. Not only did all her old friends—and they were hundreds —write to express their delight, but all sorts of public bodies, from village councils upwards, wrote to her, and another of the marvellous £1,000 gifts for the cause was presented to her " in honour of the honour." Scores of women whom she had never seen took this opportunity of telling her that she had altered and influenced their lives, and there was an outpouring of gratitude and affection which touched her deeply. Nearly every letter begged her not to answer ; but on the top of each one stands the scrawl @, proving how she disregarded this suggestion ; and to one and all she expressed the same feeling, that " IT " was given " for my suffrage work, and that makes me feel that all my old colleagues have a share in it."

CHAPTER XV

THE FINAL VICTORY, 1928, AND DEATH

Eightieth birthday—Championship of the young—The second victory in the Lords—The Royal Assent—The portrait—Queen Elizabeth—Age of Marriage Act—Visit to Ceylon—Luncheon to women M.P.'s—Illness and death.

DAME MILLICENT FAWCETT's eightieth birthday was in June 1927, and many things were done to celebrate the occasion. One of them, which brought her mixed feelings, was a garden-party at Aubrey House, on Campden Hill, the very place where, sixty years before, she had attended the first Women's Suffrage committee meeting which was ever held.

Much had happened in the world, and in her private life, in those years, and as she looked round at the friends who were with her she must have remembered a great deal of the past. She must have missed the faces of many who had shared the early days : Mrs. Peter Taylor, whose home it had been ; her sister Louie, with whom she had so often visited it, and above all Harry, whom she had first met at that very place. These thoughts did not make her melancholy, for that was not her nature. But they were in her mind when she rose to speak, and they led her to dwell a little on the past, but even more on the future. So much had happened since those early beginnings ; the cause and all it stood for had travelled such a long way, and the friends who were gone, and those who were still with her, had put so much of their best into the movement. And now there lay new and even better things ahead, for women were taking up their freedom.

That very year, that very moment, the final victory of Women's Suffrage was approaching. Mr. Baldwin,

the Prime Minister, had announced early in the year
that he was about to extend the vote to women upon
equal terms, and there was no reason to fear that the
delays and difficulties of the former struggle would be
repeated. So Dame Millicent, speaking there with
her memories fresh in her mind, bade the women's
movement look forward and justify its past.

The proposal to complete the enfranchisement of
women which came to the front in 1927 and was carried
into effect the following year did not pass altogether
without opposition. Ten years had gone by since the
first instalment of votes for women, and none of the
disasters the antis had predicted had come about;
but there were still a few timorous people to say that,
although women of thirty seemed fairly safe, young
women of twenty-one must be dangerous, and that
their enfranchisement would be a national disaster.
This view, which received more notice in the Press than
the number of its upholders warranted, roused all Dame
Millicent's fighting spirit, and she sprang to the defence
of "the blessed young" with enthusiasm. In letters
to the Press and in interviews with reporters, as well
as in private talk with young and old alike, she eagerly
praised and defended the young women of the new
generation. She liked their looks, their dress, their
short hair and their healthiness. They had, she said,
more independence and sincerity than those of her own
generation, they were more frank and outspoken; and
these things, she maintained, " lead to better manners
and a more charming demeanour than formality and
repression," so that she loved to think of their freedom.
" The wisdom and experience of age," she added,
" which everyone values and appreciates, may be
accompanied by drawbacks; the old are sometimes
slow to learn, may even become sordid and callous.
But we don't disfranchise them. Let us give the young
a chance. They will grow old quickly enough; but
let us benefit from their youth as long as it lasts for

helping to the right solution of the great problems that
lie before us."

The Bill, which finally conceded the vote to women
" on the same terms as it is or may be granted to men,"
was introduced as a Government measure in March 1928,
and its Second Reading was carried by the overwhelming majority of 387 to 10.   Dame Millicent was in
Jerusalem at the time, paying her fourth visit to
Palestine, and the telegram which brought her the
news rejoiced her heart.

"The majority," she wrote, " is really farcical. I don't
know," she added, with the caution of all her years
of experience, " if the abstaining hundred or so have
any darts up their sleeves to aim at us later, but I
should think not.   No M.P. can wish to antagonise
a large proportion of his future constituents. This I
imagine made the antis abstain from a hostile vote.
The attacks upon ' the young ' have been very futile
and silly, and ' the old ' have not particularly distinguished themselves of late ! "

During the later stages of the Bill, no " darts " came
from the anti side, and on May 21 and 22, Dame
Millicent had the happiness of sitting again in the House
of Lords while a Bill enfranchising women was passed
with a substantial majority.

" For the next two days," she wrote to Miss Gwen
John, " I am very full of engagements, and shall have
to hover round the H. of L. and hear what their Lordships have to say against Women's Suffrage. They will
wish to take it out of us after our tremendous victory
in the H. of C., but I don't think they will seriously try
to defeat us."

The occasion was curiously different from that of ten
years earlier. This time no agitated anti-suffragists
sat by Dame Millicent's side : only her friends and her
supporters had come to listen, and all the bitterness
seemed somehow to have melted away. There was
indeed plenty of speaking of the good old-fashioned

kind, and many of the Peers were still repeating that women's place was the home, and that their enfranchisement was the ruin of the country. But these speeches had a despairing note, and the issue of the debate was never for a moment in doubt. And then there came the concluding speech. Again, as on the former occasion, the Leader of the House, who rose to wind up the debate, was a strong and unconverted anti. It was not Lord Curzon this time, but Lord Birkenhead, and he began, as his predecessor had begun, by saying that he was opposed, and always would be opposed, to the enfranchisement of women. But, just as ten years before, their Lordships were told that the majority in the elected House was too strong, and that they could do nothing against it ; and Lord Birkenhead's final advice was even more contrary to his declared judgment than Lord Curzon's had been ; for he urged them, " in a spirit of resignation," to vote for the Bill.

Dame Millicent went home from that debate with a thankful heart. She had known, ten years before, that the first instalment would lead to the next step in due time ; but it was splendid to see her knowledge come true. As she wrote that night :

" It is almost exactly sixty-one years ago since I heard John Stuart Mill introduce his suffrage amendment to the Reform Bill, on May 20, 1867. So I have had extraordinary good luck in having seen the struggle from the beginning."

A few weeks later, on July 2, 1928, the official seal was set upon the final victory, when the Royal Assent was given to the Representation of the People Act. Dame Millicent was eager to be present on this, the very last of all the Women's Suffrage occasions, and took great pains to find out the exact time of the ceremony, and to secure tickets for herself and her friends. And as she heard the words, " Le roi le veult," she must have said in her heart the words of Simeon and of Anna the prophetess, who " gave thanks likewise unto the Lord."

The summer in which the Act was passed contained many joyful ceremonies in which Dame Millicent took part. There were services of thanksgiving which she attended both at St. Martin's-in-the-Fields and in the Roman Catholic Cathedral, and there were victory breakfasts and private meetings, and on July 8 a magnificent garden-party, given by Lady Astor at Cliveden. In all these functions Dame Millicent was, necessarily, the leading figure, and many were the joyful speeches she had to make, and the armfuls of flowers she had to carry home after these occasions. Although they tired her, Dame Millicent would not refuse to go to any of them, because they were, as she knew, her last possible service to her cause ; and besides, exhausting as they were, she loved them. She was glad to see her fellow-workers again, and to meet the new younger ones who were coming into the movement ; and she wanted to tell them to " go on, and go on, and go on," until everything which the movement included should be accomplished.

There was one of the congratulations which she received which gave her particular pleasure, and that was one which came from the newly enfranchised young women. A year or two before, her own society, Women's Service, had established a Junior Council of women who were just entering upon business or professional life, and no one had taken a greater delight in their energetic progress than their President. And now, when they brought her an illuminated address, she was both touched and pleased. The letter which she wrote in answer told them that they were " the very embodiment of our dreams."

" It is very splendid," she continued, " to see you taking up your responsibilities and carrying on our work into the new fields where it must now be pursued. . . . I look upon the formation of your Council and its achievements with the greatest pride, and I feel that the future of the movement will be safe and triumphant in your hands. I believe, of course, that it will change and develop ; you will probably find new methods and new needs, and your ways will be the ways of full citizens instead of the way of beggars and outcasts as ours for so long had to be. But I feel confident that you will find, as we did, that the cause of the real freedom of women is a great one, worth one's best service, and that you will never lose sight of it even amidst your new opportunities.

" It is not the only good cause in the world, nor the only one you will care for. But it does lie with you to care for it ; and for all its changes it is the same as that which we older women cared for. And it does lie close to our hands, as women, and it must not be forgotten until it is wholly achieved. You know from your own experience that equal pay and equal economic opportunity are still withheld from us.

" I shall expect to see you individually and collectively putting your shoulders to that wheel and pushing the car of progress along in your generation as we tried to do in ours ; and I know you will find that, in this struggle, there is enjoyment, pleasure and real interest as long as you believe in your cause and in your associates. And I am firmly convinced that justice and freedom for women are things worth securing, not only for their own sakes, but for civilisation itself.

" Believe me, with warm interest and great expectations
" Yours sincerely,
" M. G. FAWCETT."

Although the suffrage victory and the celebrations which followed it took up much of her time and thoughts during 1927 and 1928, Dame Millicent did not let them crowd out the other things which occupied and amused her, and her life was as full and almost as active as ever.

Many hours in 1927 were taken up by the sittings for the portrait which her friends had absolutely insisted on having painted. Dame Millicent disliked the idea of this very much indeed ; but when it came to be done she found much entertainment in it, and made great friends with the young artist, Mr. Lionel Ellis, who painted it. When it was finished, and was both admired and criticised, as portraits must be, it was presented to her at a special party arranged by Lady Astor. And, in spite of the fact that she had to listen once more to all sorts of variants of the theme of her praises, and then to make a speech of her own, Dame Millicent enjoyed this occasion.

There was a little act of homage to one of the great women of the past which she carried through this same winter from which she derived a great deal of pleasure. Dame Millicent had always had a special admiration for Queen Elizabeth, whom she was fond of using as an example of what women could do if they were given a chance, and she had read a good deal about her, and had very definite theories as to her character and gifts. Towards the end of 1927 she received a copy of a new life of Elizabeth sent to her by the author, Miss Gwen John, and she was so much pleased with the book that a friendship at once began between the two admirers of the great Queen. They met, and they exchanged letters, and they looked up the relics of Elizabeth which were to be seen, and presently the idea came to Miss John that the contemporary statue which stands outside the church of St. Dunstan's in the West was in need of care. She suggested this to Dame Millicent, who immediately asked her if she could " get an estimate from some competent person as to the cost of washing and cleaning our great Queen." This was done, and the Vicar was consulted, and also the Society for the Preservation of Ancient Buildings (of which Dame Millicent had been a member from its formation) ; the necessary sum was provided, and the work put in hand, and finally, at the end of July, Dame Millicent herself unveiled the renovated effigy of Elizabeth in the presence of what she called " a very jolly friendly little crowd."

This whole episode gave Dame Millicent immense pleasure. She collected the Press cuttings of the ceremony, and the still more welcome eulogies of the Queen which the occasion brought into the Press, and she kept a photograph of the statue always at hand to show to anyone who had not seen it, and talked and smiled over the enterprise for many weeks. She collected, too, a little endowment to ensure that Elizabeth's face should, from time to time, be washed, and her ruffles kept in order, and she was as proud of the statue as she could be.

Dame Millicent and her sister spent the summer of 1928 at Salisbury, and while they were there the Greek elections resulted in the return to power of M. Venizelos. Ever since the time of the Peace Conference Dame Millicent had known him to be one of the true friends of the women's movement, and she at once thought that this would be a good moment to make an approach to him on the subject of votes for the women of Greece. It was not easy to secure the proper signatures to an official letter during the holidays, but she worked perseveringly at the task, and first drafted a letter, and then dealt with the various amendments suggested by the proposed signatories, and finally got the memorial into shape and sent it off.

" I think," she wrote, " that it will not do any harm, even if it does not do any good. It is something to remind him that we are observant of that ' duty to one's neighbour ' which is sometimes described as ' keeping an eye on him ! ' "

This was direct suffrage work, very familiar and very congenial to Dame Millicent ; but for the most part her occupations concerned other feminist objects which were not yet secured in her own country. It was on her initiative, and in response to her pressure, that the Age of Marriage Act was passed in May 1929. The state of the law which allowed boys of fifteen and girls of twelve to contract legal marriage, though it was largely a dead letter in Great Britain, seemed to her a disgrace ;

and when she had once called attention to it, not only the big women's societies but the general sense of the House of Commons was found to agree with this view. No doubt Dame Millicent stored up this fact as another proof of the value of enfranchisement ; no doubt she added it to the long list of benefits which the years since 1918 had conferred ; but there were so many of these that they were hardly to be counted.

On that eightieth birthday, when the Aubrey House garden-party had been held, yet one more of her £1,000 gifts had been offered to her. This time it was intended for Crosby Hall, the headquarters of the International Federation of University Women, and it was devoted to equipping and naming one of the study-bedrooms which were available for international graduate students. This gift had given Dame Millicent the keenest pleasure. It combined the international work, which she knew to be so important, with the higher education which she had herself done so much to promote in the early days. When she spoke of these things Dame Millicent had to throw her mind a long way back, and to call up memories of a past which was distant, but not dim in her mind. It was a thing she liked to do, because the past had been so full of strong and honest effort, and the present was so full of its achievement.

Besides the university work, the Elizabeth Garrett Anderson Hospital, which was the memorial of her sister, was very often in her thoughts, and she went gladly to take part in any of its ceremonial occasions. There, too, the early work was developing and expanding, and its fruits were plain to be seen. Wherever she looked Dame Millicent saw progress and success ; and it made her very happy.

But she was over eighty, and at last she began to be conscious that she was growing old. She was not ill, or ever bored, but she felt at times a little tired, and a little lonely. Her dearest sister Agnes was still with her, but most of the other brothers and sisters were

setting up of the new Indian constitution. As she said later, she had strongly sympathised with the effort to include women in the electorate from the outset, but when it had been decided to leave their inclusion to the new Indian Legislatures, she had not been disheartened. In some ways it would be better for the women to be brought in by the decision of their own countrymen ; and when, in a surprisingly short time, this actually took place she was jubilant. But in India, as everywhere else, enfranchisement was not the whole story ; and Dame Millicent was positive that no stable solution of any of the social problems of India could be reached until there had been a radical change in the position of women. And now, in 1928, there were signs of rapid progress in that direction, and the women of India themselves were coming forward so magnificently that she felt profoundly encouraged. It was a thing she had not thought she would live to see.

It was perhaps partly this interest, and partly her unconquerable energy which made her decide in the course of this winter to go all the way to the Far East herself. In January 1929 she and her sister Agnes sailed for Ceylon, intending to meet there their niece, Dr. Louisa Garrett Anderson, who was returning from Australia, and to travel back again in her company.

This voyage was the longest Dame Millicent had ever undertaken, and her letters from the ship seem to reveal that the sea part of it was a little too much protracted for her liking. She made the best of it, as she always did.

" It is so nice to be warm without taking any violent steps to become so," she wrote to one friend ; and to another she said, " You give us credit for activity we do not deserve ; for a sea voyage is a wonderful and delightful time of rest, with no newspapers and no letters, the heads of important news by wireless, and in fact everything to encourage absolute rest, coupled with good food and the opportunity of seeing places one has never seen before."

But rest, though it might be what Dame Millicent needed, was not what she enjoyed. She fretted over the absence of news, and was proportionately delighted when they reached Ceylon and found newspapers and a picturesque Women's Suffrage deputation awaiting them. They had only twelve days in Ceylon before the Australian boat which they were meeting came in ; but in those twelve days Dame Millicent managed not only to stay with the President of the Cingalese Suffrage Society, to visit Kandy, and to do a lot of sightseeing, but also to attend and speak at a public meeting to help forward the dear familiar cause.

" The people here are on the point of winning Women's Suffrage," she wrote to her daughter, " although they have only just issued their FIRST annual report, while we were in our sixty-second year ! "

From this agreeable, but no doubt exhausting, round of activity, the two old ladies were snatched away by the arrival of the boat they were to return on.

" Our time was all too short," Dame Millicent wrote. " We did not realise before we arrived how much there was to interest us in Ceylon. Ignorance, you see, sheer ignorance."

The return voyage was prosperous, but the arrival at home, which Dame Millicent had so much looked forward to, was saddened by two misfortunes. Miss Garrett, after travelling in safety half-way round the world, slipped and fell in her own sitting-room the day she got back, and badly dislocated her shoulder. It was an exceedingly painful injury, and although it slowly got better it was a long and very trying business ; and her sister was deeply concerned and distressed. At that moment, too, their youngest brother George died at Snape, and they grieved for him very sincerely.

These troubles weighed heavily upon Dame Millicent ; but nothing could diminish her impulse to " stand and stare," and all through the spring she found comfort and distraction in the progress of public events. The General Election, which took place at the end of May, roused her greatest interest, and she was very glad of the opportunity which was offered to her of writing to the electors of Cambridge University recommending them to vote for her own and Edmund's old friend Sir John Withers. She enjoyed, too, the process of recording her own vote, though she would not tell anyone for whom she had cast it.

On election day she wrote to one of her distant correspondents of the women's movement, telling her how it was going forward.

" This is the day of our General Election," she wrote. " Everything at present is very quiet, but of course party feeling will run high. Many of us have done what we could to ensure that whatever party is returned to power, the paramount importance of WORLD PEACE will be ensured. I believe this will be one of the results of the women's vote."

The second return of a Labour Government which resulted from this election interested Dame Millicent very much, and she was delighted by the increased number of women who had become M.P.'s. When Miss Bondfield was included in the Cabinet she wrote at once to express her joy, and she took much delight in speaking of " the Right Honourable Margaret." Everything was going even better and faster than she had hoped ; how could anyone have believed, twelve years before, that such a thing could be ?

During the following months Dame Millicent continued her usual activities, and she heard a great deal of music. " I thought the two Mozarts *most* lovely," she wrote after one concert towards the middle of July. " It made me think of ' He restoreth my soul and leadeth me into paths of righteousness.' I wish I had had Agnes with me."

This wish of sharing what she enjoyed with her sister was fulfilled very soon after, when they both attended a public luncheon given in honour of all the new women Members of Parliament by the National Union. It was a tiring function for both of them, but a very happy one. There was the Right Honourable Margaret herself, and among her companions Miss Eleanor Rathbone, and several others of Dame Millicent's former colleagues of the suffrage days ; and there was Lady Astor, who had " held the fort with a Joan of Arc gaiety and courage " in the days, already remote, when women were a novelty in Parliament. Dame Millicent loved to see them all, and to hear their quick clear speeches ; and it was not her optimism, but her faith which told her that the future of her cause was safe in their hands.

This, the last of Dame Millicent's meetings, was on July 18. Three days later she confessed to feeling tired when she came back from the Temple Church. The next day she still felt tired, and consented to stay in bed. She hardly knew that she was ill ; but her friend Dr. Jane Walker saw that it was so. Her illness increased, gently and quietly, but irresistibly ; and on August 5, 1929, she died.

" The Lord hath done great things for us ; whereof we are glad."

INDEX

NOTE : In this index the usual initials are used for the various societies referred to and H. F. & M. G. F. are used for Henry Fawcett, and Millicent Garrett Fawcett, respectively.

25*

Women Doctors for India, 163

Women Justices of the Peace, 337-8

Women M.P.s, the first, *see* Astor, Viscountess; increase in, M. G. F.'s delight at, 359

New, the luncheon to, M. G. F.'s last public appearance at, 360

Women Suffragists, amateurishness of, 154-5; ideals and aims of, 178; insults to, 159, 160

Women's Anti-Suffrage Society founded, M. G. F.'s utilization of, 233; proposal of, in 1914, 271

W.A.A.C.'s, W.R.A.F.'s, and W.R.E.N.'s, the, 295, 324

Women's Employment Bureau, the, and its founders, 10-11, 18, 41

Women's Enfranchisement Bill, The, 1907, introduced by W. H. Dickinson, M.P., 246 *sqq.*

Women's Liberal Federation, 123; M.G.F.'s attitude to, 122, 123; the split in, 155

Women's Liberal Unionist Committee, 145; and the South African War, 185

Women's Party, a, 333

Women's Property, a farmer's view on, 83

Women's Rights, introduction of the idea of, 8 *sqq.*

Women's Service Bureau, *see* London and National Society for Women's Service

Women's share in War, M. G. F. on its compensation, 280

Women's Social and Political Union, militant methods of, 210 *sqq.*, increase in, 256, and the "Cat and Mouse" Act, 267; M. G. F. on, 218, 268; Mrs. Garrett Anderson and, 219 *sqq.*; protests against, of N.U.W.S.S., 217, 218, 232; opposition of, to the Government (1908), 249

Women's Suffrage, as the key to all improvements in women's status, in M. G. F.'s view, 121, 166, 225, 245, 323

Women's Suffrage. A Short History of a Great Movement (M. G. F.), 218, 343

Women's Suffrage Amendments to Reform Bills of 1867, moved by Mill, 42-3 1884, moved by Woodall, 95 *sqq.*

Women's Suffrage Appeal, the, shown in Westminster Hall, 160-1

Women's Suffrage Bills
1870, 48-9
1891, 156-7
1897, 172 *sqq.*
1907, 246 *sqq.*

Women's Suffrage Committees, formation of, 43; difficulties of, 44-5; disillusionment of, 97

Women's Suffrage Movement, the, the start of, 18-19; the first Petition on, 41-2; in the '60's and '70's, 41 *sqq.*, in the '80's, 97 *sqq.*, helped by Philippa Fawcett's success, 145; in the '90's, 152 *sqq.*; in the early 20th century, rush and hurry of, 244 *sqq.*; international character of, 242; spread of, M. G. F. on, 240; attitude to, of British Suffragists, 243-4; M. G. F.'s efforts to keep to a non-party course, 122 *sqq.*, 249, 252, 259; militant methods started by W.S.P.U. (*q.v.*), 210 *sqq.*; new recruits, 207; odd suggestions for furthering, 239-40, 271, 319; position of, on defeat of the Conciliation Bill, 265, 267; value of, gradual extension of belief in, 240, 241 *sqq.*; varied aspects of, problems due to, 44-5; War, the, as affecting, M. G. F.'s anticipations, 275; final victory of, and celebrations of, 346 *sqq.*, results anticipated by M. G. F., 323, 333

Printed in Great Britain by
Hazell, Watson & Viney, Ltd., London and Aylesbury.

THE LETTERS OF QUEEN VICTORIA

A Selection from Her Majesty's Correspondence and Journal
from 1886 to 1901

Published by Authority of His Majesty the King

Second Volume (1891–1895) of the Third and Final Series

Edited by GEORGE EARLE BUCKLE

This volume covers five important years in the interval between the
two Jubilees of Queen Victoria, and includes the sudden and premature
death of the Duke of Clarence, the second phase of Mr. Gladstone's
Home Rule Policy, the death of Mr. Parnell, Lord Rosebery's Ministry,
and the formation of a Coalition Ministry with Lord Salisbury at
its head.   With Photogravures.   25s. net.

First Volume (1886-1890) of the Third and Final Series. With Photogravures. 25s. net.

FROM MY PRIVATE DIARY

By DAISY, PRINCESS OF PLESS

Edited, with an Introduction and Notes, by Major DESMOND
CHAPMAN-HUSTON

'No one can read this book without falling in love with the gay
tomboy who wrote it.'—*Evening Standard*.   'Indiscreet, but the
charm of the personality so skilfully revealed makes indulgence
inevitable.'—*Spectator*.   With 31 Illustrations.   21s. net.

'DAISY, PRINCESS OF PLESS,' by HERSELF. With Illustrations. 21s. net.

A WOMAN OF THE TUDOR AGE

By LADY CECILIE GOFF

From the Letters of Katherine Willoughby who, at the age of
fourteen, became the fourth wife of Charles Brandon, Duke of Suffolk.
'Lady Cecilie Goff must have devoted untold patience and time to her
story.   Her book is an enthralling addition to historical literature.'—
Sunday Referee.   Illustrated.   18s. net.

BOYS IN TROUBLE

A Study of Adolescent Crime and its Treatment

By MRS. LE MESURIER

'I should wish it known to everybody, studied by everybody, and,
after careful consideration, acted upon by the State.'—*News-Chronicle*.
6s. net.

MATTERS THAT MATTER

By DAME HENRIETTA BARNETT, D.B.E.

'These articles by Dame Henrietta contain a great deal of autobio-
graphical material.   It is refreshing to read a book so clear-cut, so
direct, so free of sentimental or emotional appeal.'—*The Times*.
Illustrated.   7s. 6d. net.